To the kindergarten teachers and children

of the

Boston Public Schools

who have allowed us to learn with and from them

Martha Horn & Mary Ellen Giacobbe

Talking, Drawing, Writing

Lessons for Our Youngest Writers

Stenhouse Publishers · Portland, Maine

Stenhouse Publishers
www.stenhouse.com

Credits:

Page 75: From *My Big Brother*. Text copyright © 2005 by Miriam Cohen, illustrations copyright © 2005 by Ronald Himler. Used by permission from the publisher, Star Bright Books.

Page 166–167 and 246–248: Adapted with permission from "The Writing Workshop: Support for Word Learning" by Mary Ellen Giacobbe. In *Word Matters* by Gay Su Pinnell and Irene Fountas. Copyright © 1998 by Gay Su Pinnell and Irene Fountas. Published by Heinemann, a division of Reed Elsevier, Inc., Portsmouth, NH. All rights reserved.

Page 167 and 249: Alphabet Linking Chart adapted with permission from *Word Matters* by Gay Su Pinnell and Irene Fountas. Copyright © 1998 by Gay Su Pinnell and Irene Fountas. Published by Heinemann, a division of Reed Elsevier, Inc., Portsmouth, NH. All rights reserved.

Page 213: From DIM SUM FOR EVERYONE! by Grace Lin, copyright © 2003 by Grace Lin. Used by permission of Alfred A. Knopf, an imprint of Random House Children's Books, a division of Random House, Inc.

Library of Congress Cataloging-in-Publication Data
Horn, Martha, 1956–
    Talking, drawing, writing : lessons for our youngest writers / Martha Horn, Mary Ellen Giacobbe.
    p. cm.
    Includes bibliographical references.
    ISBN-13: 978-1-57110-456-4 (alk. paper)
    ISBN-10: 1-57110-456-9 (alk. paper)
    1. Language arts (Primary) 2. Creative writing (Primary education) 3. Drawing—Study and teaching (Primary) 4. Storytelling—Study and teaching (Primary) I. Giacobbe, Mary Ellen. II. Title.
LB1528.H67 2007
372.62'3—dc22

2007007752

Cover design, interior design, and typesetting by Martha Drury
Cover photographs by Martha Horn and Mary Ellen Giacobbe

Manufactured in the United States of America on acid-free, recycled paper
13 12 11 10 09 08 07   9 8 7 6 5 4 3 2

Contents

Talking, Drawing, Writing

Mini-Lessons by Chapter

Acknowledgments

ONE AFTERNOON IN THE FALL of 2000, we sat in the library of the Everett School in Dorchester, Massachusetts, with Maryanne Martinelli, program director for early childhood education in Boston Public Schools, and Catherine Marchant, a literacy coach, planning professional development in the teaching of writing for kindergarten teachers in Boston. Now, seven years later, we have put the finishing touches on a book that has evolved from that work. So it is first to Maryanne and Catherine that we say thank you. Your invitation to Boston brought us to a place we never imagined.

Throughout the writing of this book, we have felt supported on a variety of levels both in Boston and in other places:

At the district level . . .

Maryanne Martinelli's wholehearted belief in teachers and in our work is what started and continues to sustain the Writing in Kindergarten project. The Massachusetts Department of Education Quality Full-Day Kindergarten Grant helped provide the means to do this important work. Maryanne wrote the grants, trusted our ideas, and continued to ask, "When are you two going to write a book?"

Sid Smith, director of curriculum and instruction for Boston Public Schools, looked at the work that teachers and children were doing, took seriously our proposal for an assessment tool that reflected that work, and gave us the freedom and the space in which to try it out.

Ann Deveney saw the need, and made it possible to continue this work with first-grade teachers.

At the school level . . .

Kathleen Armstrong, Kyle Dodson, Jeanne Dorcas, Olga Frechon, Nicole Mack, and Janet Palmer Owens, Boston Public Schools principals, generously opened their schools and found space for us to meet with teachers even when there wasn't any extra. Janet Palmer Owens welcomed us year after year, creating a second home for us at the Mason School in Roxbury.

At the classroom level . . .

Rina Cimino, Mayra Cuevas, Jennifer Friedman, Amelia Greiner Gorman, JoAnn Jones, Megan Sinclair Joughin, Joyce Malfa-Cady, Caitlin McArdle, Marina Miranda, Laurie Myrick, Bebhinn O'Connell, Kathryn Peterson, Keri Purple, Connie Redden, Tara Remy, Lesley Ryan, Sue Seabrook, Patty Smith, Sarah Trantina, and Lois Williams-Blades freely shared their students and their classrooms as demonstration sites for our work. We also thank the many other teachers in those schools who sometimes "moved out" of their rooms for the day so that teachers attending the workshops would have a space to meet.

Special thanks to Caitlin McArdle, Bebhinn O'Connell, and Megan Sinclair Joughin, who read and responded thoughtfully to a final draft of this book.

Teachers and colleagues outside of Boston . . .

Nancie Atwell, Nancy Canastrari, Helene Coffin, Joyce Craw, Carroll Garland, JoAnn Portalupi, and Patty Rock listened, encouraged, and offered their clear thinking. They showed us that this work has a life beyond the city of Boston.

We have learned from many other teachers over the years—writers and colleagues, some whose names we've mentioned in this book. Donald Graves is at the top of that list—or maybe it makes more sense to say he's at the bottom, because all of what we've done in the past twenty-nine years stands on his original work. We wouldn't have written this book without him.

The people at Stenhouse . . .

Philippa Stratton, our trusted editor, believed in this project right from the start—and waited patiently. Erin Whitehead and Jay Kilburn treated our work with great care and delighted in the work of the children on these pages. We love how Martha Drury's design captures the work of these young writers and presents it so respectfully—and playfully.

Our families and friends . . .

Too many and too diverse to mention individually. It was the dinners, the phone calls, the listening, the invitations away, the common sense, the wisdom, and the laughter that nurtured us as we worked on this book.

Teachers in Boston . . .

This book would never be without the teachers in the Boston Public Schools. We thank you all for allowing us to learn in your company:

Margaret Foley Aslane
Lauren Austrian
Connie Avellino
Debbie Aviles
Gladys Babalola
Patricia M. Bain
Susan Barrett
Jessie Beaubrun
Sharon Watson Beck
Leah Blake
Matilde Bobadilla
Felica Parker Bobbitt
Kate Bowker
Cindy Browne
Ellen Buchanan
Heather Buzby
Deborah Carr
Jennifer Carrol
Alicia Carroll
Joyce Cassidy
Donna Cavanaugh
Dianne Celona
Paula Cerqueira-Goncalves
Joan Chisholm
Sandra Christison
Rina Cimino
Diane Cloherty
Ruth Molta Cohn
Linda J. Collins
Shanon Connor
Margaret Conway
Iris Coronel
Stephanie Anne Cousens
Christina Crawford
Shannon Crocker
Mayra Cuevas
Maureen Curran
Nilda Diaz
Nicole DiLeo
Deborah Dorman
Melina Evangelinos
Carolyn Fahy
Marionette Fennell
Jeanne Ferris

Christine Fitzgerald
Catherine Flores
Jennifer Friedman
Alice Fulgione
Nancy Gilson
Debbie Greene
Rosalie Guglielmi
Emily Harmon
Susan Harrington
Ann Hawkes
Donna Hill-Harris
Marilyn Horan
Katie Husgen
Elsa Jackson
Linda Jackson
Loretta James
Celeste Janey
Lena Jar
Joyce Johnson-King
Leslye Jones
Megan Sinclair Joughin
Marsha Kaminsky
Danita Kelley-Brewster
Pat Kelliher
Patricia Kinsella
Amy Kwan-Chan
Genteen Lacet
Jean Larrabbee
Christa Lau
Andrew Lawler
Brian Patrick Leahy
Susan Leary
Mary Ellen Lewis
Aristy Liousas
Lisa Llorente
Jean Lucas
Denise Lupianez
Kara Lysy
Maureen Mahoney
Paula Mahoney
Joyce Malfa-Cady
Amy Martin
Adelina Mateo
Beth Matlin

Caitlin McArdle
Joanne McCormack
Barbara McGinnis
Sharon McLaughlin
Sharon McRae
Maria Mehdizadeh
Marina Miranda
Awilda Molina
Bridget Molinari
Lillian Morales
Paula Morton
Erin J. Murphy
Janet Murphy
Barbara Najjar-Owens
Shellie Nee
Barbara Nowell-Haines
Ciara O'Connell
Bebhinn O'Connell
Aine O'Malley
Elsa Olmedo
Kelley Garvey Pellagrini
Vicki Permatteo
Kathryn Peterson
Isabel Pina-Britt
Megan Mahoney Polcaro
Rosemary Powell
Darrel Powell
Susan F. Quigg
Connie Redden
Jocelyn Rivera
Maureen Roach
Sarah Robinson
Marilyn Rodes
Nieves Rollin
Jackie Rosario

Mary Rudder
Lesley Ryan
Jan Ryerson
Peg Sands
Cristina Santos
Sue Seabrook
Janet Sherman
Janice Shuman
Amy Sicairos
Patty Smith
Amy Sprott
Lauren Staffiere
Jennifer Stahl
Kelly Stevens
Jeanette Sullivan
Kelly Tassone
Romaine Mills Teque
Christiana Theodosiadou
Natalie Loving Thomas
Sarah Trantina
Carolina Tucker
Joyce Udler
Janice Vazuqez
Kathy Vierbickas
Maureen Walker
Shakera Walker
Cheryl Waller
Nick Weisskopf
Jessica Wheaton
Robin Williams
Cindy Wilson
Jessica Wolf
Agnes Wong
Andrea Wong-Peterson
Kathleen Wood

Most importantly, we thank our greatest teachers: the kindergartners in Boston Public Schools past and present who continue to teach us that looking and listening are the essence of our work.

Introduction

THIS IS A BOOK ABOUT LOOKING. About listening. About teaching young children the craft of writing by beginning with what they know. It isn't a book of lessons to be followed but rather is our way of saying to teachers, "Come along with us as we observe children in classrooms, listen to their stories, study the work they put on paper and use what we learn to inform our teaching."

The idea for this book has been percolating for a long time, its roots dating back to the Atkinson study of 1978–1980. It was then that Donald Graves and his two research assistants, Lucy Calkins and Susan Sowers, embarked on their seminal research, "How Children Change as Writers," at the Atkinson Academy, a public school in Atkinson, New Hampshire. Those of us who were fortunate enough to be part of that study or to watch these teachers and researchers at work, often look back to it as critical in the history of education as well as a formative time in our own development as teachers. What was so instructive had much to do with the way the work was done. By looking to the children to teach us *what* they knew and *how* they knew it, we saw how to make learning meaningful.

This book is situated in work we're doing now, almost thirty years later, with kindergarten teachers in Boston Public Schools.

Maryanne Martinelli, program director for early childhood education in Boston, listened to her kindergarten teachers' laments that primary-grade professional development was always geared to first and second grades; rarely did they have a chance to look closely at issues particular to kindergarten. She asked us, "What can you offer to kindergarten teachers in the way of teaching writing?" Thus, in January 2001, the Writing in Kindergarten project was born.

Writing in Kindergarten is a classroom-based professional development project, led by the two of us, in which teachers, along with their principals' support, commit to a dozen or so workshop days throughout the year to explore the teaching of writing. This work is supported by the Massachusetts Department of Education Quality Full-Day Kindergarten Grant Program. In each workshop session teachers reflect on what their students are doing as writers, observe a lesson that the two of us teach in site classrooms, and talk about what they observed and how it applies to them and their students. To support them during the weeks between the workshop sessions, we visit their classrooms and work alongside them as they focus on issues, questions, and topics that are particular to their setting. Although our focus in this project is kindergarten, we also work with first-grade teachers, and we continue to find that the implications reach right up through the grades.

This book is a story of that work. It is a vehicle through which we can share what we've been learning over these past seven years and offer a way for readers to peek into classrooms and see the extraordinary work that the teachers and children in Boston are doing. With close to fifty combined years of experience in this field, we began this project thinking we had a good understanding of young children, teaching, and writing. But like any teaching experience, when we leave ourselves open to be instructed by our students, we're always enlightened and often surprised. Most enlightening has been what we've learned about the roles of talking and drawing in learning to write.

In writing conferences, we have always focused mostly on the content—on helping children figure out what they want to say and how to say it. But in this project we discovered that talk, in and of itself, plays a more powerful role in the beginnings of writing than we had considered in the past. "You can't know what you mean until you hear what you say," Berthoff tells us (1982, 46), and we have found that when children have a chance to talk their stories through first, they have a better sense of what they want to put on paper. Their ability to write clear, full, detailed stories has everything to do with having the language with which to say it. So, in the name of writing, we carved out a formal storytelling time, a chance for our students to hear what they have to say—and so we could hear them, too. At some point in our initial planning, we decided that, in the beginning stages, storytelling would *be* the writing workshop.

We made a similar decision about drawing. We had long held the belief that young children enter the world of writing through drawing, but we hadn't looked closely and carefully enough at the important place of drawing as a way of making meaning. In this project, we made a conscious decision to make time for drawing, not just during writing workshop, but throughout the day. Yes, we focused writing mini-lessons on drawing, but we also built in a regular time for the whole class to sketch together, set up a drawing center in the classroom where children could sketch during independent work times, and fostered the conversation that naturally grew up around drawing in all other aspects of the curriculum. Through this work we have been reminded that drawing is not rehearsal for writing: drawing *is* writing.

We've designed the book around actual lessons we've presented to children. It took a while to figure out just how we wanted to do that. For years we'd been resisting teachers' requests for a book of lessons, believing that teaching grows out of what our students show us they know and need to learn, and that we outsiders can't possibly decide what other teachers need to teach next. But that reasoning is (at least somewhat) flawed, because we know that not all lessons are homegrown; there are some that we present no matter what children are sitting in front of us. At the beginning of the year, for example, we model how to use and care for materials, where we keep our writing and how to get it and return it when writing time is over, how to reread their work in order to know what to do next, and how to listen for sounds in words so they can write independently. There is some information that we want all children to know so they can work independently, and we find ourselves going back and fine-tuning those trusty lessons that worked well.

It was the teachers in Boston who helped us understand what so many other teachers had been asking all those years. One afternoon we gave them a copy of the lesson we had presented to children earlier that day and their immediate response was "Do you have any more of these?" By listening to their comments we came to see that they weren't asking for a recipe to follow or a script of what to say, but for a point of reference: having a lesson in hand served as a helpful guide. It may very well be that they were asking, "What are those foundational lessons that make it possible to get the writing classroom up and running, and can we have a reminder of how you say it so that children understand?" In that case, we are happy to share some lessons here.

We believe, however, that what we are presenting is something much bigger.

We've come to believe that the more critical question teachers were asking had to do with how to look at children's writing and name what they see. Since we teach in response to what children are doing—or not doing—we need to know what we're trying to respond *to*. This can take some practice, especially when we haven't had much, and most of us haven't. We weren't taught how to craft writing in our own schooling, so it's hard to know what elements of craft to look for in children's work. Also, most of us didn't learn how to teach writing during our teacher education programs. We didn't spend time looking at children's writing and saying what we saw, most likely because there wasn't a lot of writing to look at. Our hope is that, by revealing our thinking behind these lessons and situating them in the contexts of real classrooms, you will better understand how you might develop *your* lessons for *your* students.

How This Book Is Organized

You will notice, throughout the book, that we use the pronouns *I* and *we* without ever saying who's who. That's because we did so much of the thinking and planning together and it just made sense to write it that way.

You will also notice that the lessons are written in a particular format:

Title of the specific lesson
Background
What's going on in the classroom
What's next
Materials needed

The Lesson
This is what I noticed . . .
Let me show you what I mean . . .
So, today as you write . . .

Resources
Why we chose this book
Suggested other books
Other possible lessons

We came up with it by paying attention to how we presented mini-lessons and then putting our own, ordinary words to what we were doing. It's a format that works for us. Each lesson consists of three parts: the background, the lesson, and resources. The background helps readers know the context for the lesson. In the first section, **What's going on in the classroom**, we list what we noticed our students doing—or not doing—which led us to pinpoint the one aspect we wanted to address in the lesson. **What's next** explains just that: here's what the lesson will be about based on what we observed. **Materials needed** speaks for itself.

The next section consists of the actual words we say to students. This, too, consists of three parts: **This is what I noticed . . . , Let me show you what I mean . . . ,** and **So, today as you write . . .** We don't actually say these words to children; they are headings that, we discovered, capture the essence of how we were naturally organizing our words.

In the section called **This is what I noticed . . .** , we reveal to our students that what we're about to teach them comes from our observations of them as writers. We let them know that we've looked at their work or watched them as they worked and noticed something that is important to mention. Most, but not all, lessons follow this design. There are times when we present information that is not necessarily based on their work but is something we want them to know. Then, **Let me show you what I mean . . .** is the part of the lesson where we give a concrete example to make the idea understandable to our students. In choosing the example, it's important to make sure it is clear. Then we want to connect the lesson to their writing. **So, today as you write . . .** is a reminder that what we've just talked about is something they can use as writers—if not now, then at some point.

Last, the resources. **Why we chose this book** explains the reasoning behind our choices, and **Suggested other books** acknowledges that the books we chose are not the only ones. We've suggested some we like; you will know others. Later, in Chapter 8, we add another resource—**Other possible lessons**—in which we begin a list of lessons we could imagine following up with, based on having presented this particular lesson. We don't list them all, of course, because we can't know what they will be. Mini-lessons are generative; once we present one, we see possibilities for another and another . . .

In this book we've focused on telling, drawing, and writing stories, which means we haven't addressed poetry, informational texts, and other genres that are flourishing in many of these classrooms. That's because each year as we begin work with a new group of teachers, we start by getting them to tell stories with their students. Children's own stories form the heart and soul of our work, and we think they are important enough for a whole book.

We invite you now into classrooms across the city of Boston, which includes the neighborhoods of Roxbury, Dorchester, Jamaica Plain, and others, where teachers are getting to know their students through their stories.

CHAPTER 1

Storytelling

DANITA KELLEY-BREWSTER CLOSES the picture book and leans in toward her twenty-one kindergartners, who sit "crisscross applesauce" on the rug in front of her. Well, most of them do. It is the second day of school, and in this classroom in Dorchester, Massachusetts, it's writing time. They have just finished reading *The Ugly Vegetables* together, a story by Grace Lin about a city neighborhood where all the families plant gardens—but one is different from the rest. Throughout the read-aloud the children made sense of the story the way five-year-olds do—asking questions, pointing out things they noticed, making predictions—and as she read, Danita watched, listened, and set out to learn all she could about them as language users, thinkers, and knowers-of-things.

"Boys and girls," she says, standing the book on the shelf next to her, "Grace Lin wrote and illustrated this book about planting a garden of Chinese vegetables because it's something she knows. That's what writers and illustrators do: they write and draw about what they know. In this classroom this year, you're going to get to tell and draw and write about things that you know, too. As we were reading Grace Lin's story, I got thinking about something we used to do in my house when I was a girl, but my story isn't about planting a garden."

She leans in close to the children, her brown eyes dancing from one to another as if to say, "You won't want to miss this!" And she begins.

"In our house, Saturday morning was cleaning day. My mother would get up and go into the kitchen and have her tea while my brother and sisters and I were still asleep. Then she'd turn on the record player. We didn't have CDs when I was little, we had records. They were round like CDs, only black and much bigger"—she rounds her hands to show the size—"and you'd pile them, one on top of the other, and this rod would hold them up in the air, and one would drop down, and it would play. When it was finished, the next one would drop down and it would play . . . I'll show you a record player sometime. Well, my mother would put on a stack of records of her favorite singers—Barbra Streisand, Natalie Cole, Chaka Khan—and when we heard the music, we knew: time to clean the house! She'd turn the music up loud and start cleaning the living room, and my brother and sisters and I would get out of bed and go into the kitchen and have our breakfast, and then we would have to start cleaning our rooms—picking up our clothes, putting all our toys away.

"My job was to take the sheets off all the beds, sort the laundry, and put it in piles in front of the washing machine. That meant going down three flights of stairs, because the washing machine was in the basement and we didn't have laundry baskets, so I'd just carry that big pile of dirty clothes down in my arms. A few things always dropped on the way, so I'd have to go back up all those stairs and pick up all the things I'd dropped. Sometimes my brother and I would start playing, throwing dirty socks and dirty underwear at each other, and my mom would yell from the living room, 'Stop foolin' around!'

"And now in my house we do the same thing, only I put on 1090 AM—WILD. It has Motown music, you know, oldies but goodies! I get up early and I have my coffee, then I put the radio on and Aja, Che, and AJ, they know what that music means. AJ is usually the first one into the kitchen, and he says, 'Oh man, it's time to clean again?' and pretty soon he's cleaning his room and taking the sheets off his bed . . ."

Two girls who, moments earlier, were playing with some loose threads in the rug are absorbed in Danita's story. A boy who had bounced his way through *The Ugly Vegetables* is sitting, looking up at her. There is a stillness as she weaves her story masterfully, every ounce of her being assuring them that in this classroom, telling our stories is what we do and that this is a safe place to do it.

Danita is teaching writing. She is teaching her kindergartners that we all have stories to tell, that we tell stories about what we know, and that the most engaging stories are often about ordinary, everyday things. She is surrounding them with the sound and the language of story through the books she reads aloud and the stories she tells, language they'll be able to draw on as they craft their own stories on paper. She is setting the stage for the writers in this classroom to be known to each other and to themselves. And she does it by first making herself known to them.

In this kindergarten, and in so many kindergartens across Boston and beyond, writing begins with the oral telling of stories.

Why Oral Stories First

Seven years ago, as we sat down to plan our work with the kindergarten teachers in Boston, we spent time thinking about how we wanted to begin writing with young children. We had no doubt kindergartners could and would write; we had both worked with enough young children over the years to know that they have things to say and would readily say them in pictures and in words. But we also knew what was involved in setting up an environment where five- and six-year-olds work independently, and we knew what could happen when structures that support learners and their work are not in place. We'd seen, too many times, what happens when children are expected to work for too long, too soon, independently:

They head off to the tables, excited about telling their stories on paper, and sit right down and begin drawing. Some even write letters and words. There's a soft hum in the room and you think, *This* is really nice, so you sit down next to a child to ask about his story, but before long you feel a tug on your sleeve and you turn and a child is standing there holding up her booklet as proud as can be, saying, "I'm done!" She's filled every page with drawings all done in purple and can't wait to show it to you, and behind her comes another, and another—a line is forming with kids announcing, "I'm done!" Out of the corner of your eye you catch a glimpse of a child coloring over his gorgeous picture with black crayon swirls, and you want to go and find out what his story is about, but you can't because you have all these kids coming up to you and the noise level is rising and you know you've got to do something because writing time is unraveling in front of your eyes.

Any teacher of writing, it seems, has experienced a moment like that. It can happen for many reasons. One could be that we begin with our vision of the end, rather than building toward it over time. We knew, for example, when we began this project that we were headed toward an hour-long workshop where children would meet for a quick lesson, work independently for thirty to forty minutes, and come together to share, but experience had taught us that to begin there would be problematic. We knew that for young children to work independently on their writing, they'd need to know what we mean by composing on paper, they'd need to be familiar with the tools we were asking them to use, and they'd need to know what we expect of them when they go off on their own to work. If children haven't had opportunities to use crayons and colored pencils or other writing tools, if they haven't learned how to take things out and put them away just the way they've found them, if they haven't had opportunities to share materials with others, we could be setting them—and ourselves—up for a scene like the one described above.

So as we thought about how to begin writing with classrooms of twenty-plus kindergartners, we asked ourselves, "What *can* they do when they come to school?"

It was Donald Graves who taught us to ask this question. It was he who had looked at the children in Atkinson, New Hampshire, back in 1978 and noticed, first, what they *could* do. We had taken on this way of looking ever since and had placed it at the heart of our work. So in response to our question, "What *can* they do?" we decided, they can tell stories. "Human beings are natural story-tellers," Peter Johnston tells us. "We constantly tell stories about ourselves to others and to ourselves, and the stories shape who we think we are" (2004, 30). In a random aisle in the grocery store, in the faculty room at school, on a porch where we're gathered with friends, stories abound.

Stories abound in kindergarten classrooms—if we make room for them. A little girl arrives on the first day bubbling with the events of her first ride on a school bus. A boy unpacks his lunch box and tells how, when his dad takes him to school in the morning, they go to Stop & Shop to buy Lunchables. Another tells about his new baby sister who "cries too much." For so many children, telling stories is naturally what they do.

There are some children, of course, who don't come to school telling stories. It may be that they haven't been invited into conversations about what matters to them, haven't been read to, haven't been told stories. Some may have a physiological or psychological reason why talk is hard, and they may need extra support. Some, it seems, don't know that they have something to say. All it usually takes is for us to notice the colorful barrettes in their hair or the sneakers with an orange stripe or the bandage on their knee. "Look at this necklace you're wearing" brings forth a story about a grand-mother who sent it from Colombia because in her country "it means good luck, and if you wear it, you have good luck." We notice the tattoo on the back of a child's hand and he tells us, "My brother got tattoos for his birthday. You put it in the water and then you put it on your hand and you have to hold it." We read *City Signs* by Zoran Milich, a wordless picture book filled with photographs of scenes of the city, and when we get to the page with the front windows of the ice-cream and pizza shops, the talk bubbles out:

"Yum! Pizza!"

"He's putting it in the thing to cook—I do that at Nick's!"

"I don't like the pepperonis, but my mom does, so I take them off and she eats them."

"Once I got ice cream and it fell off, right on my shoe!"

There's laughter. There's a natural exchange of words. And we notice that the child who hasn't yet spoken is talking to the boy next to him. Through their talk, children let us into their worlds, so we listen, pay attention, and continue to carve out space where they can talk their way into stories in the company of an audience who values what they have to say.

Because storytelling, or, more basically, talking, is what just about all children can do when they come to school, we decided to start there. We didn't know exactly what it would look like and we had no idea where it would lead us, but it made sense because it brought us back to that which is most essential: the child.

Receiving the Story

Across the city from Danita, and through the tunnel into East Boston, Marina Miranda is teaching writing, too. In a gentle, calming voice she is telling her students a story about growing up in the Dominican Republic. As she speaks, she watches for understanding in their eyes.

"When it rained in Santo Domingo, it was such a treat. All the kids in the neighborhood, we would put on our bathing suits and go out to find the best water spouts—you know," she says, looking out the window, pointing, "those things on the top of the house that catch the water? What's the word here—gutters! In Santo Domingo they weren't as fancy as they are here. Sometimes it was pieces of metal that would channel the water to come out at a certain spot, and we would look for the best ones in the neighborhood, the ones that were the biggest, like waterfalls, and we would just stand under those downspouts of water and we'd let the rain come over us. Sometimes we'd sing,

> "'*Que llueva, Que llueva*
> *La bruja está en la cueva . . .*'"

Children chime in and sing along with her.

"And then, in front of the house we had a *galleria*, like a small deck or porch, and when it rained, there was a spot where the water collected, like a pool because the porch was tipped, like this"—she slants her forearm and hand—"and we'd slide down the porch into that pool of water. We would be so happy it was raining! And when it rained, my mother would make the best *sancocho de habichuelas*—that's what we call bean soup. When it rained, it was the best time to have soup."

The boys and girls on the rug in front of her are captivated. Some recognize what Marina is talking about because they've lived in her country or one like it. Others don't understand some words because she is telling the story in English and all but three speak a language other than English at home. When she sees confusion on a child's face, she clarifies with the word in Spanish so they'll understand. When she is finished, she says, "That story I read to you this morning about Elizabeti and her doll, that's something that

Stephanie Stuve-Bodeen knows. And the story about playing in the rain in Santo Domingo—that's one that I know. I wonder who wants to tell a story about something you know."

One, then two, then three hands go up. Marina reaches for the basket with the clothespins clipped around the edge—each with one child's name on it—and she looks from the clothespins to the children.

"Let's see," she says, her voice almost singing out the names of those who haven't yet told a story. "We have Melanie, Devianna, Kelvin, Carlos . . ." Carlos's hand shoots up when he hears his name and Marina says, "Carlos, you have a story you want to tell us?" He jumps up and plops himself on the chair, facing the children.

"Can you find your name?" she asks, holding the basket out to him.

"Found it! Found it!" he says, pinching the clothespin and dropping it into the basket. Marina places the basket back under the easel.

The children on the rug ready themselves with a few reminders from Marina about how to listen when someone else is telling a story. This is, after all, only the second week, the seventh day of school.

"What is your story about, Carlos?" Marina asks. Carlos gets down off the chair, walks over to the easel where Marina has placed *Elizabeti's Doll* (1998), and he opens it to the picture of the baby on the title page.

"This one. He livel," he says.

"The baby is little, isn't he," Marina says gently back to him. Thinking that the picture must remind him of something, she asks, "Do you have a little baby at your house?"

"No. I have two babies."

"You have *two* babies!" she says, surprised, edging in closer to him.

"One ih Yenne-fer and one ih Ongola."

"Jennifer and Angela!" Marina repeats, giving back his words.

"Yeah. Two babies."

Marina sits facing Carlos, her chair a little lower to the ground than his. That is purposeful: she wants him (and all the other storytellers of the class) to have the seat of honor when they tell their stories. He is facing forward, reveling in the moment. (See Figure 1.1.)

"Are they little babies? At home?" Marina prods, cradling her arms as though holding a baby.

"No," Carlos says. "Yenne-fer and Ongola ah kool."

"Jennifer and Angela are at school?"

He fast-forwards into an explanation of how they were going somewhere together—maybe walking to school—"and Yenne-fer and Ongola go around and around and they play in the rain" (most likely a reference to Marina's story). Then he ends with "I got a kooter and I got a bike."

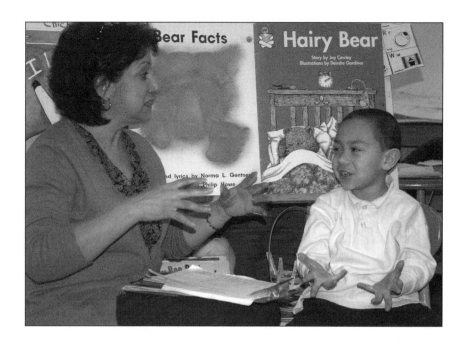

"So you have a scooter and a bike?" Marina says, switching gears along with him.

"Yeah. My dad give me my bike."

His ideas are flowing—it's as though he's just figured out what this storytelling time is for, and Marina is working really hard to stay with him.

"So Carlos," she says, "you have a lot of stories, don't you! You were telling us about Jennifer and Angela, and now you're telling us that you have a bike and a scooter."

"My dad gave it to my sister," he says excitedly.

"He gave the bike to your sister?" Marina asks, puzzled.

"He doesn't show it to me," Carlos says, working hard to put the story in words. Marina gives back his words as best she can with each new piece of information, but it's not easy. The story seems confusing, the way he tells it, yet clearly he has something to say. Marina wants to understand how he got this bike, and she also wants him to choose *one* topic so that she might help him shape it into a story.

"So it sounds like you have two stories. Which one are you going to tell us? Are you going to tell us the story of Jennifer and Angela, or are you going to tell us about your bike?" she asks.

"My bike," Carlos says. "And my kooter!"

"Okay," Marina says.

It has taken eighty seconds to find the direction for the story, which, when you're in it, can feel like a very long time. Actually, a lot happened there. Marina learned things about Carlos that she didn't know: there are two little people in his life who matter to him, he is willing to talk and share about himself, and he needs support as an English language user. In less than a minute and a half she has been instructed by him, and this data will inform how she continues this storytelling session as well as how she designs next instruction for him. What may be most important is how Marina allowed Carlos the time and provided the support he needed to find his way into his story.

Marina continues, trying to make sense of what Carlos has told her. "So your father gave your bike to your sister—he didn't show it to you. Did he buy one bike for you and your sister? One bike to share?"

"No," Carlos says. "My sister have a bike," and Marina asks if his sister showed him how to ride the bike.

"I know how to ride the bike!" he says indignantly, and then adds, "My kooter can go faster!"

His talk is fast, and to us, the story seems to jump from here to there, but the children understand. They call out from the rug, "Is it a motor scooter?" and "I got a scooter, too," and Carlos responds to them.

Attempting to keep the story moving forward, Marina interjects, "Is the scooter the kind that you put one foot on the scooter and one foot . . . ," but before she gets her whole question out, Carlos cuts in.

"No, it's two feet. Like this!" He jumps down from the chair, turns sideways, and plants one foot on the floor. Lifting the other foot, he says, "You pull it back and back and back . . . ," and each time he says "back," he pushes off with his free foot, the way you do on a scooter.

"Oh yes, I see," Marina says seriously while at the same time delighting in his wholehearted attempt to help us understand.

He keeps going, telling us, "I was playing by myself, then my sister, she was riding her bike, then we was playing a race," and Marina takes all of the pieces in, trying to make meaning for herself as well as for Carlos and all the children.

"So let me see if I understand Carlos's story," Marina says, looking at the children. Then, turning to Carlos she says, "And Carlos, you tell me if I've got this right, okay?"

He nods.

"Your father got you a bicycle. And your sister had a bicycle, too. And you know how to ride your bicycle. Sometimes you ride it by yourself, and sometimes you ride with your sister and you have a race. Tell me, does your bicycle have the training wheels, those little wheels on the back, you know, those little wheels to hold it . . ."

Carlos jumps in. "No."

"No training wheels?"

"No. I don't have the wheel. You hold it like this"—he gestures holding both hands on the handlebars—"and then you lift the thing." He raises one foot up and cradles it with both hands, pushing his foot into his hands.

"The pedal?" Marina asks. "You lift the pedal?"

Carlos says, "Yeah." Then, as though exhausted of all his words, he says, "And you have to come to my house if you want to see it."

"You know what," Marina says, her eyes smiling at him, "we can not come to your house to see your bicycle, but you can draw a picture of it and we can see it. Maybe you can show us what color it is . . ."

"It's orange!" he exclaims.

"It's orange, ooh . . ."

Feeling the need to bring the session to a close, Marina says, "Thank you for sharing that story about your orange bike, Carlos. And right here, on this chart," she says, taking her clipboard with her conference notes, "right next to your name, I'm going to write that you told a story about your bike and your scooter." She points to where she's writing so they all can see, and then, specifically to Carlos, she says, "I'm going to say that you have lots of other stories to tell, too. I love when I hear you boys and girls tell stories about what you do at home, because I didn't know these things, and now I know, now we all know, Carlos, that you have a bicycle and a scooter, and that your sister has a bicycle, too, and sometimes you race with her, and sometimes you ride the bike by yourself near your house."

"*Si!*" Carlos says, hopping down from the chair. "I can speak Spanish!"

It takes eleven minutes from start to finish for Carlos to share his story, and in the end Marina is still left with questions. But what matters is that Carlos has learned that he has something to say and that others want to hear it. Most likely, he'll want to do it again.

Why It's Important for Children to Tell Their Stories

You may be thinking, This is what we do during a one-to-one writing conference in the writing workshop, so why don't they just tell their stories on paper? After all, when children put their marks on paper, they show us a lot about who they are and what they know. Why is it so important for them to tell their stories orally?

First, because inviting children to talk about themselves and about what they know honors them for who they are. They don't need a picture. They don't need to know how to write letters. They don't need a spectacular event to share. They are valued for themselves, for using the words they have to say what they know. Marina encouraged them to tell what they know by intentionally telling a story on a topic that was very different from the one she had just read to them. The connection she made between the two stories had to do with how writers work, rather than content. The message she was giving her students was this: here's someone telling a story about something she knows; I have a story about something I know, too. It is very important that we not tell a story on the same topic as the topic in the book we just read. If, after having read *Elizabeti's Doll*, Marina had told a story about a doll, the children would have gotten the message that we listen to a story about dolls and we tell a story about dolls. And for sure, we'd get a *lot* of doll stories. Instead, the message was, This writer/illustrator knows things, this story-teller knows things, and you do, too. Most likely, our stories will all be different. (In Chapter 8, Lesson: Noticing Ideas for Writing, this idea is addressed again.)

Second, by telling stories orally, members of the class immediately become known to each other. Certainly children learn about each other through their writing, but it happens sooner through the oral telling. This self-revelation helps build a climate of respect and a culture where each member is known as "one who . . ." Carlos has told a story, but more than that, he has been introduced to his class-mates as "the one who knows about riding his bike and his scooter" and he will hold that place, that expertise, for a long time. As more children tell stories, the class comes to know John as the expert at Game Boy, Angelica as one who loves to wear clothes with flowers on them, and Tracy as one who went to visit her friends who "live in the Haitian world." Being known and having a place among members of a learning community help individuals become known to themselves. It is quite possible that some children will learn for the first time that they have something to say.

Third, telling stories acknowledges talk as having an essential place at the core of writing. According to Vygotsky (1978), talk is one of the basic symbol systems, along with gestures and drawing, that children use to communicate before they ever put words on paper. These young "symbol weavers"—to borrow Dyson's term—move fluidly among these systems as they make meaning (1986, 381). Although talking and telling stories is what young children do natu-rally, carving out a time for formal storytelling gives them an oppor-tunity to tell a story with support. Many times, children make public their thinking about a particular topic for the first time right there in the storytelling chair. Through talk, they "unfold" their thinking for an audience that needs to understand, and in doing so, they come to understand it better, themselves. According to Elena Bodrova and Deborah Leong (1996), this is because "When children become capable of thinking as they talk, speech actually becomes a tool for understanding, clarifying, and focusing what is in one's mind" (98).

Fourth, telling stories orally allows children to learn about elements of craft before they ever put them on paper. As they craft stories with their words, they begin to understand the following:

Writers are specific in their information. Marina pushes Carlos for more information and then for more *specific* information by asking questions when she doesn't understand or when she needs clarifica-tion. In this way she is modeling for all of the students that story-tellers use specific, detailed information because it is through the specifics that listeners come to know and understand.

Order and organization are important in that they allow listeners, and eventually, readers, to follow a story line that makes sense. As she listened, Marina periodically told Carlos's story back in a logical order that was sometimes not exactly the order in which Carlos had said it. She didn't assume that her "reordering" of the events was right, so she'd ask, "Is that right?" By retelling the pieces in order, Marina was showing her students that it is important to organize the information so that it makes sense. She was teaching them that writers consider the readers of the text.

Audience matters. Through the audience's immediate response—body language, facial expression, clarifying information, telling back what they heard, and asking questions—the teller (writer) finds out that what is interesting to him can be interesting to others. They also learn how the listeners (readers) heard their story and begin to learn that they have to include certain information if they want their readers to understand.

Talk can help you think your way into the story. When children have the chance to talk through their stories before they sit down to work, they tend to have a clear sense of how to organize that information on paper. We want to teach children how to use talk as a strategy for figuring out what they want to write and how to write it.

Composing involves revising. The story Carlos started out telling and the way the story ended up are very different, yet the two images seemed to lead naturally into the other. Carlos revised in the following ways:

- adding information (He does this throughout.)
- clarifying (First he said that his dad got him a bike, then that he gave it to his sister, and then that his dad didn't show it to him. Although we still don't fully understand, he was working to clarify with each new bit of information.)
- changing the focus (He began by talking about his sisters, then moved to talking about his bike and scooter.)

Carlos had the opportunity to change his focus and find his way into his story because he had someone listening closely, wanting to understand, and modeling how he could use his words to shape his story. Over time, Carlos and the other children will learn how to be both teller and listener, writer and reader, making changes based on their own rereading of their texts.

We say the children are "learning" these elements of craft, but really we're putting forth, implicitly, a lot of information about craft that we hope they actually will learn throughout the year. Once children begin telling their stories on paper, we'll get a glimpse of what they actually are learning, and from that, we'll find out what we need to teach more explicitly. At this point we are planting seeds for what they will be doing as composers of written text.

A Vision for Telling Stories on Paper

In a classroom at the western edge of Boston, Pat Kelliher and her twenty kindergartners sit listening to Trayshawn, who commands his peers' attention with his story of how he gets on the city bus at Dudley Square and rides across town to Allston. He tells about how his aunt takes him and his brother to the bus and how when they get to the Jackson Mann, they get off the bus and a lady crosses them. Hands go up when he finishes. He leads the response as his classmates tell him what they understand.

"I understand you ride the MBTA bus to school," Aine says.

Trayshawn nods and says, "Alan?"

"I understand that your aunt takes you to the bus," Alan tells him.

"Yeah," Trayshawn says. "She buys us a doughnut."

"Your aunt buys you a doughnut when she takes you to the bus?" Pat asks, picking up on the new information.

"Just sometimes if we have time," Trayshawn fills in, and then he calls on Jimmy.

"I understand that the lady crosses you," Jimmy says.

Trayshawn nods. "Shakila?"

"Does the lady wear a orange thingy?" Shakila asks.

"No," Trayshawn says.

"What do you mean, an orange thingy, Shakila?" Pat asks, picking up on something that needs clarification for all of them, even Shakila.

"Like, when you cross the people," she says, pointing across her chest.

"Do you mean one of those orange vests that the crossing guards wear?" Pat asks. Shakila nods. "A reflective vest, that's what that's called," Pat says, and then she turns to Trayshawn. "Do you understand what Shakila is asking?" He shakes his head. "She wants to know if the lady who crosses you is a person whose job it is to stop the traffic so the people can cross."

"No, she's on the bus," Trayshawn says.

"Oh, you mean the lady is someone who rides the bus just like you do?"

Trayshawn nods, and says while pointing, "She goes that way, and me and my brother go that way to the school."

"So she makes sure you get across the street okay? That's nice of her." Pat turns to the children on the rug and continues. "So Shakila, I'm wondering if you asked Trayshawn that question because you've seen someone do that before. Is there someone on your bus who gets out at each stop to cross the children?"

"At my other school," Shakila says. "She holds her hand like this"—she sticks her arm out as though stopping traffic—"and the cars stop."

"So you asked Trayshawn that question because you wanted to find out if the lady on his bus had the same job as the person at your other school?" Shakila nods. "And Trayshawn's answer helped us understand how the lady on his bus is different from the person at your other school, didn't it?

"Boys and girls," Pat says, looking at the rest of the children, "I noticed that Shakila didn't just tell Trayshawn something she understood about his story—she asked a question. She wasn't sure about something in his story and she wanted to understand. So she asked a question. Now we know two ways that we can respond to the person telling the story. One way is to say what you understand, the way Alan and Aine and Jimmy did, and another way is to ask a question if you're not sure about something, or you need more information, the way Shakila did."

Forty years ago, James Britton advised that "many of the problems of the infant and junior schools would be solved if we could have more adults or older children to engage in talk, for it is above all talk with an understanding older person that is wanted, talk that arises directly out of shared activity in and around the classroom" (1967, xiii). The need for talk with "an understanding older person" is needed as much today, if not more so, and the storytelling session provides one formal structure within which that can happen. In this interaction with Trayshawn, Pat doesn't lead the storytelling session or the response to it as Danita and Marina did, because by now the children know the routine, yet she is an active participant who takes seriously her role as teacher. She listens, pushes for more information, clarifies so the listeners understand, and models how, when you respond to the storyteller, you do so because you genuinely have something to say. By providing opportunities for her students to make meaning and by giving language to what they do, she is doing what Britton advises, "patiently exercising the special kind of leadership [needed] to build a talking community" (xii). She is also helping them see possibilities as writers.

Helping Children to See Possibilities

Holding a booklet like those the children will eventually write in, Pat brings the share session to a close by planting a seed for what is to come over the weeks and months ahead.

"So, Trayshawn," she says, "if the story you just told us was in a book, it might go like this:

"Here on the front, there would be a title—just like on Charlotte Voake's book it says *Ginger*. Maybe your title would be here at the top, maybe it would be in the middle or even down here, wherever you'd decide to put it, and somewhere here, on the cover, readers would see your name."

She opens the cover of the booklet and, proceeding through, uses his words to tell back his story, one part on each page.

"On this first page, you'd tell the first part of the story. What was the first part of your story?" she asks, looking like she's trying to remember, then quickly answers her own question. "Oh, this is about going with your aunt to get the MBTA bus." Then, lowering her voice a few decibels she says in her fun-loving way, "That's because you missed the school bus, isn't it?" Pat knows that Trayshawn rides the MBTA bus because he's too late for the school bus almost every morning, and she engages playfully with him. But that's not part of the story Trayshawn has chosen to tell.

"So here," she says, pointing to the space for an illustration, "maybe there'll be a picture of you going to Dudley to catch the bus, or maybe of you and your brother and your auntie Cora walking . . . Does your aunt drive you to the T stop or do you walk?"

"We drive," he says.

"So maybe it would be a picture of you and your brother and your aunt, driving there. Then here"—she points to the space below—"maybe there will be some words. Who knows, maybe it'll say something like, 'I go to Dudley to catch the bus,' just the way you said it to us."

She flips the page and continues, as though retelling a well-known story from memory. "This next part is about getting a doughnut, so we'd probably see a picture of that. Maybe the words would say, 'Sometimes, if we're not late, my auntie Cora buys us a doughnut,' just the way you said it to us."

She moves the story along, recapping each part, modeling how each page is about a different part, but she doesn't leave time for Trayshawn to explain what he plans to put on each page because she isn't going to give him the booklet right now. Her intent is to show the children a possibility, one of many, of how these stories they tell with words might be told differently—more permanently—later on. She's setting the stage for what is to come, elevating the work they're doing by using their words to help them see how one day, a story they tell could become a book like those on the bookshelves next to them.

When the story is told through, Pat closes the booklet and looks at Trayshawn. There are a few seconds of stillness, the way it is when you've just finished a really good book. And they have. Storytelling is taking on a new meaning. They're beginning to see that telling stories is part of something bigger.

Danita, Marina, and Pat are teaching writing, their students are "writing" their stories, and no one is using pencil, crayon, or paper—yet. By helping them deepen their ability to use words to say what matters while putting it in a context of something much bigger, we're giving them a vision for how they might put their thinking and their words on paper when they actually sit down to write.

In her reflection at the end of her yearlong participation in the Writing in Kindergarten project, Pat wrote about storytelling as one of the most important aspects of writing. "Their ability to learn how to tell a story orally has a direct influence on the children's ability to write a story later. It was including those details in telling a story [orally] that enabled all my kids to be successful writers." During our last session of the year, Pat told her colleagues, "Here's what I've learned: the more detail in the telling, the more detail in their drawings; the more detail in their drawings, the more detail in the words when they write their stories" (2001, written and oral communication). We haven't systematically collected and analyzed the data to prove this, but we have the observations of this thirty-five-year veteran kindergarten teacher and those of many other thoughtful, wise teachers. And we value that.

When Teachers Tell Stories with Their Students

So, what do teachers need in order to tell stories with their students?

First, they need to believe in the place for oral storytelling in the teaching of writing, and to carve out a time and a place where it can happen. If we really believe that the oral telling of stories has a place in the context of our writing instruction, then we make time for it every day. On the first day of school, what we call writer's workshop might be a combination of what Danita and Marina did: read aloud as children interact with the story, tell a story of our own, and ask a child to tell a story of his or her own. This usually takes somewhere between thirty-five and forty minutes. On the next day, the teacher may not tell her story, but instead, after the read-aloud, might ask one or two children to come up and tell their stories. As they do, she listens for opportunities to model how these stories they say with words might sound as a book, as Pat did with Trayshawn.

The forty-or-so minutes that we call writer's workshop at the beginning of the school year looks very different from a typical writer's workshop. Mostly, the composing is oral and the group works together as a whole. We surround children with the language of story through read-alouds, by inviting them to tell stories and listen to those of their peers, and by modeling how to tell stories on paper (see Introducing the Drawing & Writing Book in Chapter 2). On a daily basis we continue this language support through more read-alouds, interactive writing lessons (see McCarrier, Pinnell, and Fountas 2000), conversations between teacher and student, and by creating opportunities for children to talk with each other as they play and work together.

Eventually—and by *eventually* we mean maybe the second week, maybe the third week, whenever the teacher deems it appropriate— the children begin telling their stories in their Drawing & Writing Books (see Appendix B for sample teacher plans). Over time, writing no longer begins with a formal storytelling session because the oral telling takes place during one-to-one writing conferences. What we want to make clear is that although the format for storytelling changes over time, what doesn't change is that we build in time for it every day.

Second, teachers need to know that they have stories. When we tell teachers that we want them to use their own stories as models, it's not uncommon for them to say, "But I don't have stories" or

"What would I tell?" or "That's the most difficult part for me—coming up with a story to tell my students." That usually reflects a perception of storytelling as a crafted performance—the kind that people sometimes do for a living. Yet once we model for the teachers how we tell one of our stories to children, they see the ordinariness of it and realize that not only do they have stories but they tell them to their students all the time.

As teachers become aware that the everyday stories they tell in passing are actually stories they could tell in this context, they begin to listen for them and collect them. Danita Kelley-Brewster has a strip of chart paper on the wall next to where she sits at the meeting area, at the top of which she has written "Stories to Tell . . ."

"I'll be in the middle of a story" she explains, "and I think of something I want to tell them and I'll say to the kids, 'I just thought of another story I want to tell you sometime,' and I jot it down right then." Not only is she making it easy for herself to find her stories when she needs them, but she's modeling for her students that writers are always seeing possible stories and that they usually have a place to collect those ideas.

Third, when choosing a story to tell students, we want one that is accessible to them. By that we mean one they will be able to relate to, one that matters to us, one that as they hear it, causes them to say, Hey, I could do that. We sometimes ask ourselves questions such as these when thinking of stories to tell our students:

- What is a recent happening that I've told others about?
- What's an ordinary, everyday happening from my childhood?
- What personal stories do I tell my own children at bedtime?
- What stories of my childhood do I keep coming back to, the ones that cause people to say, "Tell the one about . . ."?
- What's a moment, a seemingly simple happening, that I hold dear?
- Who do I know and care about and what stories do I have about him or her?

It is by beginning with ordinary, everyday topics that we make it possible for all of our students to feel they can enter in.

Sometimes we mess up, too. We choose a story that, although appropriate to tell young children, has a more sophisticated meaning that isn't accessible to them. In other words, what makes a story powerful may be the poignancy that is so appreciated by adults but not necessarily understood by children. Unfortunately, we don't usually find that out until we're in the middle of the telling! In those cases, we make adjustments along the way so the children can connect to it, or maybe put it aside and choose another story.

We've found that it's not uncommon for a child to sit in the chair and say, "Once upon a time . . ." and proceed to tell about a dragon or a princess, or retell a Yu-Gi-Oh adventure in which they are a main character. We honor their story, of course, listening, taking them seriously, and, most important, expecting their story to make sense. Yet, as they listen to the stories we tell and as they continue to listen to classmates tell theirs, we help them see that it's easier to tell a story in which they can reveal their inner thoughts and feelings when it's based on something they know firsthand.

It's also not uncommon for children to be hesitant because they don't have access to the words they need, especially when English is not their first language. Marelen, a kindergartner, told about going to Kmart and Stop & Shop on Father's Day "to get the things for a cookout." When I asked her what she ate at the cookout, she hesitated, then couldn't seem to find the words. I saw quickly that it wasn't that she couldn't remember, but rather that she knew the words only in Spanish—tortillas, carne, arroz, and frijoles—and that the person who asked her—me—did not speak her language. Unlike Marina, who could fill in the Spanish word for her students, I could not. What happened was what usually happens: the other children joined in with explanations and translations. This incident taught us that Marelen—and other English language learners like her—needs us to welcome her attempts at using her new language and to try to understand her. By listening closely and really wanting to know, we have an opportunity to introduce them first to themselves, and then to each other. Marelen came to see herself as a teller of stories, as a knower of things that many of us didn't know.

Children learn to tell stories that are personally significant, include specific details that evoke emotion, and reveal feelings when they hear stories that do those things. The stories that Danita and Marina told their students were effective because the topics were accessible to young children: they were about ordinary, everyday things, and they were told with specific information that revealed the tellers and their feelings. If we begin by telling students about our trip to Cancun or breaking a leg, children think they need an extraordinary event to have a story to share. We want to tell about ordinary things so that as students listen, they'll say to themselves, I have a story like that, too.

Despite how ordinary we make our stories, sometimes teachers say, "My students really don't have any experiences outside of school. They go to day care before and after school, and at night they watch TV, then go to bed. They don't go to the park. They don't ride bikes." So one thing we need to do is consider the environment in which the storytelling and writing take place. What experiences are we providing in the classroom that could spark topics for writing? How do we design our yearly curriculum so that children are exploring and discovering and playing and engaging with each other? How do we model that the way we spend our time together might be worth writing about? When children spend time in classrooms where they're actively engaged in learning, they naturally write about what they do: building a tower with blocks, playing at housekeeping, hatching chicks, observing tadpoles, playing at the park across the street, watching the construction workers dig up the pavement to repair the road in front of the school. These school-related happenings tend to find their way into children's stories no matter what their experiences outside of school.

Finally, we must believe that every single one of our students has something to say, and we must believe in our ability to help them find it and say it. Not all children are going to come to school telling stories the way Trayshawn did. In fact, early in the school year Raquan, who was waving his hand furiously to tell a story, sat in the storytelling chair, looked self-consciously down at the floor, and said, "Ice cream." I had just told my own childhood story about the ice-cream man and it seemed that he was doing what children sometimes do when they don't think they have stories: try on someone else's. Right away I knew he would need help finding a story of his own, but first I wanted to acknowledge what he brought to the storytelling chair.

I responded, "So, Raquan, you have an ice-cream story, too! Tell us your story." I looked at him, eager to hear what he had to say. He stared out over the heads of the boys and girls and then at his feet, unsure about what to do.

"Tell us about getting ice cream," I said eagerly after what seemed like an unusually long eight seconds.

"My dad," he responded.

"Oh," I said, trying to understand, "so is *your* story about *you* and *your* dad getting ice cream?" He shook his head. Three seconds passed, then four, five, seven. "Tell us about your dad," I broke in, thinking he might speak more easily if I simplified his topic.

"My dad work," he said, not making eye contact with anyone.

"Oh, your dad is at work?" I asked. He nodded. "What else do you want to tell us about your dad?" I prodded.

He looked down; the room was silent.

"What does your dad do at work—do you know?"

"My mom home," he said. I could see that Raquan had something he wanted to say, but it seemed he needed help finding the words and needed help building his story around his words. So I used his words to elicit more of his story: "So let's see, there's you and your dad and your mom . . ." and I waited. Each time he added another little bit of information, I'd give back his words, piecing them together to form a whole. "There's you and your dad and your mom and your little brother . . . ," I said, waiting for him to continue. But when he didn't, I got specific, while keeping the questions open-ended: "So tell us, what kinds of things do you and your mom and dad and your little brother do?"

By listening intently, giving back his words, and mostly, believing in him, Raquan's story came out. It was a simple story, seemingly created as he went along, but it was his. And it had nothing to do with ice cream.

In his book *Ireland*, Frank Delaney tells of a *Seanchai*, the last of his kind, who roams the country bringing stories to the people. In his last words the storyteller says this to his audience:

Talking, Drawing, Writing

The one joy that has kept me going in life is the fact that stories unite us. To see you as you listen to me now, as you have always listened to me, is to know this: what I can believe, you can believe. And the way we all see our story—not just as Irish people but as flesh-and-blood individuals . . . that's what we own, no matter who we are and where we come from.

That's why I spent my life as I did—because that was all I ever owned, stories. Indeed our story is finally all any of us owns. (2005, 560)

Storytelling Beyond the Classroom

It is a July morning. Twenty teachers sit crowded around a table in the library of the Curley School in Jamaica Plain, reflecting on the year they spent learning about teaching writing in kindergarten. The talk moves back and forth, and when it ebbs, Paula Cerqueira-Gonsalves, a kindergarten teacher at the Otis school in East Boston, enters in:

"The person in charge of parent outreach in my school asked me to speak at one of their breakfasts about what I was learning about writer's workshop in kindergarten. She had been asking me all year, and I kept putting her off because I don't like to speak in front of people. Finally it was the last one of the year and I thought, I know what I can do—I'll show them the wonderful books we've been reading and talk about how important it is to read to their kids at home.

"There were about twenty-five parents there, Spanish-, Portuguese-, and English-speaking. I had decided to read *Bus Route to Boston* because I figured they'd relate to a story about growing up in the city, so I get up there and start reading, and after a few pages I could see their eyes glazing over. First one, then another, I could see them falling away. So I put the book down. I didn't even finish reading, and I said, 'You know, reading aloud to your kids is important, but you don't have to have these books, because you can *tell* stories. Everybody has stories.' And then I told them mine.

"'I'm an immigrant like you. I came to this country when I was seventeen months old. My parents could speak English a little, but they couldn't read or write in English. They both got jobs at the Colonial meatpacking factory—you know, where they make Fenway Franks—and they worked opposite shifts so one of them would be home with us. My father would come home in the morning and my mother would be getting ready to leave for work, and they'd sit talking at the kitchen table—I'd hear their voices from my bedroom. We called it the coffee hour, but really it was only a few minutes.'

"I told them how my grandparents lived next door on the second floor, upstairs from my aunt, and I would go visit them, and my grandfather always had those colored Life Savers in his pocket. We'd say, '*Vovo, posso ter gama?*' which was, 'Grandpa, can I have candy?'

The word for candy (*gama*) and bed (*cama*) are close in Portuguese, and my grandfather would tease us, saying, '*Queres ir para cama?*' which was, 'Oh, you want to go to bed? You can go to bed if you want!'

"As I told my stories, something happened. You could see it. Their faces started to change, and they sat up, and I could see they were with me. When I finished, I asked if anyone wanted to tell their story, and some of them actually did. One man got up and told about coming to this country from El Salvador. A woman told about how they were really poor and didn't have books, but her grandmother, who couldn't read, lived with them, and every night before bed she and her brothers and sisters, they'd go to the grandmother and she would tell them stories.

"Then, a man I didn't know raised his hand. He said, 'I wasn't going to come today, but I'm glad I did. All this time I didn't think I could help my children with their homework and be part of what they do at school because I can't read. But now I know I can help my children because I have stories. I can tell them stories.'"

Indeed, our story is finally all any of us owns. Once our students know that, we have what we need to help them write.

Talking, Drawing, Writing

CHAPTER 2

The Drawing & Writing Book

Putting Stories on Paper in an Environment That Supports Writers and Writing

As children come to expect a time each day for sharing oral stories and see that they have stories to tell, we want them to know there is another way to tell their stories: on paper. We have prepared and made ready spiral-bound books with blank pages on which children will "write" their stories and a larger version for the teacher. We call it the Drawing & Writing Book (Figure 2.1).

The Drawing & Writing Book makes sense as a starting place for kindergartners because the format is

Inviting. It has a beautiful cover and thirty heavyweight, drawing paper–quality pages inside that beckon children to draw.

Appropriate. The pages offer space on which children can tell their stories through illustrations, which is something most if not all of them feel they can do. At the start, we invite them to work on one page; there is no expectation for a continued story or written text— at least not at first.

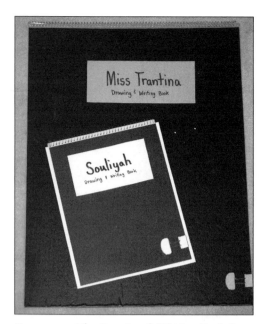

FIGURE 2.1 The Drawing & Writing Book for students and a larger version for the teacher. The clips in the lower right-hand corners are used to mark the page they are working on.

Organized. The children's work is contained all in one place, in the order in which the child does it. This collection will become a record for the teacher and for the child of the child's growth over time.

Manageable. Through one page of work we can see at a glance what children can do independently and use that information to teach them more about how to acquire a writing process:

Planning—such as how to choose topics, what to include in the drawing and where to put it on the page, and what words to write.

Writing—such as how to represent stories using words and pictures on paper.

Rewriting—such as how to reread your work from the previous day to help you remember where you left off, as well as to make decisions about what to add, change, and get rid of, and when to move on.

Editing—such as where to place periods to let readers know to stop.

We know there are children who come to school able to write letters and words, who are already reading, and would relish the opportunity to write whole books, and certainly we will offer that option to them. But we give all of our kindergartners a Drawing & Writing Book to start with because it allows us to begin on common ground. On the pages of these books children reveal their voices. They show us what they know about telling stories on paper, and they ease their way into writing words with confidence. It is a medium through which we can support children who haven't had many experiences with pencils and paper, extend children who have, and celebrate what all of them can do.

At some point during the first few weeks of school, once we've established the routine of reading aloud and telling and listening to stories, we take our enlarged, 18-by-24-inch Drawing & Writing Books and one of the caddies (a container that holds colored pencils, crayons, felt-tip pens, and so on) and model how we go from the oral to the written.

 Lesson Introducing the Drawing & Writing Book

What's going on in the classroom	• Children have been telling stories on a daily basis, for the first nine days of school.
	• They are comfortable telling and listening to stories and have a sense of how to work on their own at the tables, because that is how they work during other times of the day. It seems likely that they could work for ten minutes, independently, on a story of their own in their Drawing & Writing Books.
What's next	To show them how writers include specific details, write with voice, organize the information, and other aspects of craft, we start with a

medium that is appropriate for beginning writers: drawing. We model how to choose one part of a larger story and draw that part.

This lesson is longer than usual and is organized in two parts: Purpose and Procedures.

Materials needed

- teacher's enlarged, spiral-bound Drawing & Writing Book (18 by 24 inches)
- a Bind-it Flag Clip to mark the page
- a container with colored pencils for drawing (including multicultural pencils)
- knowledge of stories that children have told, as a reference

This is what I noticed . . .

"Since the first day of kindergarten, you've been telling stories.

"Jerrod, you told us about your cousin's kitten that you petted and fed, how you played with him and his toy mouse, and how you let him sleep on the floor right next to you.

"And Ana Marie, you told about how you went to the park with your mom but then your mom changed her mind and you went to the beach. Then afterward you went to your cousin's party, and then you came home and took a shower.

"Other people have told stories, too, like . . ." (I refer to a couple of others from a while back.) "Using words to tell a story, the way you do when you sit in the storytelling chair, is one way to tell a story. Another way to tell a story is to tell it on paper."

Let me show you what I mean . . .

Part I: Purpose for the Drawing & Writing Book

"Remember the story I told you about how on Sunday, my niece Abby came over with her new dog, Bella, and we took Bella for a walk? Well, I like that story, so I'm going to tell it in my Drawing & Writing Book. You can see that this is my Drawing & Writing Book because my name is right here, on the front," I say, referring to my enlarged book standing on the easel. I open the book to the first page.

"Inside, there are blank pages where I can draw and tell my story. And see this clip at the bottom of my page? That lets me know that this is the page I'm working on.

"So I have this big page to tell the story of Abby and Bella and me, and I'm thinking of what I want to draw. I can't really tell the whole story because that story has lots of parts and I have this one page to work on, so I'm thinking of telling about one part. ✉ Let's see," I say as I hold up one finger for each part. "There's the part about

- "Abby calling me to go for a walk with Bella;
- "how hard it was to hold Bella's leash;
- "how Bella would say hello to every dog she saw;
- "then, when she said hello to Cody, Cody bit her; and
- "now she has a sore eye and has to wear a cone and I feel sad.

"I'm trying to decide which part to tell on this page. Hmm . . ."

As I am thinking, kids call out suggestions. I acknowledge their desire to help but don't follow their suggestions, saying, "I could draw

---

✉ **Note to the Teacher**

Since our goal is to help students craft writing that includes detailed information, we begin by modeling how to do that on one part. We believe that if young writers can learn to go into depth in their telling of one part of a story, they'll be more likely to bring that level of specificity to a story that includes many parts.

---

that part . . . That's an idea . . . Actually, all of those are good ideas, but here's what I'm thinking I want to do. I want to tell a part that happened right near my house, when Bella was pulling Abby and Abby had to hold the leash tightly." I intentionally don't take their suggestions because I want to model that each writer makes decisions about how to tell his or her story. I want them to understand that this is my story and there will be decisions that I'll have to make, just as when they write their stories, there will be decisions they'll have to make.

"So let's see . . . First, I have to decide how I want my book to go. This way?" I point to the way it is standing, vertically. "Or do I want it this way?" I turn it so it's horizontal. "I think this way, horizontal, will give me more room to fit Abby, Bella, and me. Right here I'll draw Bella running," I say, using my hand to point, "and here," I say, moving my hand to another place on the page, "I'll draw Abby holding the leash while Bella is pulling her, and here, I'll draw me.

"Now, boys and girls, I've never drawn Bella before. In fact, I'm not sure I can really draw a dog, but I'm going to try my best. I'm going to close my eyes, because sometimes it helps me to first get a picture in my mind of what I want to draw."

I close my eyes, think, then begin. As I draw, I say things such as:

"Now I want to make her look like she's running, so the front legs would be bent like this . . ." I use my hands and arms to model.

"Let's see, I want it to look like Bella was pulling Abby, so I want to try to draw her looking like this . . ." I stand up and act out what it looks like to be pulled into a running position with your arm outstretched.

"So first, I'm going to draw Abby's face. And look, in this section of the caddie there are these multicultural, colored pencils. They're all different shades of brown." I lift a few out, one at a time, reading the labels. "This one is called mahogany, and this one is called cinnamon, and this one is called peach. This one is tan, and we have them so we can make people's skin look real—because skin comes in lots of different shades, doesn't it? Let's see," I wonder out loud as I scan the skin colors, "which of these shades is closest to the color of Abby's skin?" I hold the point of one against the back of my hand. "No, that's my color, and her skin is a little bit darker than mine. I think it might be this one." I take one out and shade in her face and hands.

"You know, boys and girls," I say, leaning back and squinting, taking a critical look at what I've drawn, "I'm not sure I've got the shade of her skin just right. I might have to mix in another color with it—like this one." I hold up a darker color and lay the point against what I just colored. "But I think I'll come back and do that later.

"Now, over here, behind where we were walking is the water, so, let's see, I'll need the blue pencil and the brown, because sometimes the water looks bluish and brownish and I want to make it look the way I remember it."

The children talk to me as I work: "You draw good!" and "That looks like a dog!" and "What about Abby's mouth?" I respond, "Well, thank you," and "I sure am trying," and "Oh yes, I do need to give her a mouth, don't I!" all the while keeping my focus on my illustration. I work for six or seven minutes, thinking aloud as I draw, and intentionally don't finish it in that sitting. My goal is to help the children see how to go from the picture in my mind to the picture on the paper. I also want them to see that it is important to represent the story on paper as it looks in my memory. By recalling the color of the water, by standing up to act out how to draw someone being pulled by a dog on a leash, by closing my eyes to imagine what a dog looks like when it's running, I let them know that I take this seriously and do all that I can to stay true to my story.

"Well," I say, assessing my page and then looking at the boys and girls, "I have a lot more left to do, but I'm going to leave it for now. Tomorrow I will come back, look at what I've done, and ask myself what else I want to do. As I was working on my story, you might have been thinking about the story you want to draw in your Drawing & Writing Book. I'm sure you won't be writing about Bella, because that's my story, and you have your own stories. And tomorrow, you're going to have a chance to start your story in your Drawing & Writing Book."

I hold one up. "Yours is like mine, only smaller. When you get it, you'll see your name on the front of your book, just as my name is on the front of my book." I open the cover as I talk. "Inside, yours has blank pages, too, where you'll be able to draw your story. The pages are a beautiful kind of paper special for drawing." I touch the page gently and with awe. "When you get your book, you can touch the pages and see how beautiful they feel. And in your book you'll see a clip at the bottom of your page, just as I have a clip on mine. It's there to remind you: this is the page you're working on today, and it will help you find the page easily. ✉

"Who thinks they know what they might draw in their Drawing & Writing Book?"

I ask a child to come up and tell her story. I help her tell her story, pushing for specifics as we do during storytelling.

"So of all those parts," I say, raising one finger for each part as I retell, "what part do you think you'll draw in your Drawing & Writing Book?"

She chooses the part. Then I take the book with her name on it and ask her to open it to the first page. I undo the clip and invite her to feel the page as I comment, again, on what special paper this is. I put the clip back on, saying, "I'm going to put the clip on for now; later we'll talk about how to use it. As you work in this book, you just look for the clip and that will tell you what page you're working on that day."

Then I ask her to use her hand to touch the places on the first page of her Drawing & Writing Book to show where the different parts of the drawing will go. I prompt her, asking things like, "And where will you draw that part about . . .?" or "What will be over here, behind . . .?" pushing her to include specific information. "So when we get ready to work in our Drawing & Writing Books, you know just what you're going to do!"

She goes back to her place on the rug and I ask, "Who else thinks they know what they will write about in their Drawing & Writing Book?" Another student comes up and tells his story. Taking the Drawing &

✉ **Note to the Teacher**

The clips we refer to here are Staples Bind-it Flag Clips, and we use them to mark the page the child is working on. If we don't give them a concrete way to easily find the page they're working on, they often open up to any random page and begin drawing, which makes it difficult to keep track of the order and document their growth over time. Or worse yet, they fill in every page of the book!

Over the years we have tried different systems for marking the page (thick rubber bands, numbering the pages, Bind-it Flag Clips) and we find that the combination of Bind-it Flag Clips and numbering the pages works best. (See Figure 2.2 in the color insert.) We like the Staples Bind-it Flag Clips best because they are easy for young children to manipulate and provide one more way for us to color-code. Also, they come in the same four colors as the plastic bins in which the children will store their Drawing & Writing Books, and later, their folders.

Writing Book with his name on it, I ask him to use his hand to show us where he plans to put the parts of the drawing.

Part II: Procedures for Using the Drawing & Writing Book

"Boys and girls, these are beautiful books, aren't they? We want them to stay beautiful, so we have this special place to keep them." I walk over to the writing center and have them turn toward me. I show them the colored plastic file holders and explain, "If your name is written in red on the cover of the Drawing & Writing Book, it will go in the red file, right here. And if your name is written in blue, it will go in this blue file right here, just like Gabriel's. Gabriel, would you come up and show us how carefully you will place your Drawing & Writing Book in the file holder the way you think it goes?"

Gabriel comes up and places the Drawing & Writing Book in the container. (See Figure 2.3 in the color insert.) We talk about how they're arranged: all going the same way so they will be easy to find when they need them. Then I call another child, and another. Once everyone has had a chance to see and touch and place their Drawing & Writing Book in the file holder, I say, "Now, let's imagine it is time for writing. How do you think you might get your Drawing & Writing Book from the file? "Tatiani, do you remember what color your Drawing & Writing Book is?"

"Yellow!" she says, hopping up, ready to participate.

"Would you show us how you're going to find your Drawing & Writing Book, take it carefully from the yellow file, and bring it to a table where you think you might work?" As we watch her, I make comments like the following:

"Look at how she is carefully looking through all those other books to find hers.

"Look at that—the book next to hers was coming out when she lifted hers out, but she was so careful. She held that other person's Drawing & Writing Book in place so it wouldn't fall out.

"I see she is carrying that book like she really cares about it, and she's placing it on a table that she thinks will be a good spot for her to work.

"And now, Tatiani, would you pretend the music✉ has started, which means it's time to put the caddies and the Drawing & Writing Books away and come to the rug? Would you show us how you're going to do that?" We watch as she places it carefully in the file.

"So now, boys and girls, you know about the Drawing & Writing Book. You know where we keep them, how to find yours, how to treat it carefully, and where it goes when it's time to put it back. And you know that when you work on a page, you think about how to do your best work. During the rest of the day today at school, and maybe tonight before bed, and then in the morning while you're eating your breakfast with your friends here at school, you might think about your story and what part you'll tell on that first page. Because tomorrow you're going to get to work on that first page!"

This lesson illustrates one way to introduce telling stories on paper. Mostly, it is about establishing procedures, routines, and expecta-

✉ **Note to the Teacher**

In this classroom, the music is the call to clean up and come to the rug. Most often it's a CD of a playful, happy song to which the children can—and do—sing along. It makes sense because it lasts about three minutes, just enough time for children to put their things away and have a chance to move about—and even dance—before being expected to put their attention to what will take place at the rug.

FIGURE 2.4 Caddies containing tools writers need arranged in various containers.

tions that will help the independent work happen smoothly. To ask twenty five-year-olds to go off and work independently with purpose and to follow the expectations of the learning environment requires a vision of what we're asking them to do and how we expect them to do it.

They need to know what these books are for, where they're kept, how to use them, and how to treat them well. If they have had a chance to touch them, see where they go, and actually take them out and put them back before they are expected to do all those things *and* make decisions about what they'll draw on the page, they'll be more likely to do it all, independently, when the time comes. When they have the chance to watch an adult think through and model her own purpose for writing, they are more likely to approach their work purposefully.

And of course, in order to tell their stories on the pages of these books, children need tools for drawing and writing. We assume that by the time we invite children to tell their stories on paper, they will have had opportunities to use those tools and become familiar with them. Because young children usually tell their stories through drawings first, they need the best materials we can afford to give them so they can craft their stories well: colored pencils, which makes it possible for them to draw the smallest of details, which is necessary to make drawings look life-like; multicultural pencils, so they can make the skin of the people in their pictures look real; and felt-tip pens⌧, for writing letters and words, as well as for outlining and putting fine details in the drawing. In most of these kindergarten classrooms, children share the tools that are arranged in various containers called caddies that they carry from a central spot to the tables they work at each day (see Figure 2.4).

Introducing Materials to Students

The caddies (all but one) are usually empty as children arrive on the first day of school. The teachers show children the one filled caddie so they can see what it is and what it looks like when it houses the wonderful tools that writers and drawers in this classroom will be using. They may then ask the children for help opening the materials and filling the empty caddies with some basic tools: crayons (including ones for multicultural skin tones) and pencils. Over the next few weeks, teachers gradually introduce colored pencils, multicultural pencils, and felt-tip pens, and as the children explore the new materials, teachers and students build those caddies together. They decide how to organize them, how to care for them, and how to ensure that each item is in its proper place at the end of each work time. When children take part in filling each caddie, have a say in

---

⌧ **Note to the Teacher**

By felt-tip pens, we mean those like Paper Mate Flair pens. We don't use markers for writing because they can bleed through the paper and get all over tables and hands, but mostly because we have found that the children do high-quality illustrations with high-quality colored pencils (see Appendix C). Initially, we introduced the felt-tip pens because we found that when we'd make copies of children's work, their pencil markings often weren't dark enough and didn't copy well. Introducing felt-tip pens for writing text solved that problem while offering something more. The children loved writing with these "grown-up" pens, and, although they didn't color with them as we requested, some used them to outline and make precise details in their illustrations. We welcomed the way they chose to enhance their drawings, making them even more stunning than they already were.

establishing the rules for how to use them, and share them as a class, they tend to take good care of them.

Although it would have been perfectly reasonable to send the children off to work in their Drawing & Writing Books on that first day, we made a different choice. It was based on our knowledge of these children and this classroom at this point, but it was also based on how we value this work. We want these five- and six-year-olds to see that this work is worth doing, to look with anticipation toward what will be a vital part of each workday, and to feel that they can't wait to get their hands on their books.

As written, this seems like a long lesson, but the children stayed engaged. They were excited about the prospect of what was to come and enthusiastically participated in walking through the procedures. And yes, they were disappointed when we told them they weren't going to write that day, but the following day they arrived eager to begin work in their Drawing & Writing Books.

 ## Lesson Getting Started: Telling Your Story on Paper

What's going on in the classroom

- Children have been telling stories orally at the beginning of writing time.
- They have been introduced to the Drawing & Writing Books.
- They know where they are kept, how to get them, and how to return them when they're finished.
- They have seen the teacher model how she moves from an idea in her head, to choosing a part, to beginning to put it on paper through drawing.

What's next

- It's time for them to put their own ideas on paper using the Drawing & Writing Books that were introduced the day before.

Materials needed

- teacher's Drawing & Writing Book
- children's Drawing & Writing Books
- caddies with colored pencils, etc.

This is what I noticed . . .

As the children come to the rug, I have my Drawing & Writing Book open on the easel and I am continuing with my illustration from the previous day. The children ask questions and make comments, and I respond to them while continuing to work as they settle themselves in.

"What's that?" one child asks, getting up and pointing to the background. I keep working as I respond, "Those are boats. Abby and Bella and I were walking near the water and I want people who read my story to know that, so I put some boats way out in the water." Once they're all on the rug and ready, I stop drawing and turn to them.

"While I was waiting for you to come to the rug, I opened my Drawing & Writing Book to the page I worked on yesterday and I asked myself, Now, what else do I need to put in so that when people read my drawing they'll know what my story is about? I decided to put this grass here because we were walking on the sidewalk next to some grass. And I made the boats small because they were so far away. I want it to look just the way I remember it. That's important, you know, because you want readers to know what your story is about when they look at it. That means putting in the information that will help them understand. I think I'm going to put a house here because there is one on the corner, but I'll work on that later, because right now it's time for you to work in your books. In a couple of minutes, you're going to get your Drawing & Writing Books and begin your story. You'll be making decisions about your story, just as I've been making decisions about how to tell my story."

Let me show you what I mean . . .

Getting Your Drawing & Writing Book

"Remember yesterday, when we talked about the Drawing & Writing Books? Frank, do you remember how to get your Drawing & Writing Book? Would you please get it and bring it over here?"

As he takes his book from the files, I say what I notice:

- "Just like Tatiani did yesterday, Frank is looking through the books in the yellow file. It looks like he's found his.
- "I see he's taking his book out carefully.
- "Look at how he's fixing the other books so they'll be nice and neat for the next person."

Frank stands next to me with his Drawing & Writing Book.

Planning What Will Go on the Page

"Would you open your book to your first page?" He opens his book and we can see the clip. "Look, the clip is already there so you'll know the page you're working on. Frank, yesterday you told us what you planned to draw on the first page in your Drawing & Writing Book, remember? You told us . . ."

I remind him of what he had explained the previous day. "Is that still what you want to do?"

He says, "Yes" and I proceed. If he had said, "No," I'd have asked him to tell us what he wanted to write about instead, then proceed. In this way I let the children know that they are not locked in to the idea they chose the previous day. ⊠

"Put your hand on the part of this page where you'll draw the basketball hoop." I ask him to show us where the different parts of the illustration will go, and he places his hand on the page accordingly. "It seems like you're ready to get started."

Getting Started Writing

"This is what all of you boys and girls need to do as you go to your tables to work in your Drawing & Writing Books:

"Choose a Spot Where You Can Do Your Best Work. When you choose a spot, you want to make sure it's a place where you can do your best work. You might see a table where one of your friends is sitting

---

⊠ **Note to the Teacher**

Sometimes children grab on to an idea because they hear those around them coming up with ideas and they think they're supposed to have one. To hold them to a decision they may have made impulsively could put them in a position of having to spend time on something they're not invested in. We want them to know that there is room to rethink their decisions. At the same time, we watch to make sure that changing one's mind does not become a pattern that prevents them from seeing a piece of work through to the end.

---

and you think, I want to be near my friend, but then you might think, Hmm, but I can't always do my best work next to that friend. He likes to talk a lot and I can't always concentrate. That happens sometimes, so you need to make a good choice about that. You need to ask yourself, Where will I be able to do my best work? and you need to find that spot and work there."

"Plan Your Story. Just like Frank did, you'll need to think about what story you want to tell. You may have lots of parts to your story, but since you have this one page to work on, think of one part you want to tell about. Then think about what you'll draw to show that part of the story, and use your hand to plan where things will go on the page."

"Work Quietly. Writers need quiet so they can think and try to remember what they want to draw, just the way you were quiet when I was working on my story. That really helped me do my good work."

"When Writing Time Is Over, Join Us on the Rug. You probably won't be finished with what you're working on, but when you hear the music, you'll need to find a place where you can stop until tomorrow, put the writing tools in the caddies just the way they go, and then put the caddies and your Drawing & Writing Books away and come to the rug for share."

Because I can imagine possible bottlenecks, I ask a child to model where and how they will return their Drawing & Writing Books, and pose possible situations:

- "What if someone is in front of you, putting her Drawing & Writing Book away? What should you do?"
- "What if they're taking a long time and you just want to get to the rug? Can you just reach over them to put your book into the file? Why not? What else could you do?"

So, today as you write . . . "So, as I call your name, you may get your Drawing & Writing Book and I know you'll remember what to do. If you don't, I'll help you."

Writing in the Context of Classroom Expectations

We don't expect all students to incorporate the information from every mini-lesson into their writing, because children will be at different places and might not need, or be able, to incorporate the newly presented piece of information right then. This belief holds for lessons on craft and conventions and process but not for lessons that address procedures. We want all the children to incorporate the expectations in the classroom—tone, routines, and responsibilities as writers. We also realize that some children will need us to help them remember.

FIGURE 2.5 Jared works at the castle bench in the meeting area.

FIGURE 2.6 Ana-Marie works at the sketching nook.

FIGURE 2.7 Gabriel works at the sign-in table.

FIGURE 2.8 Jazmine and Eldon write at the table in the house-keeping center.

What is probably evident is that these first two lessons are situated in an environment conducive to writing. We can ask children to find a good work space because they've been talking about what makes a good work space in their classrooms since the first day of school. By *work space*, we mean the place where children sit and do their work. Sometimes they work at typical classroom tables, each one seating four or five children, but we have found that it is quieter and there are fewer distractions when teachers creatively spread the work spaces throughout the room. In Danita Kelley-Brewster's classroom in Dorchester, the castle bench at the meeting area doubles as a desk during writing time (see Figure 2.5). In Caitlin McArdle's classroom in Roxbury, the sketching nook and the sign-in table (furnished with its very own frog lamp) offer work carrels, each with room enough for one (see Figures 2.6 and 2.7), and the kitchen table in the housekeeping corner provides space enough for two children with a caddie to share (see Figure 2.8).

Although the expectations we have for children during writing time are the same expectations we have for them throughout the day, we need to make explicit how they look in this context. So as children begin writing independently, our conferences first acknowledge and reinforce the expectations of how to work:

- "Tyriq, I notice how you chose a place to work that isn't near your friend Deandre, and it seems that was a good choice, because I see that you are working hard on your drawing. Tell me about this part . . ."
- "I just watched you put that pencil in the container, Lynasia. Then you must have noticed it was upside down, so you took it out and turned it so the pencil tip won't break. You're remembering to take good care of the materials in the caddies."
- "Yanniel, I saw you open the cover of your Drawing & Writing Book—you had it lying across the table—and then you saw it was in Sana's way, and without anyone saying anything to you, you flipped the cover underneath to give Sana room for her book."

In these first days and weeks, as we are setting the tone and the expectations, we look for opportunities to pick up on the things individual children are doing, things we want all children to do to make the room run smoothly. We say neither, "Thank you for putting the pencil back," nor "I like how you . . ." Instead, we say, "I notice how . . ." or "I see you are remembering . . . ," which acknowledges behavior we expect and reinforces a way of being that will allow us to move forward in the work we want to do with them. Throughout the day as well, we look for ways to acknowledge these behaviors so that they become part of the way we all live in the classroom, not just as the children are writing.

For example, during the share at the end of an independent writing session early in the year, I acknowledge what I saw: "Let me tell you what I noticed Yanniel do with his Drawing & Writing Book today . . . He was being considerate of other writers at the table."

During a math lesson early in the year, Caitlin McArdle acknowledged how a child was carefully using the tools in the caddie, then turned that moment into a learning opportunity for the whole class. As they gathered at the rug at the end of the work time, she said, "I want to tell you what I saw Richard do . . . When we take care of the colored pencils the way Richard did during math, it means that our colored pencils will be in good condition for each other, and for when we work in our Drawing & Writing Books, too."

Basic Information We Address Early On

As we move about the room talking with children, we're paying attention to not only how they're working but what they know about how to represent their stories on paper. In other words, are they drawing a person that looks like a person? Are they putting any words on the paper? Are they making everything the same color? We're finding out what information they'll need from us to tell their stories as best they can. But we also have some basic information that we want to teach them early on, no matter what we observe. It is information that we think most children can take on with a degree of success, information that is not dependent on their knowing letters and sounds. We want them to know how to

- reread their work. Begin each writing time by rereading their drawings and words from the previous day and asking themselves questions that will help them know what to do next.
- draw. Tell a good story by giving detailed information in the pictures.
- write words. Represent the story with words using sound spelling.

We address these topics in many lessons in a variety of ways because we know that to internalize new information, learners need to hear it and see it over and over. And we use a variety of resources to do it.

Children's literature is one resource that we draw on for many of our lessons because we know that showing our students the work of professional writers and illustrators and talking about how they practice their craft will help them envision their own stories. However, from our concentrated work in kindergarten during the past seven years, *we believe more than ever that our own pieces of writing and the writing of other children, including their published pieces, are most powerful in providing them with a vision for how to approach their own writing.* In the lessons that follow, we draw on these three resources in presenting basic information that young writers need to know.

Thus far, the lessons we've presented give children a vision for how to proceed when they get their Drawing & Writing Books. We have modeled that people who draw stories decide what to draw about, plan where the information will go on the page, and try to represent, honestly, the image they are trying to portray. Basically, we're asking them to tell their stories; they have been doing it with words, and now we are asking them to do it with pictures on the page. In these early lessons that focus on procedures, routines, and expectations, we weave in information about things authors consider as they craft their stories through their drawings. Although we may mention things such as skin color and background almost incidentally, it is important information that we want our students to know, and we will make it more explicit in lessons to come.

Rereading Your Work

The following two lessons illustrate a strategy for going back and rereading work from the previous day to make decisions about what to do next. At this point, rereading will most likely mean looking at drawings; some will be looking at drawings and words. In these lessons we are once again modeling how to reread your work and are also teaching them why. We want them to know that when we write stories, we write them so our classmates can understand them, just as when we tell stories, we tell them so our classmates can understand them.

Lesson Questions to Help You as You Reread Your Work

What's going on in the classroom

- Children began work on the first page of their Drawing & Writing Books.

What's next

- They need to know how to continue with what they started.
- They need to know a strategy for rereading what they've done previously and considering what else they need to do to help the reader understand.

Materials needed

- two or three Drawing & Writing Books open to the page the students worked on
- one Drawing & Writing Book where the child may have more to add
- my Drawing & Writing Book
- a caddie

This is what I noticed . . .

"Boys and girls, yesterday you started working in your Drawing & Writing Books, and these are some things I noticed." I hold up each book as I speak, so all children can see.

"Flevor, you started writing about going to the movies. Here we see you and your dad, and here we see the movie theater, and you really tried to show that you and your dad were walking, didn't you. We can see how you made those legs bent like that so they look like you are walking!

"And remember how Imani shared her story yesterday at the end of writing time? She told us about how she and her mom were watching TV and her mom was on the bed, and Imani, you were standing on your tippy-toes so you could get the remote, right?

"And Tà-Shayla, on this page, it looks like some water here?"

"We were going to the beach!" she announces.

"Oh, I can't wait to hear more about that!

"You all worked hard in your Drawing & Writing Books yesterday, and today you'll get to work on those stories some more. I want to tell you what writers do when they go back to the work they started."

Let me show you what I mean . . .

"When you go back to your table to work, the first thing you do is open your book to the page you worked on yesterday, take a good look at your drawing, and then ask yourself a very important question: What else do I need to put in so readers will understand my story? Writers

Talking, Drawing, Writing

ask themselves that question because they want readers to understand their stories.

"Remember when I went back to my story about Abby and Bella and I added the water and some boats out in the water, and I put in this grassy part?" I point to my page as I explain. "So now I'm asking myself, What else do I need to put in my story so readers understand? I'm going to draw the house that's on the corner."

I begin drawing. The children watch.

"I won't be able to draw the whole thing because I don't have enough room, so I'll just draw part of it. That way, anyone who reads my story will know that we were walking by the water and that across the street there was a house. Even though readers won't be able to see all of it, they'll know the house is there by seeing just part of it. I want them to know what it looked like there.

"Then, I also ask myself another important question: Is there anything I need to change so readers will understand? Yesterday, I made Bella's collar brown, but I forgot—it's really rainbow colors! So today I'm going to try to change that by coloring over the brown to make it look right."

I make rainbow stripes on the collar and say as I work, "It doesn't really look right—the colors don't show up very well—but that's okay. Sometimes you mess up and it doesn't come out just the way you want but you try to fix it the best way you can. And when you go back and read your picture the way I read mine, you'll ask yourself those questions, and you'll decide what else you want to do on that page.

"Imani, let's look at your page again. Would you come up here?" She stands next to me as I say, "Yesterday when you shared, you told us a whole lot more information about watching TV with your mom, didn't you? And I asked you, 'What do you think you will put on this page so that readers will understand that you were in your mom's bedroom, and that the TV was on top of the chest?' Do you remember what you said?"

She tells what else she plans to add and I respond, "It looks like you know just what you need to do in this drawing so that readers will understand your story! Why don't you get a caddie, find a good work space, and begin."

She goes off to work; the rest of us are still on the rug. "Jahaan," I say, holding up his Drawing & Writing Book. "I'm dying to know what this story is about. Will you come up and share it?" He stands next to me as I hold up his book for all to see. "So tell us your story!" I say. (see Figure 2.9.)

"It's my birthday."

"Well, tell us about your birthday!"

Jahaan points to two stick figures. "This is me, this is my brother."

"So this is you, and here's your brother. I'm wondering, what else will be in this picture about the party?" I look at Jahaan and he thinks.

"Balloons," he says after a few seconds.

"So you had balloons at the party. Where will you put the balloons?"

He points to different spots all over the page as though thinking about this for the first time.

FIGURE 2.9 Jahaan's initial drawing about his birthday party.

"Oh, so it seems like there were *lots* of balloons . . ."

He nods. He is shy and tentative and it takes time to draw the story out, but I wait for his responses that come carefully and in a soft voice.

"What else would we see at the party?" I ask, pushing for more.

"Cake."

"Where will the cake be? Will we see it on this page?"

His eyes scan the page, as though deciding. Then he points to a spot.

"So the cake will be over here," I say, pointing to the spot where he has decided it will go. "Now, tell us, what was the cake on? Was it on a table? A shelf? The floor!"

There are giggles and the sound of a few astounded voices: "The floor!"

Jahaan looks at me surprised, then says, incensed, "On the table!"

"Can you show us where you'll draw the table?"

He points to a spot on the page, near where he said the cake would go.

"When I look at you and your brother, I'm wondering what clothes you'll be wearing. Do you remember what you wore to the party?"

Jahaan thinks, and I don't wait for him to respond. I turn to the children on the rug and say, "Boys and girls, Jahaan is doing just what writers do. He is going back to the page he started yesterday, he's remembering what the story is about, and he's thinking about what else to put in that story and what else he wants to change so that readers will understand.

"And you know what? Maybe once Jahaan puts all that information in his story—the balloons, the clothes, the table with the cake on top—he'll look at it carefully and wonder, Hmm, what else do I need to put in to help readers understand? And if he thinks of something, I'll bet he'll put it in!

"What do you say, Jahaan, are you ready to begin?" He whisks the book from my hands and I call after him, "Don't forget, find a spot where you can do your good work!"

So, today as you write . . .

"Today, boys and girls, when you sit down to write, you'll do what Imani and Jahaan just did. You'll open your Drawing & Writing Book, read the picture you worked on yesterday, and ask yourself those questions writers ask:

- "What information do I need to add to this page so readers will understand my story?
- "What do I need to change so readers will understand my story?

"And try to make your story the best that it can be."

These children went off to work independently for the second time, having observed three different writers revisit their work: me the previous day, and Imani and Jahaan today. Before the lesson, I had thought carefully about which students might provide models for what I wanted the children to do. I wanted someone who would be comfortable talking and thinking aloud in front of their peers and who probably had more to include in his or her story. Imani seemed a logical choice in that she had already verbalized, at the share meeting the previous day, what else she planned to add to her page. I figured that would serve as a reminder for her, a jumping-off point for this conversation today. Jahaan seemed like a good choice, too, because first of all, I didn't know what his story was about, so my response would be fresh and the children would see my genuine desire to understand his work. Second, it looked like he had just gotten started and probably had more to add to the page. Third, it would provide support for him as he set off to work.

This public conference with Jahaan, or oral storytelling, seemed to give him the chance to discover what he actually wanted to say. It gave the other children a chance to see one of their peers revisiting his work, and it gave me a chance to teach the children, implicitly, what illustrators may consider in crafting their stories.

My questions imply that of course he'd want to return to his work and attend to these specific elements of craft.

"Where will you put the balloons?" implies "I assume you're planning to draw them." I neither ask, "Do you want to put the balloons in?" nor do I say, "You should put them in." By asking where they will go, I'm saying, "Readers expect to understand your story, and you need to include the details that will give them the information they need to understand."

"Where will the cake be? Will we see the cake on this page?" implies "You have a choice about what to put in and what to leave out." Implicit as it may be, we are teaching the children another element of craft: writers and drawers select what to put in and leave out.

In asking him to place his hand where he plans to draw the balloons, the cake, the table, he begins to see that authors have a responsibility to think through where the information will go and that the placement of things needs to make sense. In other words, authors attend to order and organization.

Lastly, by asking, "What clothes were you and your brother wearing at the party?" I'm implying, "I expect you'll put clothes on your stick people because you want your story to look real." In asking that question, I am implying that you want the drawing to be true to the story.

Jahaan may not attend to any or all of the aspects of craft implicit in my questions and that is okay; that's not my goal. The goal is to plant the seeds for a way of thinking about crafting. Eventually, we will present these elements of craft, explicitly, in lessons of their own. Sometimes children tell us, eloquently and in great detail, how they could add to the story, but when they go back, they seem to "forget" those glorious details and add what we adults might consider one little thing. That, we believe, is cause for celebration. It is the returning to the work and seeing other possibilities—and acting on them—that we want them to learn how to do. By adding one little thing this time (which is the beginning of revision), they show us that the possibility exists for adding more as time goes on.

In the end, we see that Jahaan was working like a writer—adding the balloons, the cake, and the clothes (see Figure 2.10 in the color insert).

Moving On to the Next Page

You'll notice that at the end of this lesson, we didn't talk with the children about moving on to the next page if they finish. We knew if we showed them how to release the clip from the page and move it to the next page, some children would move on without taking time to think some more about the work they had started. We wanted to first build in the practice of returning to work you've started, to know how to reread it and to learn the value of making it better. We help them take that practice on in two ways: by modeling how we do that with our own writing and by keeping the independent writing time short. We want to end the writing time before they have a chance to finish so they'll have reason to return to that page the following day.

But even if that works for the first session or two, there will come a time when the children need to know how to move on to the next page. We find most success in showing children how to do this individually, during conferences. "Once you've added that part about the birthday cake, what else will you do?" might elicit, "I'm done." That being the case, I might say, "Well let me show you what to do. We're going to undo this clip—here. And the way we do this is to flip these two colored tabs around and squeeze them. Look, you've opened the clip! Now you slide it off the page, turn this page that you've been working on, and here's the next page. Squeeze the clip so it opens up and slide it right on to this pile of pages so it's all ready for your next story. Now," I say, flipping the first page back again, "when you've added that part about the birthday cake on this page, you can just turn the page and the clip is right there, marking the page for your next story. I wonder what your next story will be about?"

I get up and move on to the next conference, not even waiting for a response. That's because it's not the response that matters, but rather setting him up for thinking about the next story.

It's not until I've modeled this with some of the children that I would present it as a lesson to all of them. Still, there are some children who will have a difficult time manipulating the clip on their own, opening it wide enough to fit around that many pages, or finding the next page in order. It's a lot to ask of some children, and you may come up with a better system.

Lesson Moving on to the Next Page in Your Drawing & Writing Book

What's going on in the classroom

- Children began work on the first page of their Drawing & Writing Books.
- Some have gone back to reread and make changes, and if they're not finished already, they will be soon.

What's next

- They need to know how to move on to the next page.

Materials needed

- my Drawing & Writing Book with the page finished
- a child who has finished his page, and his Drawing & Writing Book

This is what I noticed . . .

"Boys and girls, I'm looking at this story I've been working on, and I think I'm finished. I've added the water and the house and I've fixed Bella's collar. I think I've done everything I can to make this the best story it can be. As you work on your stories, at some point you're going to decide what I just decided: I think this is the best I can do. It's just the way I want it for now. So let me show you what you do."

Let me show you what I mean . . .

"First, I undo the clip that marks the page I'm on. To undo it, all you do is lift this colored part up and bring it around—it's really easy. I reach over here on the back to the other side and do the same thing, bring the colored part around. Then I squeeze these two colored tabs, and when I do, this part that's holding my pages together is going to open up. Watch."

The children watch as I slowly squeeze the clasp open.

"I just slip it off this whole stack of pages, turn over this page I just finished, and then clip it on this next page so I'll know that this is the page I'm working on. I squeeze tightly so it opens really wide—see how wide? Then I hold the book with this hand to keep the pages together and I just slide the clip right on. That can be tricky! Now look, the tabs are sticking out! I don't want to leave it like that because the book doesn't lie flat when they're sticking out. So I just gently fold them down. Watch.

"Yesterday, Jeremy was working on his story about his baby brother and he had some parts he was going to add to his page. Did you add those parts, Jeremy?"

He says, "Yes," so I ask him to come up. He stands next to me.

"Why don't you tell us what's happening here on your page?" I can see that this is another opportunity for storytelling.

Jeremy tells the story, I ask for clarification and information about some parts, and he decides he is finished with the page. I walk him through the process that I just modeled using my Drawing & Writing Book as the other children watch.

"Since you've decided that there's nothing else you want to do on that page, you're ready to begin your next page. Do you remember how to fold these tabs over so you can squeeze them?" I say. Then turning to the children on the rug I say, "I'll bet he knows just how to do it because I saw Jeremy watching very closely when I was showing you boys and girls how to do it using my book."

Jeremy squeezes the tabs and slides the clip off.

"Do you remember what you need to do next?" I ask. Someone from the rug calls, "Move the page over!" just as Jeremy is flipping the finished page over.

"Now comes the tricky part," I say. "Sometimes it's best to use both hands to open that clip wide enough. Here, I'll hold the pages so they're all together. You can slip it on right here." I point to the bottom of the page. He slides the clip on with ease.

"You know, boys and girls, Jeremy was able to do that so easily, and maybe it's because I was helping him by holding the page. If you decide you're finished, and you want to move your clip onto the next page, I probably can't help you with yours because I'm probably going to be talking to another boy or girl about their story, which means I can't be interrupted. But if you need help, you could ask a friend sitting near you. I'll bet they'd be able to help you just like I helped Jeremy."

So, today as you write . . .   "So today, when you take your Drawing & Writing Book, you'll open it to the page you've been working on. And you'll know that page because the clip is there. Then you'll decide what else you're going to do to make your story just the way you want it. If you decide that you have your story just the way you want it, you can open the clip the way Jeremy and I just did, flip the page, and put your clip on the next page so you'll be ready to start your next story."

Once again, since this was the second day that children worked independently, they worked for only about ten to twelve minutes. During these first days of independent work, we're still setting the tone, putting expectations, routines, and procedures in place, and we know we can do that best by keeping the work engaging and the work time short.

During that workshop we noticed children adding to and changing their drawings, so we asked one of them to share. We used that piece of writing in the lesson the following day as a way to help children see how another writer/drawer considers the information readers might need.

Lesson Learning About Drawing Stories from Each Other

What's going on in the classroom

- Children have begun working in their Drawing & Writing Books.
- They have seen the teacher model rereading her story and asking questions to figure out what to add or change.
- Some children have revisited their work and have included more specific information: clothing, background, skin color, hairstyles.

What's next	• We want to use a student's work to help other children see what one writer considers as she includes specific and detailed information in the illustrations.
Materials needed	• student Drawing & Writing Book—a page where a student began a piece of writing the previous day, then added on.
This is what I noticed . . .	"Remember yesterday, when we talked about how writers go back, read their stories, and ask themselves some important questions? We said they ask these questions:

• "What do I need to add so readers will understand my story?"
• "What do I need to change so readers will understand my story?"

"Yesterday, Janaya went back and asked those questions and made some changes in her story. Janaya, you said we could look at your page, right? Why don't you come on up here?"

She stands next to me. I have her book open to the page she worked on.

Let me show you what I mean . . . "Would you tell us the story?" I ask, and she tells about how her mom dropped her off at her friend's house to play and went to work, and then later, her dad picked her up and took her to McDonald's (see Figure 2.11).

FIGURE 2.11 Janaya: My dad picked me up and took me to McDonald's.

"And yesterday, when Janaya went back to work, this is what was on the page: there was the picture of you, over here, and the picture of your dad, here, and your friend's house, here, right? And then Janaya added some other parts."

I point to the yellow car. "You added this, didn't you? Tell us about this."

"That's my dad's car when he came to pick me up."

"Oh, so your mom dropped you off at your friend's house."

Janaya points to the blue car near the top of the page and says, "That's my mom's car. She's leaving to go to work."

"Oh, so here's your mom's car—you added that, too—and she dropped you off and she's driving to work?" She nods.

"Then later, your dad came to pick you up in his car?" She nods.

"And I see you added this part, where your dad is standing. Tell us about this."

"It's the thing where you walk."

"Oh, the sidewalk? I can see the lines, just the way they look in the sidewalk. So he got out of the car to get you and he's standing on the sidewalk!" She nods.

"Boys and girls, we can tell where this story is happening, can't we? We see the sidewalk, the flower, the outside of the house, and the cars, so we know the story takes place outside. And we know something about the people, don't we? We know this is Janaya and this is her dad. You know, Janaya, before you even told us who these people were, I just knew this was you! You know how I could tell?"

Kids call out, "She's small and that one's big!" and "She has a dress!"

"Well, yes, it seems that this would be Janaya because she is small and that this would be her dad because he's bigger, but also, I could tell because of the hair. You made your hair look just the way you wear it, with a ponytail like that. And I'll bet your dad's hair is like this?" She nods.

"And you made yourself small and your dad big, so we could guess that this was a little person who was with a big person, like a kid with a mom or dad.

"You know what I think?" I say, looking at the children on the rug. "I think Janaya wanted her readers to understand her story about her mom dropping her off and her playing outside and her dad coming to pick her up in his car. She added information to help readers understand: she made the people's hair look the way it looks, she made them dressed the way they dress, and she made it look like it was happening outside because we can see the outside of the house and the cars and the flower.

"Janaya, I notice that you didn't color in the faces of the people. Don't forget that in the caddies we have these different shades of skin color so that you can make the skin of the people look real."

So, today as you write . . . "Today as you work in your Drawing & Writing Books, you'll do what Janaya did. Open it up, reread your story, and ask yourself these questions:

- "What information do readers need in order to understand my story?
- "What do I have to add or change so readers will understand?

"You might think about whether or not readers will know if your story is happening inside or outside. You might think about the kind of clothes the people in your story wear and how their hair looks and the color of their skin, because that information helps readers understand."

The lessons we've presented in this chapter are what we consider to be important first lessons in teaching children how writers work. By watching us put one part of our story on paper, listening to us think aloud as we work, and observing as their peers make decisions about their work, children learn that writers and drawers are intentional about how they craft their stories. They're learning how to use and care for materials, how to look at work they've done, and how to think about what to do next—some first steps in becoming independent writers and thinkers.

Most important, the message we're giving them is this: I respect you enough to make the work meaningful, to give you the time to do it, to teach you what you need to do it well, and to trust you with the very best materials so your work will be the best it can be.

We've ended this chapter with a lesson where children learn about drawing from one of their classmates. In the next chapter, we take a closer look at the important place for drawing in beginning to write, and explore how we teachers might better support our student writers through understanding the role drawing plays.

CHAPTER 3

Drawing

BEFORE OUR WORK IN BOSTON, we realized that, although we had always honored and valued drawing as a way of expressing oneself, we had never quite honored and valued it the same as the written word. We delighted in the drawings and helped children include more information by adding details and the many other things drawers might do to express their thinking on paper. What we did *not* do was provide *information* to help them with their drawing. In our work in kindergarten classrooms we realized that we spent time, both in and out of the writer's workshop, helping children learn how to *say* words slowly, to *listen* for sounds, and to *write* letters to represent the sound/s they hear in order to write their stories. We helped children work toward accurate spellings. However, we were reluctant to help them learn how to *observe* carefully and how to *identify* lines and shapes so they could accurately *draw* pictures that represent their thinking. Perhaps deep inside we were afraid to interfere with the "creative self."

Over time that changed.

As we began thinking more about the place of drawing in beginning writing, we went back to our beliefs about drawing and named them:

- Most children like to draw. Given something to write with and something to write on, that's what they do.
- Most children come to school already drawing. It's something they feel they know how to do.
- For young children, drawing is writing; it gives them opportunities to do what writers do: to think, to remember, to get ideas, to observe, and to record.

If we really believe that drawing is writing, then we need to give our students information about how to draw well, just as we do with writing words.

In the past, we had offered our own students help with drawing. Usually, if a child wasn't pleased with how he or she had drawn something, we'd show how illustrators of children's books had drawn that object or we'd send them to the class artist for "instruction." But we hadn't honored drawing enough to make it the focus of mini-lessons. Because we hadn't been doing it ourselves, it's not surprising that we didn't talk with teachers about how to provide the information that children need as they represent their thoughts on paper through drawings. In this work with kindergartners, we came to see our roles as including instruction and encouragement in both drawing and writing, and not just for children, but for their classroom teachers as well.

Drawing with Teachers

With this in mind, on the third day of our initial workshop with a new group of teachers, we displayed an 18-by-24-inch sketchbook on an easel and provided sketchbooks and pencils for each participant. Within moments, the room was buzzing with comments from both enthusiastic and reluctant teachers:

"What's this for?"

"Are we going to have to draw?"

"I can't draw. I never could. I'm awful at it."

"I love to draw."

"Why are we going to draw?"

Heather, one of the new teachers, announced, "This is the part that I've dreaded the most. I almost didn't want to take this workshop because I knew I was going to have to draw."

Using *Talking with Artists* (Cummings 1995), I referred to a story by David Wisniewski, children's author and illustrator, and read to the teachers: "When I was little, my mother showed me how to connect circles and ovals to form human bodies" (82).

As I turned to the easel, I said, "Let me show you what he means." So began the lesson of how to draw a person. Step-by-step, accompanied by observing and thinking aloud, followed by drawing, the human body standing, sitting, and running appeared on their pages. Using the ovals, some even experimented with drawing

FIGURE 3.1 Teachers' drawing of people using ovals.

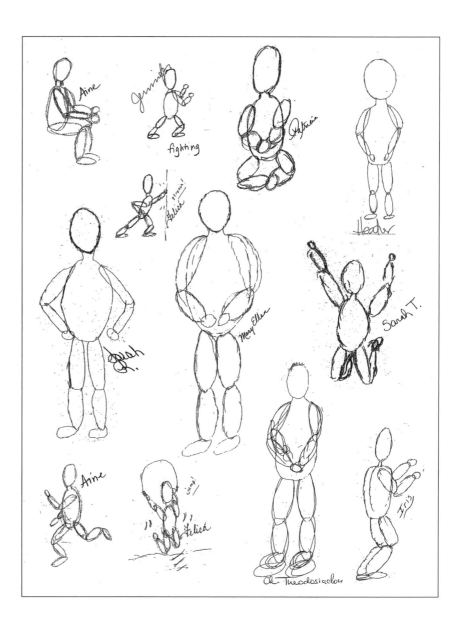

people kicking, doing a split, and stretching against a wall (see Figure 3.1).

Exuberantly, tentatively, critically, they let us in on what they were feeling:

"Wow, I can't believe I can do this!"

"I'm not really happy with how this looks—his body is too wide."

"Well, my head's too big."

As in any classroom of learners, some teachers thought of themselves as people who could draw. They made comments like, "I think of the body as in sevenths, the head being one-seventh, the torso as three-sevenths, and the legs as another three-sevenths."

Together, we looked in picture books and noted that even though we could not actually see circles and ovals—and perhaps those illustrators didn't even use them—all the illustrators who drew people knew something about the circles and ovals that Wisniewski wrote about: the head as an oval; the torso a large oval connected to the head; the upper part of the arm (shoulder to elbow) and lower part (elbow to wrist) made up of two thinner ovals, one joined at the shoulder and the other connected to the upper arm at the elbow; the leg made up of two ovals, one to represent the upper part of the leg (thigh) and the other the lower part (from the knee to the ankle). The hands and feet are two ovals at the end of the arms and legs. Because the human body is symmetrical, the same ovals are made on opposite sides of the body. Although the people on the pages of the books didn't all look the same, they were for the most part people-like. They have versions of a head, body, arms, hands, legs, and feet.

We also observed how when people sit, ride a bike, run, or jump they still had those parts. People from the side or back also had those parts, although sometimes you might not be able to see them. As we continued drawing, we paid attention to what makes a person a person. The teachers were absolutely delighted with their newfound abilities and knowledge about how to draw a person as well as how they might talk with their students about how to draw a person.

"And to think I used to draw stick figures for people. Now I know how to make them look more real," one teacher commented as she studied, with pride, her real-looking person on the page. Although an adult learning to draw, she was confirming the thinking of Mona Brookes, author of the enlightening book *Drawing with Children* (1996). In it, Brookes argues for the need to give children information, saying, "Only the rare child learns how to draw representationally or realistically on his own. It is just like learning to play piano, learning ballet, or learning to write stories. Children need information about the subject and guided instruction" (47). We saw that as teachers acquired more information about how to draw, thus feeling more confident as drawers, it was possible for them to provide guided instruction for their students. When we sketch with children, we do it the same way.

Drawing with Children

It's the second week of school. Megan Sinclair's nineteen kindergartners are sitting on the rug in the meeting area, talking with one another as they wait to begin their second sketching lesson of the year. My 18-by-24-inch sketchbook is set on the easel along with a cup of pencils (without erasers). Nearby there's a tub containing a sketchbook for each of the children.

"Boys and girls, I was looking at your sketchbooks and noticed how carefully you included so many details as you sketched this monkey yesterday with Ms. Sinclair," I say and I point to the book with a picture of the monkey on the cover. "You saw the round shape of the face and the half-round shapes for the ears. And look at the tail with a long, curvy line. It seems to me as though you must have been using your eyes to look closely at that monkey and tried to make him look real. That's what we do when we sketch: we use our eyes and look closely and try to notice the shapes and lines and then use them to make our drawings look real. When we look closely, we call that observing—paying attention to what we see.

"Today we're going to do some more sketching. We're going to observe, look real closely at a person's face, and draw it." I decided this lesson would be on drawing a face, because children are familiar with faces, and in most instances, the stories they tell have people in them. In other words, they'll be drawing many people this year.

"We'll need a model," I begin, and immediately Olivia calls out, "My sister's going to be a model when she grows up."

"And what will she do as a model?" I ask, following her enthusiasm and acknowledging as well as wanting to find out more about what she knows.

"She'll put on cool clothes and people will look at her."

I add, "And *look at the clothes*! They'll look very carefully to see how the new clothes are different from the clothes from last year. They want to remember the new things about the clothes so that when they go shopping, they can look for the latest fashions!

"We're going to look carefully at our model, too. We're going to look at her closely and see as much as we can about her face. But"— I put my finger up as if to say, Listen up, this is important—"we're going to do something else: we're then going to *draw* what we see and make it look as real as we can. And maybe you'll remember some of the things we see today on her face for when you are drawing faces at other times."

When we ask children to look at a model and try to make their drawings look real, it is called representational drawing because the object is represented realistically. This is different from the drawing that children do on their own, called symbolic drawing (Brookes 1996). In these sketching lessons, we give children information on how to draw and encourage them to do representational drawing, but we do *not* expect that every face from this point on will include all the features we talked about in the lesson. Instead, we give them information about drawing along with lots of opportunities for practice, and changes begin to occur over time.

Teachers may be wondering if giving children information about drawing interferes with their more spontaneous drawing. Brookes assures us that "children can do both symbolic and realistic drawings without either activity interrupting the benefits of the other" (47), and that has been our experience, too. When it's time to draw during other times of the day, sometimes they include aspects of what they remember from a sketching lesson, and sometimes they don't.

"I've asked Ms. Lider [the student intern] to be our model because models have to sit still for so long and I know that she'll be able to do that." Ms. Lider sits down in a chair set back just a bit from the rug so both the children and I have a front view of her face.

"On Monday when you sketched the monkey with Ms. Sinclair, she drew a part of the picture and then you all drew that part on your page. Then she drew another part and you drew that part; she drew another, and you drew, and that's how you did the whole picture. Today, with your help observing and telling me what you see, I'm going to do the whole drawing of Ms. Lider's face and I'm going to talk to you about what I'm thinking as I draw. Then Ms. Sinclair and I will give you your books and a pencil so you can draw Ms. Lider's face in your sketchbooks.

"Let's look carefully at Ms. Lider's face," I say, studying her closely. "What do you think I should draw first?"

Many voices call out, "Her head!"

"Yes," I say. "I think we'll need to draw the head so we can then draw the other things on her face. When I look at her head . . ." I pause, observe, then ask, "Ms. Lider, could I move your hair back from your face so I can see the shape of your head?" She agrees and I carefully lift the ringlets framing her face. I study her face for about three seconds and then ask the children, "What do you notice about the shape of her head?"

Some children say, "It's round," and others say, "It's a circle."

"You know, that's what I thought until I started looking more closely. But now I think the head is round*ish*, and not really a circle. I'm noticing Ms. Lider's head starts out round at the top but then is a little longer on the sides and roundish on the bottom where her chin is. Turn to the person sitting beside you and, very carefully with your hands, place their hair back from their forehead so you can see the shape of your friend's head. Then, without touching their face, trace along the shape with your finger." Most of the children let the hair go and, using both index fingers, start at the center of the top of the head and trace down to the chin. Then their partner does the same thing.

"You know, boys and girls," I say as I begin to draw a large oval covering half the page in my sketchbook, "when I was a little girl, I used to draw a circle for the head. But when I began looking more closely, I began to see what you're seeing, that a face is not a perfect circle like the smiley faces we see everywhere. A face is more like a long circle, which some people call an oval, or egg shaped."

I begin to draw an oval, and some children say, "I can't see it."

"Well, that's because when I first draw, I do it very lightly with little strokes, and then when the head looks the way I want it to look, I make it darker, just like this."

"Now I can see it," Jaidah says, feeling satisfied.

"I still can't see it," Deliahenid says, getting up on her knees.

We reposition some seats so that everyone can see as I continue.

"Next I'm going to draw her eyes." We closely look at her eyes and the children name what they see.

"They're round."

"There's a black dot in the middle."

"She has eyelashes."

"And eyebrows."

"Her eyes are green."

As they call out each feature, I point to it.

As the children observe, think, and name the parts of the eye, they're learning more about eyes. Child psychologist Venger says that "Drawing can increase a child's awareness of her thinking," and "as the child learns more about the object, his drawings will change, reflecting his newfound understanding" (cited in Bodrova and Leong 1996).

"You're noticing many things about her eyes, and I notice one more thing: the shape of the whole eye." I trace it (from a safe distance) with my finger. "I sometimes think of the eye as a football shape. Some people think it looks like an almond. Look at the person sitting beside you and see if you notice the football-like shape that holds the round part of the eyes. Be careful not to poke anyone in the eye, and trace around that outside part of the eye." I lean in to study Ms. Lider more closely and then say, "Actually, as I'm looking more carefully, I'm noticing that this bottom part of the football shape isn't as round as the top part; the lower part of the eye is flatter, dipping down just a little bit.

"I think I'm ready to draw the eyes now," I say, bringing their attention back to the drawing. "Hmm, where shall I put them?"

I'm expecting them to say "at the top" because that's where most children place the eyes when they draw a face. I want them to see that they are not at the top at all, so I show them how to notice where they are.

"Along with looking at a model to see *what* to draw, a drawer also looks very carefully at the model to figure out *where* to place things in their drawing. I'm going to place our model's hair off her forehead again to see just where her eyes are. Are they at the top of her head? Hmm, no. Her eyes are not down low. Ms. Lider's eyes are just about in the middle of her head, perhaps just a bit higher than the exact middle."

As I begin to draw, I continue to think aloud about what I'm doing. "I think this is the middle right here," I say as I find the middle and point to it with my finger. "And I want to go just a little higher." I find the spot and begin to draw the eye. "I have to remember it's shaped like a football, but a little flatter on the bottom. I also have to leave some space to draw the other eye. I'll look at my model to see how much space to leave."

I turn and look at Ms. Lider and say, "Hmm, the second eye isn't real close to the first eye. There seems to be enough space for the top of the nose in between the eyes. And her other eye looks just like the first eye—the same shape, the same size." At this point, the children can see the shape of the head and the two eyes.

"Theys don't look like my eyes," Jordan says.

"No, they don't look like your eyes. They don't even look like Ms. Lider's eyes yet, because we haven't drawn all the things that would make her eyes look real. My hunch is that once we try to make her eyes look more real, they will look a little more like your eyes, too. So, what are some of the things you notice about Ms. Lider's eyes?"

"They's green."

"Yes, hers are green and that colored part of the eye is called the iris. Since I'm only doing my sketching with a pencil, I think I'll turn my pencil a little on its side and just shade in the iris so that someone looking at it knows that her eyes are a color."

"You has to make a black dot for the eyeball," Joshua contributes.

"Thanks for helping me remember about that black part, the pupil of the eye," I say as I draw and darken in the pupil.

Closely observing our model's eyebrows, the children notice that eyebrows are little hairs across the tops of the eyes and that the eyelashes are little hairs on the tops and bottoms of the eye sockets. They also notice that Ms. Lider's eyelashes are short. As they notice, talk, and name what they see, I add each feature to the drawing. I don't rush, but rather show children how I observe carefully and take my time to do a good drawing. And there's something else I want them to notice.

"Boys and girls," I say, "have you noticed how still Ms. Lider is sitting? I just knew that she was going to be a good model."

"What about her nose?' Jayden asks with concern.

"Oh, yes, her nose," I say. "When I was little, not only did I think the head was a circle like the smiley faces we see everywhere, and the eyes were up at the top, but I used to make a circle for the nose and draw it right in the center of the face like this." On the corner of the paper I do a quick sketch of a circle with circle eyes in the top of the circle and a circle nose in the center.

They giggle and shout, "Like at Wal-Mart!" and "That's how I do it."

"But, when I look carefully at Ms. Lider's nose, this is what I notice." Careful not to actually touch her, I place my index fingers at the top of the nose, a little lower than the eyes, and trace along the outside of the nose, saying, "I notice that her nose begins between her eyes, just a bit lower, and moves down. As it goes down, it slants out, it gets a little bit wider and then there is some fullness at the bottom."

"Yeah, the holes so she can breathe," a child says, pointing.

"Yes, the holes—they're called nostrils—so she can breathe."

They look at each other's noses and confirm that the nose does have sides and holes—nostrils.

"Watch while I try to make her nose," I say, focusing their attention to the easel. As I look back and forth between our model and my drawing, I draw the sides of the nose and then the nostrils.

"Oh no, it looks like an elephant's nose!" Jelyia exclaims.

"I don't think that's how a nose looks," Monty adds.

Looking at my drawing and then at Ms. Lider's nose I say, "You're right, it doesn't look exactly like Ms. Lider's nose. I'm going to have to keep looking at noses and practicing how to draw them, because I want to get better at drawing noses. I know that the more I practice drawing noses, the better I'll get."

Throughout the lesson, I tell the children what I notice and how I'm going to draw it, and then talk as I draw. I keep it conversational, responding to their comments along the way.

"What about her mouth?" Jeannae asks.

"Yes, I need to make her mouth. As I look closely at her face, I'm noticing that her mouth isn't just a line across the bottom of her face but rather it's made up of two lips." Ms. Lider separates her lips and touches each one. "The center of her top lip is just below the middle of her nose. It almost starts out looking like a heart. It's a little lower, and then it comes up and goes over across a part of her face. I'm looking to see how far to make it across her face."

I study her face, then, using my index fingers, start at the outer edge of her eyes and trace, without touching, a straight line down her face. "Oh, I see," I say to them. "Her lips don't come out as far as her eyes do." On my page I use two fingers to trace two straight lines down from the outside of the eyes and say, "I'm not going to make the mouth as wide as her eyes," as I draw it smaller. "So, Ms. Lider, are you going to have your mouth open, so we can see your teeth, or closed?" She closes her lips and I draw the bottom lip directly under the top lip.

At this point they've been watching, listening, and participating for twenty minutes, and some of them are having a difficult time attending. Jaidah gets up and walks around, but her eyes never leave the drawing. Amani walks to a table and lays his head down and goes to sleep. I quickly talk about the ears and draw them. Rebekah mentions that I should draw her earrings.

The children are concerned that it doesn't *really* look like Ms. Lider, and I tell them, "That's because she doesn't have any hair yet. Everyone has eyes, ears, a nose, and a mouth just like our model. Just watch: when I draw her hair, my drawing will begin to look more and more like her." I carefully look at and talk about the direction her hair flows across her forehead as I draw it in. I notice how her hair is behind her ears and how you can see some of it from the sides and bottoms of her ears to the bottom of her chin. I then talk about the ringlets that frame her face as I draw them. The children get excited about the drawing of Ms. Lider and say:

"Ooh, that really looks like her now."

"Could you draw me now?"

"Ms. Lider, you look beautiful!"

"She *does* look gorgeous, doesn't she!" I concur. I put on the final touches as I say, "I'm going to draw her neck . . . I'll write, 'Ms. Lider' across the top of the page to give my drawing a name, just the way you did when you named the monkey you drew. Now anyone who looks at this drawing will know who it is. I'm also going to sign my name, so people will know who drew this picture. And I'm going to write the date so I can remember when I drew it."

The children are eager to make their drawings of Ms. Lider. "Ms. Sinclair has your sketchbook opened to the next page for you to do

your own sketch of Ms Lider. My sketchbook is going to be on the easel, and Ms. Lider is going to stay in her modeling chair, so you can look at them as you draw her. Remember as much as you can about what we observed about her. I'm going to come around and watch you work as drawers—people who look carefully at their model, notice shapes and lines, and try to draw them on the paper."

After the children get their sketchbooks and pencils, they spread out on the rug, keeping both Ms. Lider and my sketch in full view. And they draw.

"This isn't right," Ashley says as I kneel down next to her.

"What is it that you're not sure about?" I ask.

I respond this way, rather than saying, "Sure looks good to me!" or other automatic words of encouragement because, although I do want to be encouraging, I also want them to know that I'm listening. I trust that children know how they feel, and if a child isn't happy with what she's done, and if I give her a chance to explain just what she's not happy with, I'll be better able to give her the information she needs so she can do her best—and be pleased with it.

For the next eight-and-one-half minutes, the class is totally engaged. Although I've seen it many times throughout the years, I'm still struck by the amount of time young children attend during sketching lessons. These children had watched and participated as I sketched for more than twenty minutes and then continued to work on their sketches for another eight minutes. Some sat on the floor with sketchbooks in their laps, and others were on their knees with their sketchbooks on the floor in front of them. All of them looked from their pages to the model and back again. As they sketched, they talked softly and showed their sketches to one another.

As a way of celebrating this work, we sat in a circle and they held their sketchbooks in front of them, their drawings facing outward. We looked around the circle and marveled at what they had done. (See Figures 3.2a and 3.2b.)

Why Drawing Is Important for Young Writers

We return now to the question of why drawing is important for our students as writers.

Figure 3.3 Jordan's drawing about "going to Philly on the train."

First, drawing is one primal way that beginning writers represent and understand meaning. Most young children come to school knowing how to draw, and, in most cases, they enjoy it. So, we provide opportunities for them to practice and be playful as they make meaning through drawing. We can also help them learn some things about drawing so that they can do it better.

Second, drawing is a way for children to be heard. A student who has difficulty recognizing letters, perhaps even the letters in his name, can often draw what he knows, thinks, and feels. In September, before he knew how to write any words except his name, Jordan drew his story about "going to Philly on the train" (see Figure 3.3). In his drawing, he includes two people (one being him), and a long, narrow railroad track. The numbers on the side of the track designating different platforms not only gave him the opportunity to experiment with his newly acquired skill at writing numbers, but were also a way of representing the platforms, a word he doesn't yet have in his vocabulary. When his classmates show an understanding of his drawing, he learns that people can listen to and "read" his drawings, that what is important to him is being understood by others, and that what he knows, thinks, and feels matters.

Third, drawing is a medium through which children can develop language. In their book *Tools of the Mind* (1996), Elena Bedrova and Deborah Leong interpret the ideas of Lev Vygotsky in terms of early childhood learning. According to Vygotsky, thinking is an inner dialogue through which human beings process, compose, and develop language. For young children, thought and speech are separate at first, then merge when children "become capable of thinking as they talk" (Bedrova and Leong 1996, 98). This is the emergence of what Vygotsky calls private speech, where their talk is more for themselves than for communicating with others. For example, it is not uncommon for a four- or five-year-old who is drawing a picture to reveal his or her thinking out loud: "Here's the door of the bus. It's open. The kids is getting on. Oh, wait! I didn't made the windows!" This child is talking to himself rather than to others, and his verbal thinking allows us to peek into his mind.

At some point around school age, this private speech turns inward and becomes less audible. The conversations take place inside their heads as they engage in a task. As children try to represent meaning on paper through their drawings, they are processing, composing, and thus developing language.

Fourth, drawing allows children to go deeper into their stories. On the third page of his five-page story about going to Six Flags (see Figure 3.4), Joshua wrote, "I went on a wotrslid. I splasht into the wotr." (I went on a waterslide. I splashed into the water.) That was more writing than his usual one sentence. There is, however, depth to this story beyond what the words reveal, and that depth is in the drawing. For example, he has drawn himself coming feet-first down the waterslide in a red bathing suit (the rest of his body shaded with the appropriate skin color), and there is a speech bubble coming from his mouth with the word *We* (meaning, "Wheeee!"). He's drawn his mother standing on the top tier, laughing "Ha Ha Ha" as she dumps the bucket of water on Joshua's father, who calls out, "Oh no!" Joshua's friend is climbing the stairs past the palm tree and the fountains and we see the movement of the water (swirls of black felt-tip pen amid the blue), actions of people (sliding, walking, yelling), and we get a sense of how the ride looks at that moment. Through the drawing, he reveals information about the sounds, images, setting, characters, feelings, and little substories that were going on in his head that are not in his text.

At a later point in his literary life, Joshua might depict such a moment with words: "Next, we went on the waterslide. My father, sister, and I climbed the stairs to get to the top of the slide and there were palm trees and fountains all around—just like Florida. My mother was standing outside the fence, and when my father came by, she dumped the bucket of water on him. He yelled, 'Oh no.' She was laughing! I was the first one to go down. I put my hands up and yelled, 'Wheee!'"

FIGURE 3.4 Joshua: *I went on a waterslide. I splashed into the water.*

Right now, Joshua doesn't have the facility to go into such depth in words, but he can craft his ideas through drawing. It is the drawing that allowed him to revisit that moment and recreate it for himself and for the reader. Drawing makes it possible for him, and so many other children, to tell a deeper, more involved story than they can with text.

Fifth, through drawing, children are learning about the craft of writing. Because talking, drawing, and writing are three aspects of a complex "symbol weaving" (Dyson 1986), over time we have come to see that what children learn how to do in one mode sets the stage for and supports learning how to do it in the others. For example, when children take on the concepts of including more and being more specific in their drawings, eventually they are able to be more inclusive and specific in their writing of text. Newkirk supports this belief, saying, "The graphic challenges of inclusiveness and specificity have clear counterparts in expository writing" (1989, 55). Young

FIGURE 3.5 Britney's story in October of kindergarten. *We went to the beach.*

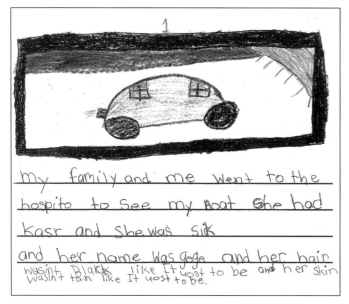

FIGURE 3.6 Britney's writing in December of first grade. *My family and me went to the hospital to see my aunt. She had cancer and she was sick. And her name was Gigi. And her hair wasn't black like it used to be and her skin wasn't tan like it used to be.*

writers show us this connection between the graphic and the written, not just in expository writing, but in other kinds of writing as well. For example, in October of kindergarten, Britney drew a picture of her and her mom at the beach (see Figure 3.5). In December of first grade, she drew and wrote about her aunt who had cancer (see Figure 3.6). We believe that the specific information she included in the text had something to do with the opportunities and support she was given to be specific in the stories she told orally and through drawing.

We also recognize that it is possible for a child to choose to write words first and, in some cases, not draw at all. This happens most often when children are reading books with fewer illustrations and more text. As readers, they understand that the message is in the words and this carries over to their own writing. In such a case, we wouldn't require the child to draw first or even to go back afterward to include an illustration. We do, however, believe that for most beginning writers, drawing gives them a starting place and a point of reference for the story they're trying to tell. Young children who only write words, or who write the words first, sometimes have difficulty remembering what they wrote. But if they've drawn first, we can point them back to their illustration. Looking at the drawing helps them remember what their words say.

Most important, drawing is part of writing because it is what young children do naturally and playfully. And playfulness that energizes, challenges, and engages is essential in our classrooms.

Ways of Supporting Young Children as They Draw

We always knew that drawing was an essential part of writing for young children, but what we've learned through this work is that we teachers have a responsibility to help children to tell their stories well, through drawing. That can be both exciting and scary for teachers. It's exciting because we finally acknowledge that what is often considered "an extra" is a core element of composing. It can be scary because many teachers feel tentative, at best, as drawers. Yet, for the same reasons that teachers of writing must write, we suggest that teachers of young writers must draw. And because we believe this, we support the teachers we work with as best we can, each time we meet. At the start of each workshop, for example, we have objects arranged on the tables (such as pinecones, gourds, bittersweet, holly and other greens, and wooden models of people), and as teachers come in, they take out their sketchbooks and draw. They notice the shapes and lines in the coffee mugs, the vase of flowers sitting on the table, the tree outside the window. For some, this may be the first time they've sketched since the last time we met; others have gotten into the practice of taking out their sketchbooks at other times, particularly when their students are sketching in order to work alongside them.

At each session teachers share what their students have done in the name of sketching, and we think together about ways to support children with sketching during writer's workshop and at other times during the day:

- Create a drawing center filled with interesting pencils, a sketchbook for each child, and interesting things to draw: a wooden human form on a stick that bends where there are joints (knee, elbow, etc.); blocks of many shapes (cylindrical, rectangular, triangular); objects for still lifes (shells, leaves, vases of flowers, stuffed animals); anything that looks interesting that children might want to study and draw. Ed Emberley's wide range of step-by-step books and other how-to-draw books are favorites of children and can be included there as well.
- Ask children to bring in familiar objects from home that they know and love: action figures, stuffed animals, rocks, model cars, animal figurines—those everyday objects they touch, play with, and even sleep with. These are the things they're probably drawing at home. Why not begin with what they already know and love?
- Get to know something by doing it a lot. Don't just draw faces once—do lots of faces. Draw the same face on different days. What changes do you notice? What is different and what remains the same? Take the same object (pumpkin, daffodil, toy car) and draw it from different positions and perspectives.
- Look at student writing and drawings and assess what children need help with in order to make their drawings better. For example, in Reed's story about the Patriots (Figure 3.7), he shows objects moving. The plane has little swish marks and the football travels in a straight line from the hand of one player to the other. He also shows people in action—he's drawn hands in the air, one player kneeling, and one lying down. Based on these illustrations, it would be helpful for him to learn how to draw a person from the side view, giving him yet another way to show people in action.
- Provide time to draw during the writing workshop. Sometimes we think children are spending too much time drawing their stories and we want to rush them to get words on the paper. When that happens, we need to ask ourselves questions such as, What role is drawing playing for this child as a person who is

FIGURE 3.7 Reed: *Go, Patriots.* 1. *The Pats are flying to the Super Bowl.* 2. *Nice throw, Tom.* 3. *Go, Patriots.* 4. *The Pats won the Super Bowl.*

trying to get text on paper? Does he have enough information and skill, along with stamina, to write all the words he needs to express his story on paper? Does he have the words to express his thoughts, or does he have only the picture in his mind?

- Provide opportunities for making their work better. When it's expected that children look at the drawings they were working on the day before, they learn how to think about other possibilities in the drawing.
- Provide lots of time and opportunities for drawing throughout the day and across the curriculum. What role can drawing play when responding to reading? In writing math problems? In the block corner?
- Enlist the help of others in your school. When Megan Sinclair was first learning about writing workshop, she discovered that the computer instructor, José, was a self-proclaimed artist. He conducted many of the drawing lessons while she watched and participated with the children. Over time, she gained the confidence to provide instruction in drawing herself. In some other instances, classroom teachers asked the art teacher to help them with drawing lessons.
- Allow for and celebrate differences in how children see things, hence the differences in their drawings.

In *Henry Moore's Sheep Sketchbook* (Moore and Clarke 1998), sculptor Moore writes about how much he loved the art lessons he had in elementary school during the last period of the week. Later in life he came to understand their value.

Drawing itself is a part of learning: learning to use one's eyes to see more intensely. To encourage everybody to draw is not to turn people into artists, just as you don't teach grammar to turn them all into Shakespeares. If every man were made to draw his wife, you might have a few more divorces come about, but that husband would start to look more intensely at his wife and he would know much more about her. He might make a very bad drawing, but that wouldn't be the point.

Because drawing is writing for young children, providing opportunities and guidance in drawing helps children "to learn to use one's eyes to see more intensely." And in that intense looking they have the opportunity to come to know something better and thus to represent it on paper the best that they can, at first through their drawings and over time through their words.

CHAPTER 4

The Craft of Drawing

ONCE CHILDREN BEGAN PAYING attention to shape and we noticed them looking closely and observing as they sketched, we hoped we'd see some carryover between the sketching lessons and their illustrations in their Drawing & Writing Books. For the most part, however, there wasn't any. They sketched exquisite, real-looking people in their sketchbooks—and seemed to enjoy doing it—but in their Drawing & Writing Books we saw the same stick people. It didn't take long for us to figure out that our expectations weren't realistic. Those few sketching lessons couldn't possibly be internalized so quickly. They'd need many more opportunities for practice, and we couldn't expect them to make those connections on their own; we'd need to do that for them. So in our mini-lessons we began to show them how to bring what they were learning during sketching lessons into the work of the Drawing & Writing Book. Modeling with our own stories we'd say things like, "I'm remembering how we sketched TJ the other day and how we used ovals to make the parts of his body. I'm going to use ovals right now to draw myself in this story that I'm working on, in my Drawing & Writing Book."

But something else was happening during those early days and weeks of school. We were showing them a way of looking at and observing the illustrations in children's picture books, and we weren't doing it just in the mini-lessons. During read-alouds, too, we couldn't help noticing and naming what we were seeing. When reading the book *Goal*, by Robert Burleigh (2001), we'd hear ourselves saying, "Stephen T. Johnson really shows these soccer players in action, doesn't he!" Or, as we read *Dim Sum for Everyone!* by Grace Lin (2001), we'd flip back to a previous page and say, "Hmm, isn't it interesting that on this page we see the whole dim sum restaurant and then on this page we see a close-up of the table? It seems that by showing a close-up or a view from far away, Grace Lin helps readers know what she wants us to pay attention to." When reading *My Mother's Sari* by Sandhya Rao (2006), we notice how the illustrator, Nina Sabnani, so often has parts or most of the people hidden. By wondering and noticing out loud how these illustrators decided what to draw and how to draw it, we're modeling for our students how to pay attention, how to name what we see.

But it was looking closely at the "Rosie" books, a collection by Isabelle Harper and illustrated by her grandfather Barry Moser, that challenged our thinking about how to talk to young children about being specific in their stories. For example, until that point, we might have addressed the importance of specific information by showing our students a two-page spread with not a hint of white space, explaining in great awe how the illustrator had filled the pages with information that was important for readers to know. And, of course, that is true. That wonderful illustration in Dav Pilkey's *The Paperboy* (1996), where the boy is in the garage in the early hours of the morning folding newspapers and wrapping them in rubber bands as his dog looks on, is stunning and filled with good information, and there's not a hint of white space. But when we looked closely at what Isabelle Harper and Barry Moser do through the marriage of their simple words and illustrations in the "Rosie" books, we could see that effective writing is not about filling the background in, but about being specific in the information you include.

"Effective writing is built from specific, accurate pieces of information," Murray tells us. "The reader wants, above all, to be informed. Whatever you are writing, you should try to make the reader an authority on your subject" (1984, 17). And don't we come away from the Harper/Moser books as authorities on how rottweilers and tabbies act, on how they spend their days and how the people who love them care for them! We come away knowing that this author and illustrator write and draw about what they know well, and love.

On each page of *My Dog Rosie* (1994), *My Cats Nick and Nora* (1995), and *Our New Puppy* (1996), Isabelle Harper and Barry Moser give readers important, specific information. For example, on the second page in *My Dog Rosie*, we see Rosie, the dog, and Isabelle, the little girl who is emptying food from a can into the dog's dish. That's it. There's nothing in the background to tell us what room they're in or whether they're inside or outside or who else is around. What we do know, however, is that the dog is eager to get at that food—we can see it in his eyes and his mouth, and just by the way he is waiting we can tell that he is kind with children. We know the girl is working hard to get that food out of the can. We can tell by the furrow of her brow and the way her hands are holding the can and the fork. We notice that she's using her left hand, and we wonder if Barry Moser did that because he knows his granddaughter Isabelle really is left-handed. We also know that she's feeding the dog cat food. In this illustration we don't learn so much about the place, but we learn a lot about the characters.

As we continue to read the books by this twosome, we see that it is in subtle but specific ways that Barry Moser lets us know where the story is happening. For example, in *Our New Puppy* there is a page where Rosie and the puppy are feasting on a hot dog that fell from an overturned grocery bag that was left on the kitchen counter. We know they're in the kitchen because of the spigot and handle on the sink above, and the cabinets underneath, and because of the grocery bag, and we wonder if maybe Rosie knocked it over. But whether he did or not, we know what the people who live with these dogs like to eat because of the hot dog links hanging from the shelf and the onion, pork sausage, and can of soup lying on the floor nearby. Atop the counter next to the dog dishes sits the cat, surveying the scene with an unsettled look in her eyes. It may be one of the most filled pages of all three books, and still there is a lot of white space. Without even reading the words, we learn about how the animals act and about their relationship with one another, about the house they live in and the people who care for them. With so much empty space on the pages of these books we still come away from reading them feeling like authorities on the subject.

Now, we're not saying that background should be sparse or that filled backgrounds aren't good—not at all. Rather, we're showing how, by stopping to really look at books we thought we knew well, we learned a whole lot more and it was information that would change the way we talked to students. It would also change the way we'd look at other books.

Earlier we said that we draw on three resources as we consider what and how to teach our student writers: our own writing, their writing—meaning students' work in progress as well as their published books—and children's books. We invite you now to look with us at these three children's books as we try to name exactly what Barry Moser and Isabelle Harper do, so that these observations might inform our teaching as well. We noticed that they do the following:

- Draw about what they know
- Draw characters in a variety of ways:
  - facing forward, from the side, from the back, in action, just a part

- Include the tiniest details:
  - the dog tag on Rosie's neck with Rosie's name (you can see that there's writing but you can't always make out the name, only when it's close enough to read)
  - the sunglasses on the face of the woman driving into the yard
- Reveal feelings:
  - the troubled look in the cat's eyes as it watches Rosie and the puppy eat the cold hot dogs
  - the skepticism on Rosie's face as Floyd tries to play with her
  - Aunt Maddy's face as Isabelle breaks the news that Floyd is here
- Reveal the place through one little detail:
  - the paper towel roll and the spigot at the sink let you know they're in the kitchen
  - the blades of grass and the shadow of the bike on the ground let you know they're outside
- Get a big message across through a single, tiny detail:
  - the cat food label on the can from which the girl is feeding Rosie (who is a dog)
- Point your eye toward what they want you to pay attention to:
  - Rosie's reaction to the puppy pulling on his ear (we see that a person is nearby, but the focus is on Rosie and the puppy)
- Use simple and honest words that sound as though the girl in the story is actually saying them:
  - "Sure enough, there he is."
  - "Our neighbor Fluffy sees us. He wasn't invited to the party because he's not nice. He likes to fight."
- Use people's exact words, which help us feel like we're standing there watching them and listening to them talk:
  - "'Grandpa,' Eliza says, 'I didn't know Floyd would be this little.' 'Yes,' Grandpa says, 'Floyd is much smaller than Rosie. He's only eight weeks old.'"
- Tell readers something, then show readers what they mean:
  - "From the start, Floyd loves Rosie. He follows Rosie everywhere he goes. At first, Rosie's not sure what to do."
- Tell one part on each page, and each part builds to create a whole
- Use illustrations and words to tell the story. They may not give the same information, but the information works together to help the reader understand.

By looking so carefully at one author/illustrator team we learn a lot about craft. We learn about being simple but precise and intentional, which is what we want to teach our young writers. Of course, we don't expect this quality of work from our five- and six- and seven-year-olds—it takes an accomplished craftsperson to do work like this. But we want them to know that writers pay attention, they notice things, and it is by including the tiniest details that they give readers important information.

Because our primary goal is to help children feel successful telling their stories on paper, most of our early mini-lessons in the

Drawing & Writing Book focus on drawing because it's something they think they can do. By representing story through pictures, we're not excluding any child who may feel unsure about writing letters and words. That doesn't mean we ignore or overlook the idea of representing stories with text. In Chapter 5 you'll find lessons in which we show children how to label their illustrations and to listen for sounds in words as well as examples of conferences in which we nudge children to include text. What we want to emphasize is that because most children already think they can draw, we begin there and use it as an opportunity to show them how to do it even better. It is by going deeper into the illustration that they learn to tell a fuller story.

What our students put on those first pages of their Drawing & Writing Books teaches us about them. We learn what they do outside of school, about the people who are important to them, and about their passions, and we learn what they know and what they need to learn about crafting stories through drawing.

In the following lessons we address in more detail some elements of the craft of drawing that we only touched on in the earlier chapters. These lessons are not presented in a specific order, but rather are some that we did early in the year, based on what we observed in the classrooms.

 ## Lesson Drawing People

What's going on in the classroom	• Children draw people on most pages of their Drawing & Writing Books. • Mostly, they draw stick people, even though they've had sketching lessons on how to draw people more "filled out."
What's next	• They need to be reminded about how to draw people so they look real.
Materials needed	• my sketchbook, open to the page with sketches of people • three or four children's sketchbooks, open to pages where they've sketched people • *My Big Brother*, by Miriam Cohen, illustrated by Ronald Himler • an overhead transparency and a black pen
This is what I noticed . . .	"Remember how we talked about drawing people—how we learned from David Wisniewski that you can make people look real by using ovals?" I show a page in my sketchbook where I drew people made of ovals. "We drew people using an oval for the head, an oval for the torso—that's this middle section—and ovals for the arms and legs. You sketched people like that in your sketchbooks, too." (See Figure 4.1a–c.) I hold up some children's sketchbooks as I point out, "You drew an oval for the head, an oval for the torso, and ovals for those three parts

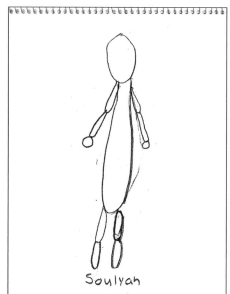

FIGURE 4.1A–C Children use ovals to sketch people in their sketchbooks.

FIGURE 4.2 Children use stick figures in Drawing & Writing Books.

of the arm—upper arm, lower arm, and hand—and ovals for the legs—upper leg, lower leg, and foot. Look at all these sketches of people that you boys and girls made just by drawing ovals! You know how to make people look real by drawing them this way. But here's what I'm noticing: when you draw people in your Drawing & Writing Books, many of you make people out of sticks, like this." (See Figure 4.2.)

I sketch a stick figure.

"I can understand why you might want to make people out of sticks—it's easy! You can make a person really quickly that way, can't you? I'm noticing, though, that in most of the books we read, the illustrators make their people filled out, the way they really look. Using ovals can help you make people in your Drawing & Writing Books filled out, so they look real."

Let me show you what I mean . . .
"Let's look at the way Ronald Himler drew people in *My Big Brother*. Right here on the first page, we see the boy and his big brother. They look real, don't they? Their bodies look more the way bodies of real people look. He made both of their heads small compared with their torsos, and their arms and legs have those parts that we talked about: the upper arm, lower arm, and hand, upper leg, lower leg, and foot. Here, on this page where they're working on the car, we can see those same parts: their heads (although we see only part of the big brother's head), their torsos, the little brother's upper arm, his lower arm, and his hand holding the wrench, their upper legs, lower legs, and feet.

"Now, I'm going to try something. I'm going to lay this clear piece of plastic—it's called a transparency because it's transparent—it means you can see right through it!" I say as I hold it in front of my face and look through it to them. I continue, "I'll put the transparency over this illustration of the two brothers on the first page, and I'm going to use ovals as I trace the shapes of their bodies with my black pen."

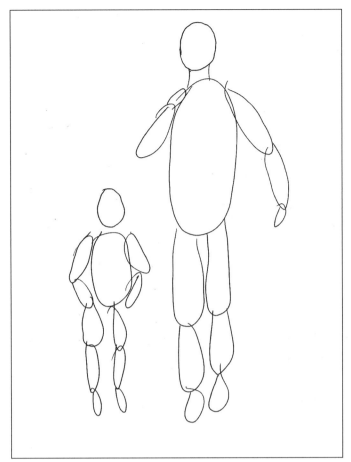

This is me and my big brother.

FIGURE 4.3A A transparency showing how the characters in *My Big Brother* could be made with the same ovals they are learning about as they make people.

FIGURE 4.3B The actual page from *My Big Brother*.

I think aloud as I trace: "Here's the oval for the little brother's head, here's the oval for his torso, and here's his upper arm, lower arm, and hand, upper leg, lower leg, and foot. Now, keeping the transparency right where it is, I'll draw the ovals for the shape of the big brother."

When I finish, I remove the transparency and lay it against a white piece of paper next to the illustration in the book. (See Figures 4.3a and 4.3b.)

"Now look! There are the ovals—the same ones you used when you sketched people in your sketchbooks! You know, maybe Ronald Himler used ovals to make the people on these pages and maybe he didn't. He may have another way to draw people. But when we look at the illustrations in this book, we know one thing: Ronald Himler tried to make the people in this story look real. Using ovals is one way that can help you make the people in your stories look real."

So, today as you write . . .

"So if you're going to draw people in your Drawing & Writing Books today, try to remember what you know about making people look real. You may want to use what you've learned from sketching people in your sketchbooks, using ovals to shape the people so they look filled out, or you may have another way to do it."

- Children often write about other children doing what children do: playing outside, playing basketball, sitting on the couch watching TV, sitting at a table eating together, and so on. In this book, there are boys playing basketball, sitting on the floor reading together, playing with trucks, and doing ordinary things.

- In this book there are some drawings of people standing. At least at first, children tend to draw their characters standing, so we wanted to start with what they know how to do.

Suggested other books

- *Matthew and Tilly*, by Rebecca C. Jones, illustrated by Beth Peck
- *My Best Friend Moved Away*, by Nancy Carlson
- *My Dog Rosie*, by Isabelle Harper, illustrated by Barry Moser

Lesson Drawing Clothing on People

What's going on in the classroom

- Sometimes children use ovals to draw people in their Drawing & Writing Books, but often they leave them as a collection of ovals, unclothed. (See Figure 4.4.)

FIGURE 4.4 Shammala used ovals to draw a person and dressed the figure by coloring it in.

| **What's next** | • They need to be shown how to put clothing on the people they draw so the ovals won't show. |

| **Materials needed** | • the teacher's Drawing & Writing Book
• an overhead transparency, a black pen, and colored pens
• one or two Drawing & Writing Books where they've drawn real-looking people
• *My Big Brother*, by Miriam Cohen, illustrated by Ronald Himler |

This is what I noticed . . .

"I see in your stories that you're remembering what you know about drawing people." I show some children's Drawing & Writing Books where they have drawn people using ovals. "Instead of just drawing stick arms and legs, you're really thinking about what we've learned about drawing people and you've tried 'filling them out' to make them look the way real people look. Some of you have tried to make their bodies look real by using ovals." I show a couple.

"But I'm also noticing that when we look at the illustrations in the books we read, like *My Big Brother*, we don't see those ovals. Usually we see people dressed in clothes. Today, I want to show you how to put clothes on the people in your stories so we won't see the oval shapes underneath."

Let me show you what I mean . . .

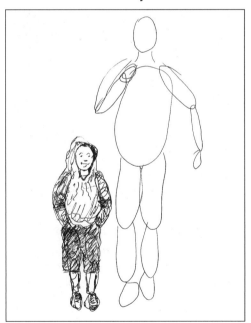

FIGURE 4.5 Returning to the same characters drawn with ovals in *My Big Brother,* we show children how to put clothing on people.

"Let's take a look at this transparency of the two brothers that I made the other day." I lay the transparency of the brothers, shaped from ovals, against a white paper. "It's all ovals, isn't it? But on this first page in *My Big Brother*, we don't see those ovals. I think it's because once Ronald Himler decided how he wanted the two brothers to look, he asked himself, Now, what kind of clothes will these two brothers be wearing? Then he made them wearing clothes. And even though Ronald Himler may not use ovals at all, a lot of you do, so you could put the clothes on like this."

I lay the transparency back over the illustration in the book and use colored markers to quickly trace over the sweatshirt, hood, shorts, and shoes of the younger brother so the ovals are covered. I do the same for the older brother.

"Boys and girls, now when I place this transparency back on the white paper, we don't see a bunch of ovals. Instead, we see two people who look the way people look." (See Figure 4.5.) "Well, actually we see some of the ovals, but that's because I had to draw the ovals with marker so you could see them. If you had done this with your colored pencils, you'd probably make the ovals lightly and we wouldn't see the ovals at all."

So, today as you write . . .

"So, today when you open your Drawing & Writing Books to the page you were working on yesterday, look and see if you've put clothes on the people you drew. If not, ask yourself what clothes these people would be wearing, and see if you can draw the clothing so readers won't see the shapes underneath, but instead will see people as you want them to look."

Why we chose this book	They know it well. We've read it, they've talked about it, and we've used it in the lesson where we talk about drawing people so that they look real. Because we want to pick up on that lesson, we return to the same book where, on most pages, the children are wearing everyday clothes, the kind the people in their stories might wear.
Suggested other books	Any book where the people are drawn in a way that makes it easy to see the shape of the body:

* *Bigmama's*, by Donald Crews
* *Two Girls Can*, by Keiko Narahashi
* *The Paperboy*, by Dav Pilkey

Lesson Other Ways to Draw People

What's going on in the classroom	• Many children are using ovals to draw people. • We've discussed the possibility that illustrators of the books we read may not draw people this way. • Some members of the class draw real-looking people and don't use ovals.
What's next	• The children need to see other possibilities for how to draw people.
Materials needed	• a large blank paper (or my Drawing & Writing Book open to a blank page) at the easel • one or two Drawing & Writing books where children have drawn real-looking people without using ovals • some books nearby so I can pull one out as an example
This is what I noticed . . .	"We've been talking a lot about using ovals to draw people so they look real. We said that you might start with the head"—I draw as I talk—"and make an oval, then those two curved lines for the neck, then another oval for the body, longer this time, and then, if I wanted to make the arms like this . . ."

I hold my arms folded on my hips, but one of the children calls—and acts—out, "No, like this!" putting her arms out to the sides.

"Okay," I say. "I could make the arms out straight like Sumiko's," and I do. "And then the legs. I make one oval, and another, then the foot . . .

"We said that was one way to make a person, and I'm glad I know that way because it helps me make my people look real. But we also said that maybe the illustrators we know didn't use ovals to draw their people." I reach into the bin next to me and take out the book *I Love My Hair!* illustrated by E. B. Lewis, and open it to a page with two people walking. "For example, I don't know if E. B. Lewis made ovals first when he drew these people. He may have a different way of drawing people.

"And I've been noticing that right in this class there are illustrators who don't use ovals to draw people, and their people look real. For example, Marisol, I was looking in your book about your first day of

FIGURE 4.6 Marisol does not use ovals to draw people.

school and I noticed this picture. It sure looks like a real person." (See Figure 4.6.)

"And I didn't use ovals!" she says with pride.

"That's what I thought."

Imani suggests, "Or maybe she used the ovals but then she put the clothes on and you can't see them."

"Well, that's a possibility, but Marisol just told us that she didn't do that. And Flevor, your people look real and you don't use ovals, either, do you? And Aisha, Jahaan . . ."

Other children call out, "Me, too!"

"Well, you're all good at making people look real, and I'm discovering that you do it a lot of different ways. So today I thought we might get a couple of the illustrators in this class to show us how they draw people. That way we'll have a few different ways we might want to try, too."

Let me show you what I mean . . .

"Marisol, I was wondering if you would come up and right here, on this paper, show us how you draw a person. Here's what I want you to do.

As you draw, I'd like you to talk out loud and explain to us what you're doing. You know how when I drew this"—I point to the oval person I just drew—"I talked out loud about what I was doing? I said, 'First I make an oval for the head, then I make these two curved lines. . .' When people get to watch and hear the words for what they're seeing, it can help them to understand it better."

Marisol comes up, takes the pencil from my hand, and says emphatically, "I don't use a oval, I use a circle."

She begins drawing as she says, "I make a circle, then I make the lines for the neck, then I go straight across and down and go across to make the arm, then I go up to make the shirt."

She stands back to show the head, neck, and shirt, and the kids erupt into applause.

She resumes drawing. "And for the pants I go down, and I go over and up a little bit, and I go back and go up."

The children clap again. One child calls out, "What about the shoes?" and Marisol puts the shoes on the person.

"Marisol," I say, once the applause has ceased, "who taught you how to draw a person like that?"

"Mrs. Baron," she says, referring to the preschool teacher.

"It seems like you learned how to draw a person already dressed—you don't start with the ovals underneath the clothes. So, boys and girls, that's another way to draw a person and make them look real.

"Now, Aisha, I was noticing how you made people, and it doesn't look like you use ovals, either, do you?"

Aisha comes up and gives a step-by-step lesson while explaining how to draw a person. Her instructions are similar to Marisol's, except that she leaves space between the legs. She says, "You come down, then over then up, then down for the other leg, and over at the bottom, and up." (See Figure 4.7.)

Flevor comes up next. He shows us how to draw a person looking like they're running, and he acts it out for us, stopping drawing to stand in the running position, pointing to his bent leg, saying, "It goes like this and down, so I make it like this and down."

"So Flevor," I say when he is finished, "it seems that you're really good at picturing the person in the position you're drawing. You try to draw it just as you see it in your mind."

He says, "I just think, The legs look like this"—he acts out a running position—"then I draw it."

So, today as you write . . .

"Today we got to see how Marisol, Aisha, and Flevor draw people differently from the way I showed you, the way we learned from David Wisniewski. You may want to try drawing people the way Marisol or Aisha or Flevor do, or you may decide ovals are the best way for you, or you may have another way. The important thing is to try to make your people look real." (See Figure 4.8.)

Why we chose this book

We refer to illustrators of books they know well, illustrators whose work we've been looking at as we've been discussing how to draw people.

FIGURE 4.7 Aisha shows her classmates how she draws a person.

FIGURE 4.8 Drawings of people by Marisol, Aisha, and Flevor.

Suggested other books	• Any book where the people are drawn in a way that makes it easy to see the shape of the body
	• *Goal*, by Robert Burleigh, illustrated by Stephen T. Johnson
	• *Karate Hour*, by Carol Nevius, illustrated by Bill Thomson
	• *Bippity Bop Barbershop*, by Natasha Anastasia Tarpley, illustrated by E. B. Lewis

 Lesson Drawing People in Action

What's going on in the classroom	• Most of the children's drawings include people.
	• Children have been incorporating information about how to draw people and how clothing can help readers know something about the people.
	• Most of the time, however, they draw the people standing straight, looking forward.
What's next	• They need information about drawing people in action.
Materials needed	• my sketchbook with people in action, made using ovals
	• my Drawing & Writing Book
	• Shammala's Drawing & Writing Book, where she drew a person in action
	• *Goal*, by Robert Burleigh, illustrated by Stephen T. Johnson

FIGURE 4.9 Shammala's drawing showing a person "in action."

"When Flevor showed us how he draws a person the other day, he drew one running. Today I want to talk to you about how to draw people so they look like they're doing the things that the story says they're doing. I think that's what you did in this illustration, Shammala." I hold up her Drawing & Writing Book (see Figure 4.9). "It looks like you were trying to show the person moving. Were you?"

She nods.

"Stephen T. Johnson's illustrations in this book, *Goal*, by Robert Burleigh, show all these soccer players in action, too." I flip through the pages of this book, which we have read together, and we talk about the actions.

"You know, boys and girls, you can do that, too. Remember when we had that sketching lesson about how to draw people in different positions? We said that when we draw people using ovals, we use those same parts no matter what position the people are in."

I refer to a page in my sketchbook where I used ovals to make people in different positions: "On this page it looks like a person is running, and I used the same oval parts: the head, the torso, the upper arm, lower arm, and hand, upper leg, lower leg, and foot. In this one, the person is sitting down, and look: head, torso, upper legs, lower legs, and feet, upper arms . . . Well, you can take what you learned about drawing people in action in your sketchbooks and use that information to draw people in action in your Drawing & Writing Books."

"Let me show you," I say as I open my Drawing & Writing Book, "how I tried to draw my people in the positions that show what they're doing.

"Remember that story I told you about my grandson Will and how when I first get to his house he kneels down and looks to see what books and things I brought in my bag? You can see that he is kneeling and bending over the bag. Here's his body. His legs are bent at the knees and his head is looking down.

"And on this page, when I drew my grandma, you can see her sitting in her rocking chair making her quilts. She's not standing up facing forward; we can tell that she's sitting because her legs go out to the side and then down.

"And on this page I wanted to make it look like I was running, so I made my legs and arms bent.

"So, I traced the people from my stories on this transparency using ovals." I place the transparency with oval-shaped people, in different positions, against a piece of white paper. (See Figures 4.10a and 4.10b.) "You can see that when I drew these people, I used the same body parts as we used when we sketched the standing up person—the head, the torso, the upper arm, lower arm, hands, upper leg, lower leg, feet—only now those ovals are in different positions. You don't see the ovals because the people have clothes on, and you also don't see the

FIGURE 4.10A A transparency shows three characters from the teacher's Drawing & Writing Book in different positions: sitting, running, kneeling.

FIGURE 4.10B The actual drawings traced over on the transparency showing three characters in different positions: sittng, running, kneeling.

people standing straight up, facing forward. I used those ovals to help me draw people in the positions I wanted them."

So, today as you write . . . "So when you go back to your work today, think about what the people in this part of your story are doing. Look and see if the people are in the positions they should be in so that the story makes sense. And remember, if you use ovals to draw your people, you'll still use the same ovals—just in different positions."

Why we chose this book • The children know the book and will be able to look at it in a more specific way.

Suggested other books • *Karate Hour*, by Carol Nevius, illustrated by Bill Thomson
• *Two Girls Can*, by Keiko Narahashi
• *Ballerina Flying*, by Alexa Brandenberg
• *My Big Brother*, by Miriam Cohen, illustrated by Ronald Himler

We could imagine a lesson after this one in which we would address how to put clothes on people in action—shooting a basket, running, riding a bike. It can be tricky for young children if they've drawn someone from a side view to have only one side of the face showing. A lesson on drawing profiles could be helpful to them as well.

We could also imagine a lesson earlier on about drawing ovals lightly, so that when you put the clothes on them, you won't see the ovals through the clothes. We haven't tried these lessons, so we don't know how students will respond. What we do know is that the more we notice about how children work, how professional illustrators tell their stories, and how to craft stories through pictures, the more possible lessons we see.

Lesson Drawing People from the Back

What's going on in the classroom

- Children are trying different ways to draw people looking real, having watched classmates demonstrate different ways to do it.
- Because children tell stories about doing things and going places, some are attempting to draw people in action, doing things and going places.
- Some members of the class have a sense of how to draw a person from the back. Some don't.

What's next

- We want children to know how it would look to see someone from behind as they're going somewhere. Since some members of the class do it well, we decided to ask a student to explain it to the others.

Materials needed

- a page from a child's story where he or she has drawn a person going somewhere, viewed from behind
- a blank page in the teacher's enlarged Drawing & Writing Book or sketchbook
- *Bigmama's*, by Donald Crews

This is what I noticed . . .

"Remember the other day when Marisol and Aisha and Flevor showed us how they draw people so they look real? And Flevor showed us how he draws a person in a running position? Well, in all of those illustrations, we could see the front of the people. We see their faces and the front of their bodies. And in most of your stories, we see people from the front. Today I want to talk to you about how to draw a person when they're going somewhere and we see them from the back. Like, John, you drew that picture of you and your dad walking into Stop & Shop in the morning before school to buy Lunchables, remember?

"Yesterday, Simone drew a picture of herself going bowling. Right here, underneath this illustration, it says . . . would you read it to us, Simone?"

She reads, "'I went to Boston Bowl.'"

"And we see the back of her, going into Boston Bowl."

I ask Simone if she would show us how she did that. "How do you draw a person when we see them from the back?" I ask her to do what Marisol and Aisha and Flevor did the other day, to say out loud what she is doing as she is drawing, because it really helps us when we can see *and* hear what someone is doing. (See photo at the beginning of the chapter, page 69.)

Let me show you what I mean . . .

Simone stands at the easel and begins, "First you draw the head." She makes an oval. "Then after, you draw little circles for the hair."

"Oh, you mean the braids?" I say, "like your braids?" She nods.

"If you want to make a neck, you make a line down, then another one down," she says, and moves on quickly. "If you want to make a shirt, you go straight across"—she draws a pencil line to the left, from the neck—"go straight down, then go to the right, go back up, go back to the right . . ." She gives us words for every line she draws. The children are up on their knees, watching.

"If you want to make the shirt, you just go down. And if you want to make the pants, go like this. This is a new way how I make the pants."

Her teacher interjects, saying, "You know, boys and girls, usually when you draw someone from the back, it is because they're going somewhere. We see them from behind. So Simone, what could you put here to show that this person is going somewhere? Like into a house or a store . . ."

"Well," Simone says as she draws a triangle shape above the girl's head to show it is in the distance of where she's headed, "you just make the roof to look like this." She draws a triangle, then says in a "voila" voice, "Then you have the roof!" She leans back, eyes her work, then continues. "You go down to make the building. And if you want to make the door open, you go like this." She adds three sides of a rectangle, attaching it to the building she has just drawn. Then she adds groupings of circles between the open door and the building, and I point to them, saying, "Tell us about these."

"Those are, um, I forgot. They open up the door."

"Oh, you mean the hinges?"

"Yeah," Simone says, continuing to add to her drawing. "And if you want a window in the door, you just go like this . . .," and she draws a circle window. Then she stands back to assess what she has done.

"Boys and girls, we can see this person walking into this doorway, can't we? Simone has shown us how to draw a person from behind, the way you would draw a person who is going somewhere. In this picture we see the person and we see where she is going. And if we look at this book by Donald Crews"—I hold up *Bigmama's*—"we can see this person going into the room. The door is open and we see him from the back. On this page we see a girl (and she has braids just like Simone's drawing!) at the edge of the pond. It looks like she's jumping. She's probably excited about the fish!" (We look through the book at other examples). "Boy, it seems like Donald Crews does just what Simone did. When he shows people going somewhere or looking at something, we see the back of the person, and we see where they're going."

So, today as you write . . .

"So today, if you're working on a drawing in your story, think about all that we've learned from the people in this class about how to draw people so they look real. And if someone in your story is going somewhere and you want readers to see where they're going, think about what Simone showed us about drawing people from behind. That might help you to think about how you'll make the person in your drawing."

Why we chose this book	• The children are familiar with it. It illustrates, in a rather simple way, what we've been talking about.
Suggested other books	• *Subway*, by Anastasia Suen, illustrated by Karen Katz • *Shortcut*, by Donald Crews • *Night at the Fair*, by Donald Crews

Lesson Specific Physical Features: Hairstyles

What's going on in the classroom	• Almost all the stories that the children are telling in their Drawing & Writing Books have people in them, but sometimes they draw the hair the same, no matter who the person is and how their hair really looks.
What's next	• They need to know that one of the details a drawer thinks about is the hair of the characters in their drawings.
Materials needed	• the work of a student where it shows attention given to hair • *Roller Coaster,* by Marla Frazee
This is what I noticed . . .	"When I was looking at Loriana's Drawing & Writing Book last night, I noticed that Loriana looked different in a lot of her pictures. And when I looked closely, I noticed it was her hair that looked different in many of her stories. It reminded me of how when authors draw pictures to tell their stories, they try to make the people look real."
Let me show you what I mean . . .	"On this page where she's at a party climbing this inflatable shoe, which was really a water sliding board, her hair was curly—just look at all those curls." (See Figure 4.11.)

"And on this page when she was cheerleading with her sister, her hair was behind her ears." (See Figure 4.12.)

"On this other page her hair was behind her ears and a curl was dangling in her face. Of course her hairdo is special because she was at a party." (See Figure 4.13.)

"And it doesn't surprise me at all that she wrote on this other page, 'My mom is so good with my hair.' Look at her again when her mom curled her hair! When Loriana draws herself, she wants her readers to see just how she looks at different times." (See Figure 4.14.)

"Marla Frazee does the same thing. When she illustrated *Roller Coaster* (2003), she put a lot of people in her story. I think she drew them so they would look like they really looked on the day at the fair. Here's a lady with short blond hair, parted down the middle; a lady with a scarf on and all you can see is her long red hair hanging out at the back with a few curls in the front; a lady with a black ponytail, tied with a red ribbon, high on her head; and way over here, twin girls with black hair, one with two ponytails, and the other with three braids on each side of her head; and a little girl with her brown hair pulled back and |

FIGURE 4.11 Loriana with curly hair. *This is me climbing a shoe with water.*

FIGURE 4.12 Loriana with hair behind her ears. *Me and my sister are cheerleading.*

FIGURE 4.13 Loriana with hair behind her ears and a curl dangling in her face. *I was at a party.*

FIGURE 4.14 Loriana after her mom curled her hair. *My mom is so good with my hair.*

made into one ponytail. Marla Frazee was trying to make the people look as real as she could, and one way to do it was to make their hair the way it really looks."

So, today as you write . . .	"So, boys and girls, as you draw your people today and every day, remember that one way you can make the people in your story look real is how you draw their hair. "Is it parted on the side? In the middle? Is it in a ponytail, in braids, or straight down? Is it orangish, yellowish, reddish? Brown? Black . . .?"
Why we chose this book	The children are already familiar with the story. In the illustrations we see a variety of hairstyles, and the hairstyles are consistent for each character.
Suggested other books	• *Subway*, by Anastasia Suen, illustrated by Karen Katz • *Come On, Rain!* by Karen Hesse, illustrated by Jon J. Muth • *We Keep a Store*, by Anne Shelby, paintings by John Ward

 Lesson Specific Physical Features: Skin, Eyes, and So On

What's going on in the classroom	• Although there are multicultural crayons and pencils in the caddies, children don't always use them. Their drawings of people aren't colored in at all or are all colored the same.
What's next	• They need to know that writers try to tell and draw their stories as true to life as they can. Making each person's skin its real color is one way of doing this.
Materials needed	• some student-published work that shows kindergarten writers attending to the skin color of the people in their stories • a caddie with multicultural crayons and/or multicultural pencils
This is what I noticed . . .	"Yesterday we said that one way of making the people in our stories look real is by drawing and coloring their hair so that it looks just like their real hair, and I noticed that's just what Alize did when she published this story when she was in kindergarten. It's called 'I Like the Park,' and right here on the cover, she was really thinking about her mom and her sister and herself. Her mom has long hair that has some curls, and it's a little bit red. Her sister's hair is black, and she wears it with one braid on the top of her head. And Alize, of course, has many braids in this picture, just the way her hair really looks. "I also noticed that Alize does something else to make her people look just the way they look in real life. She thinks about the color of the skin of the people in her story."
Let me show you what I mean . . .	"Look at Alize, her sister, and her mom on the cover of her story. Alize colored in their skin, their faces, and their hands to make them look real.

Kaja did the same thing in her book called 'When I Rented a Movie' and even colored the little bit of the legs that showed. And Audrey colored in her face and her uncle's face in this book, called 'I Went to Karate with My Uncle.' I'm noticing that the skin color of the people in Alize's story isn't exactly the same shade as the people's in Audrey's story, and Kaja's people are a different shade, too. These illustrators wanted to make sure that the people in their stories really look like themselves."

So, today as you write . . .

"So today, and every day, remember that when you color the skin of the people in your stories, it's another way to make them look real. And remember, too, that in your caddies, there are multicultural colored crayons and pencils to help you as you try to make a person's skin color look real."

Why we chose these books

The Colors of Us, by Karen Katz, addresses the topic of skin color explicitly.

Suggested other books

- *Subway*, by Anastasia Suen, illustrated by Karen Katz
- *Roller Coaster*, by Marla Frazee
- *Two Girls Can*, by Keiko Narahashi

We can also see talking with children about skin colors during an interactive read-aloud of Karen Katz's *The Colors of Us*. Through her text and illustrations, she helps her young character, Lena, notice and celebrate the many different skin colors of the people in her neighborhood and see that all skin colors are different shades of brown. By finding the right color, or mixing some (red, yellow, black, and white) together, we can make the people in our drawings look more real. (We've never tried it, but wouldn't it be a great art lesson to actually have children experiment with mixing red, yellow, white, and black paint to make different shades of brown?) Having read and talked about the book, it seems like a good book to refer to in a mini-lesson to remind children that one way to make the people in their stories look real is by making the skin colors look real.

Once we did this lesson where children mixed paints to get different shades of brown, they would benefit from knowing how to use two or more of the multicultural pencils or crayons to get the desired skin shade for the people in their stories. On another day, we could imagine asking them to sit in a circle, then rest their elbows on the rug so that their forearms and hands are touching. Then we'd talk about the different shades of brown that we have in this class. We'd bring out the colored pencils and crayons and talk about the shades that would best depict "us" using the names on them: mahogany, peach, ebony, chestnut, melon, gingerbread, fawn, toast, cinnamon, sepia, olive, and so on. We'd point out that sometimes you have to mix two of the colors together to get the exact shade you want. Then, we'd go back to one of our stories and shade in the skin of the characters, once again making the point that as you try to make the people in your stories look as real as possible, sometimes you have to mix two colors together. On another day, in another lesson, we might ask a child to show us how he mixed the shades to get his skin color just right.

The prior two lessons address two physical features: hairdos and skin colors. Sometimes, children might generalize from these two lessons and begin to pay attention to eye color as well. We could see addressing that in a mini-lesson, too.

 Lesson Clothing Helps Readers Know Something About the People

What's going on in the classroom	• Children are getting better at drawing people so that they look real. They're remembering to depict their hairstyles, shade their skin, and put clothing on them so they look the way they want them to.
What's next	• They need to know that illustrators use appropriate clothing for the people in their stories because they know that the way people are dressed helps readers know something about them.
Materials needed	• *My Big Brother*, by Miriam Cohen, illustrated by Ronald Himler • *I Am a Ballerina*, by Valerie Coulman, illustrated by Sandra Lamb • *Mama Elizabeti, Elizabeti's Doll,* and *Elizabeti's School*, by Stephanie Stuve-Bodeen, illustrated by Christy Hale
This is what I noticed . . .	"We've been talking a lot about how illustrators make people look real. We said that one way they do it is by dressing them to look the way they really looked in the story you're telling. Today I want to talk to you about how the clothing that the people in stories are wearing helps us know something about them."
Let me show you what I mean . . .	"Let's look at these people in *My Big Brother* again. The brothers are usually wearing jeans or shorts and T-shirts when they're playing around the house or outside. Then, they're dressed in really special clothes for church. It seems that Ronald Himler wants us to know that they like being comfortable when they're playing around the house, and that for church, they dress differently, in suits and ties, and the mom wears that flowered dress and that beautiful hat. It seems like he wants us to know there's something special about church. "In *I Am a Ballerina*, the illustrator, Sandra Lamb, helps us to know something about this girl and her family just by the clothes the people have on. On this page, the girl dressed up in a tutu, and it looks like she made it from her dad's tie and some feather dusters. By the way she is dressed, it looks like she has fun dressing up and pretending. And then on the next page, the dad is wearing a shirt and tie and the mom is in her bathrobe. The dad and the mom sure look different on this page"—I flip back a page—"from how they look on this page. Just by the way they're dressed, I'm thinking maybe it's early morning and the dad is going to work and the mom and the little girl aren't dressed yet.

"And then there are the Elizabeti books: *Elizabeti's Doll, Mama Elizabeti, Elizabeti's School.* The people in these stories seem to be dressed in the same clothes a lot. Elizabeti is wearing the same dress in *Elizabeti's School* that she wore in *Mama Elizabeti.* Her mama has the same dress and same turban on in all three stories. I think the illustrator, Christy Hale, wants us to know that these people live in a place where people wear turbans on their heads and use kangas to carry things. We see that they don't have lots of different clothes: maybe they don't have much money for clothes, or maybe having lots of different clothes isn't important. And they're all beautiful colors—look, we can see them hanging on the clothesline.

"I think Ronald Himler and Sandra Lamb and Christy Hale thought carefully about how the people in their stories would be dressed because they know that the kind of clothes people wear and the way they wear them gives readers a peek into their lives, which lets readers get to know the people in the stories better. And you know, Shammala did the same thing. She helps us to see what it's like in Haiti by the way she has the people in her story dressed." (See Figure 4.15 in the color insert.)

So, today as you write . . .

"So as you begin work today, look at your illustrations and ask yourself, Do the clothes that the people in my story are wearing help readers know something about them? If not, see what you can do to make the clothes, and the way the people are wearing them, help readers to know something about those people."

Why we chose these books

The clothing on the people in each of these books depicts different lifestyles, activities, classes, ethnic cultures, times in history, and so on, and we want children to learn how to reveal specific information through clothing. Also, since the children know these books well, we don't have to read them during the lesson. We can just refer them to the elements of craft that we want to address.

Suggested other books

- *Dim Sum for Everyone!* by Grace Lin
- *The Relatives Came*, by Cynthia Rylant, illustrated by Stephen Gammell
- *Matthew and Tilly*, by Rebecca C. Jones, illustrated by Beth Peck
- Actually, any book that honestly portrays the story it is telling through the illustrations reveals something about the time, the culture, the class, the lifestyle, and the bigger story of the people.

 ## Lesson Planning How to Draw Your Story

What's going on in the classroom

- Children have been telling stories orally and have a sense of story.
- They work in their Drawing & Writing Books daily.
- Most of them tell the story through drawing; some put random letters, and some write words.
- Lately we're seeing pages that look like "scribbles" or a bunch of different designs. Although students know the routine for writing, it

seems as though they've forgotten how to go from the thoughts in their heads to the pictures on paper.

What's next

- They need a vision for how to illustrate the stories they want to tell, a strategy for bringing the ideas from their heads to the page.

Materials needed

- a child, and his or her Drawing & Writing Book
- *My Cats Nick and Nora*, by Isabelle Harper, illustrated by Barry Moser
- a small mirror that children could have access to

This is what I noticed . . .

"I was looking at the books we've read since the beginning of the school year, and one of my favorites is *My Cats Nick and Nora* by Isabelle Harper and illustrated by Barry Moser. One thing I love about this book is the illustrations. When I open the book and look at the illustrations, I think, Barry Moser must have thought really carefully about how he wanted to draw them, because when we look at them, we know just what is happening. Look at this page."

I open to the page of the birthday party and point to the different parts of the illustration as I say, "We see that Emmie and Isabelle are having a party with their cats and dogs. I know, because here, Rosie is wearing a Happy Birthday hat and so is the puppy. And here, it looks like the puppy has balloons tied to her leash! Even the parrot is at the party. And here, Emmie is blowing bubbles, and look, it looks like the cats are drinking from the dish of bubble water!"

A child calls out, "He's going like this . . ." and imitates licking his lips.

"Maybe he likes it!" I say, amused.

Other children are repulsed, saying, "Eeuw!"

"You know, I was wondering if Barry Moser had a photograph of Emmie and her cousin and the pets that day and then, when he got ready to draw, he just looked at the picture and drew what he saw. I know that some illustrators have people pose for them, take a picture with a camera, and then draw from the picture. But you won't have pictures of the things you want to draw; most of the time the pictures are in your mind and you just have to remember them. So let's imagine Barry Moser didn't have a picture to look at. I'll bet he would do some things to help him remember just what to draw."

Let me show you what I mean . . .

Think hard.

"First, I'll bet he'd think really hard about what it looked like at the party."

Close your eyes and remember.

"Maybe he closed his eyes to help him remember. Sometimes I do that. He might have tried to get a picture in his mind of what he wanted to draw."

I close my eyes as I say, "Maybe he said, 'Oh yeah, I remember what it looked like. Emmie was blowing bubbles and the cats were drinking out of the bubble dish and the bird was out of the cage.' And, 'Oh yeah, don't forget the puppy with the balloons tied to her leash. And Isabelle was looking like she was having so much fun!'

"You know, I'll bet he did something like that to try to remember because he would want his picture to look just the way it was that day."

Use your hand to plan where things go.
I hold up the opened page and use my hand to point as I say, "Then maybe he planned where he was going to draw those things. Maybe he said, 'I'll put the table right here in the middle and the cats on the table because that's where they were, and I'll put Emmie over here blowing bubbles. And over here I'll make Isabelle. I'll make her laughing because I remember that laughing face. She was having so much fun! And the dogs—I can't forget the dogs. They were standing on the floor, so I'm going to make them here. We might not be able to see all of them, but I'll draw enough so readers will know they were there. And the balloons— where will I put them? Oh yeah, they were on the puppy's leash!'"

Act it out.
"I can imagine that when he tried to draw Emmie blowing the bubbles, he had to make her face look like she was blowing bubbles, right? And sometimes that's hard. So maybe he had to act it out—to pretend he was blowing bubbles so he could feel his cheeks all puffy. Maybe he had to look in a mirror and try it, like this." I take a small mirror and make my face look like it is blowing bubbles. "Oh yeah," I say, looking into the mirror, "I see how my cheeks are puffed out. Now, how would I draw that?

"Or maybe he had to go and watch someone who was blowing bubbles so he could study what it really looks like. Because it really does look like she's blowing bubbles, doesn't it? When I illustrate my stories, it helps me to do those things.

"Remember when I was telling my story about walking Bella with Abby? First, *I tried hard to remember* the parts of that story. Then, I thought about what I wanted to draw and *I closed my eyes* to help me remember what it looked like. Then *I used my hand* to help me think about where I was going to draw Abby, Bella, me, the water . . ." I use my hand to model where things would go on the page. "Then, remember how I stood up and pretended I was holding the leash and Bella was pulling it like this?" I say as I act it out. "And this arm was flying backward? *I had to act it out* because I wanted to draw her just the way she looked. Doing those things helped me plan out my story. I'll bet some of you are thinking about your stories.

"Who has a story in their mind that they plan to illustrate today?" I ask, and a student who is going to start a new page comes up.

"Tell us what you're going to draw on this page," I say, and she uses her hand to plan out where she will put the parts of her story, even acts out what it will look like when she's kicking the ball.

So, today as you write . . . "So when you begin working, you might try some of those things. When you decide what you want to draw, try closing your eyes to remember. You could try using your hand to help you plan where to draw the parts of your story. You might need to act something out or study someone who is doing what you want to draw. When you get back to your tables, don't forget those things. They might help you think about how to make your illustration the best it can be."

Why we chose this book

We chose the book *My Cats Nick and Nora* because the children knew it well. We chose this page in the book because the page had specific information but wasn't too crowded. We were looking for a familiar page to use as a model, one with enough white space yet enough detail so that it wouldn't be too overwhelming. This page had both.

Suggested other books

- *My Dog Rosie*, by Isabelle Harper, illustrated by Barry Moser
- *Our New Puppy*, by Isabelle Harper, illustrated by Barry Moser
- any book that has specific information on the page but not too much

Sometimes when boys and girls have a story in mind when they get ready to draw, they have a plan for drawing the story, but resort to what we call "safe drawing." "Safe drawing" sometimes includes, but is not limited to, a combination of the following: the outside of a house with some windows and a door, a tree on the side of it, the sun and the clouds in the sky, and maybe a person or two facing forward, all adorned with flowers, rainbows and/or butterflies. This is exactly what happened to Alena when she was trying to tell the story about going to the candy store and choosing a bagful of candy.

 ## Lesson Going Beyond Safe Drawings

What's going on in the classroom

- Children are choosing their own stories to draw and/or write about.
- In some Drawing & Writing Books, the same picture is on each page (usually a house, tree, flower, sun, and grass) even though the students tell you each story is a different story.
- In some instances, it's a "safe drawing"—they've done it lots of times, and may even have been drawing it since before kindergarten.
- They need to know that when they tell their stories with drawings, readers can tell what the story is about only by what they see on the page.

Materials needed

- Alena's Drawing & Writing Book

This is what I noticed . . .

"Boys and girls, yesterday I was conferring with Alena and I noticed that a lot of her drawings look the same even though her stories are about a lot of different things. She has a house, the sun, grass, flowers, trees"—I show them some of her pages—"but when I asked her about the story she was working on and what it was about, she told me it was about going to the candy store! She told me that there were lots of boxes of candy and that a lady was behind the cash register, and that she had to pay the lady for the candy, and that the lady gave her a bag to put it in. Do you remember, Alena, when I asked you how you might draw the inside of the store with all those things your story is about, you said all you could draw was this?" I point to her page with a house, sun, flower, and so on.

She smiles and nods.

"So of course she drew the outside because she just wasn't sure how to draw the inside. So now, if she really wants her readers to know her story about what happened when she was inside the candy store, she probably wouldn't draw the outside—she would draw the inside. And that's exactly what she did after our conference yesterday. All this got me wondering how many other boys and girls have a really good story to tell but think they just can't draw it. So I thought we'd show you how Alena drew the inside of the candy store so that her readers would know about the big bagful of candy she got."

Let me show you what I mean . . .   "Using her hand, she showed me where everything would go: the shelf with the boxes of candy, the cash register, the lady, the bag of candy— just everything. And look at what she did. Here you see the shelf with all the boxes of candy. You can even see the different pieces of candy! And here she's looking at the candy—so she's in front of it, and here's the lady behind the counter with the cash register drawer open, the dollar bill in her hand, getting ready to put the money in the drawer. Look how Alena is holding the bag of candy. Now when someone looks at this picture, they know it's about a girl in a candy store buying candy." (See Figure 4.16 in the color insert.)

"But at first, she thought she couldn't do it. So I asked her to close her eyes and try to remember how the shelf looked. And what did you say, Alena?"

"It looked like a rectangle."

"That's what she told me. She said it looked like a rectangle, so then I asked her, 'So, how could you draw the shelf?' and that's when she drew this big rectangle. And on her own, she put the box of candy on the shelf. I left her to work on her illustration and went to hear Jonathan's story, and she did the rest all by herself. I think she just needed to have a way to get started with it. Sometimes, closing our eyes and trying to remember how something looked is a good way to begin."

So, today as you write . . .   "All of you writers have interesting stories to share with readers, and you want to be sure to draw a part of the story that will really let your readers understand your story. If you draw the outside of a house or building and the story takes place inside, your readers will miss your good story. They'll think it's about someone standing outside. So sometimes, you have to take your readers inside in order for them to know and understand your story. If you think you can't draw it, just close your eyes and try to picture how things looked and try your best."

Even though we presented so many lessons modeling how to draw people "filled out," how to make people look real using skin color and hairstyles, and how to go beyond safe drawing, we often still see stick figures, no skin shaded in, and lots of houses, suns, and trees. When we observe those things, we make a note of it. Why are these children not incorporating the information? What might I do to make this information more accessible? Is what I am asking them to do realistic and developmentally appropriate?

What we discover is that sometimes what we're asking them to do isn't what they need to be doing right then. So we continue to point these things out during read-alouds, in the stories that children in the class share, and in published works that other young writers have done, and we continue to support children individually, based on what they show us they can do and need to learn.

CHAPTER 5

Writing Words

EARLY ON, AMID THE MANY LESSONS on the craft of drawing, we want to show children that text also represents meaning. Some children come to school already knowing that, but many come to school not having had experiences with letters and sounds and need lots of support with writing words.

One way the teachers in these kindergarten classrooms provide support on a regular basis is through interactive writing lessons (see McCarrier, Pinnell, and Fountas 2000). Beginning on the first day of school and each day thereafter, teachers and students, together, compose messages and "share the pen" as they put words on paper. They may write text and/or label a mural in the classroom, title a bulletin board, write letters or thank-you notes, or list guidelines about how they will work in their room. (See Figures 5.1a in the color insert, 5.1b, 5.1c, and 5.1d.) Through this direct instruction, and by participating in the act of writing according to the conventions of the language, children become more and more familiar with how letters and sounds work. In turn, their teachers show them how to take the information they're learning about writing words during those sessions, and use it as they work in their Drawing & Writing Books.

Yet the text in their Drawing & Writing Books won't look like what we see during these teacher-led sessions, at least not at first.

FIGURE 5.1B A label on a bulletin board filled with environmental print done during interactive writing.

FIGURE 5.1C A thank-you note to the principal done during interactive writing.

FIGURE 5.1D Class rules written as a list done during interactive writing.

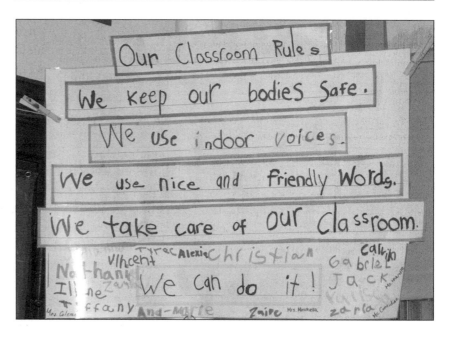

Talking, Drawing, Writing

That is because these two opportunities for writing serve different purposes. During interactive writing lessons, the children are guided as they compose a common text that looks like writing as we see it in the world, spelled and punctuated correctly. In the Drawing & Writing Book, the children work independently. They use what they know about making meaning with words, and if they don't add text to their drawings on their own, we nudge them by saying things like, "If there were words on this page, what do you think they'd say?" or "If you were going to write the word ——, what letter would you write?" or "If you were going to write one word about this story, what would it be?" Their early attempts—random letters, sound spellings, one-letter-per-word sentences with no spacing—or their hesitancy to write letters at all are instructive. Their marks on paper, and how they go about putting them there, help us see what they understand about writing words and tell us what they need to learn.

Some children, of course, show us that they know a lot about writing words, and we want to acknowledge what they can do and move them further. Others, who see their peers writing letters on their pages, often do the same but without understanding how those letters relate to the words they're speaking. These children need us to teach them that there is a relationship between the words they say and the letters they put on the page. In this first lesson, we do that by presenting a strategy for writing words.

 ## Lesson Listening for Sounds in Words

What's going on in the classroom	• Children are working independently in their Drawing & Writing Books.
	• Most children are illustrating part of a story.
	• A couple of children are labeling or writing some words; most are not.
	• A child who shared the previous day had written letters to represent parts of her picture.
What's next	• They need information about how to put text on the page.
Materials needed	• Drawing & Writing Book of a student who has some labels
	• teacher's enlarged Drawing & Writing Book with a story almost completely illustrated
	• thick marker
This is what I noticed . . .	As the children come to the rug, they see me working on my almost completed illustration. I keep working on it as they get settled. They make comments like, "Who's that?" and "That's good!" and I stay focused on my work, adding more to the drawing as I respond.
	"Well, thank you for saying that. Actually, sometimes my drawings don't look the way I want them to, but I sure am trying my best. This is

about when my nephews came to my house to stay overnight. We had so much fun. One thing we did was go to the playground near my house. That's the part I'm telling about on this page. Here is Sam on the swing, and Ben is inside the little playhouse. You can't see him, but you can see his blond hair right here."

Once I see that they're all at the rug, focusing on what I'm doing, I stop working, turn to them, and say, "You already know that one way to tell a story is by drawing the picture, the way I'm doing here and the way most of you are doing in your Drawing & Writing Books. Another way is to write words that tell about the pictures the way Jazmine did in that story she shared yesterday."

I hold up Jazmine's Drawing & Writing Book, open to the page. "Remember how she told us the story of going to the beach and building sand castles? And then here she wrote *J* for *Jazmine*, here she made an *A* for her aunt *Aida*. And here she wrote *S* for *sand castle*. She did that because she knows that when you write letters or words, it's another way to help readers understand your story.

"Today I'm going to put some words on my page to help readers know what my story is about. That's something you may want to do in your story, too.

"Now, you might be thinking, But I don't know how to spell the words, and that might be true, because when you're five or six and you're just learning about letters and sounds, you won't know how to spell a lot of the words in your story. But I'm going to show you how you can begin to *write* words—any word you want."

Let me show you what I mean . . .

"First you think of the word you want to write. I'm thinking, Hmm, what word might I want to write for this picture that will tell something about it? . . . Well, this part is really about the playground, isn't it? So I think I'll write *playground*. Now I have to find a spot on this page to write it. Let's see, where can I write the word *playground* . . . I think I'll write it right here." I point to the top, where there is space to write letters.

"Now, I actually *do* know how to spell that word because I'm a grown-up and I've been writing words for a very long time. But if I were five or six, like you, I probably wouldn't know how to spell it, so here's what I'd do.

"I'd say the word slowly, stretching the sounds and blending them together. I'd say it again, slowly, and I'd especially listen for the sound at the beginning: /p/ /p/ and I'd think, What letter makes that /p/ sound?"

Some children call out, "*P*!"

"Some of you are saying *P*, and that's what I think it is, too. *P* for /p/, so I'm going to make a *P* right here." I point to the spot where I will write the letter.

"I have to remember how to write *P*, so I'll look at this alphabet chart, or this chart with all of our names, just like we do when we're writing all together. You know, I'm so glad we have these charts, because when I'm writing and I need to know a letter, I can just look right on this alphabet chart to help me remember. Now, if I don't remember what *P* looks like, I can start with *A* and read *A-B-C-D-E-F-*

G . . . all the way to *P*. But I know *P* is for *pig*, and here's the picture of the pig, so here's the letter *P*."

I model taking a close look and use my finger to trace the letter. "Now I'll write it. I'll make a *P* right up here, for *playground*. ✉ Hey, I just noticed something! Over here is the playhouse, and /p/layhouse starts with the same sound as /p/layground, doesn't it!"

Children call out, "*P*!"

"There's a /p/ at the beginning of /p/layhouse, just like /p/layground, so I'm going to put a *P* here, next to the playhouse so readers will know. And I don't even need to look at the chart this time. I can just look at the *P* I made here," I say, pointing.

"Then, over here I want to write *Sam* so everyone who looks at my page will know this is Sam. When I say, /S/ /a/ /m/, I say it slowly and I listen to what is at the beginning: /s/, /s/. I know that *S* makes the /s/ sound because"—I point to the name chart—"I know /S/teven and /S/avaughn start like /S/am and their names start with *S*, so I'll write *S* here, right above this picture of Sam. But you know what? I know how to spell Sam's name! It's *S-a-m*, so I'm going to write his whole name right here above where he's swinging on the swing. Hey, I just heard something! /S/wing starts like /S/am, so I'll put an *S* right here, next to the /s/wing. And here's the sand on the ground under the swing and /s/and starts like /s/wing and /S/am, so I'm going to make an *S* for *sand*, right here, next to this brown, sandy part on the ground. Wow, a lot of *S*'s!

"Now when people look at this page, they can read the story by looking at the pictures but they'll be able to read it another way, too. They can look at the letters and words: *S* for *sand* and *swing*, *S-a-m* for *Sam*, *P* for *playground* and *playhouse*."

So, today as you write . . .

"Here's what I want you to think about today and every day as you write. When you're learning to write words, you can't possibly know how to spell every word correctly. But what you can do is give it your best try: First, think of what you want to say. Say the word slowly. Listen for the sounds in the word. Ask yourself, What letter makes that sound? Write the letters for the sounds you hear."

In this lesson, *writing words* means labeling parts of the illustration with a letter that represents an initial consonant sound. In thinking about what part of my story to draw, I considered what I could represent with letters whose sounds most children would know. I made sure there were a few objects that share the same one or two beginning sounds. For example, I labeled five things—playground, playhouse, Sam, swing, and sand—-five objects that begin with two sounds that are usually easy for children to recognize and letters they often know. I wrote *only the first letter* of each word, except for the name, because our goal for a lesson like this is for children to feel successful when it comes to putting words down on paper. We want every child to think this is something they can do. However, I chose to write Sam's name because it is common for children to know how to spell the names of some family members, and we want them to see that when you do know how to spell a word, you write it the way you know how.

Eventually, children will write more than one letter per word. Ultimately they will write with confidence any words they need to express their thinking. For young children to write with such abandon, they need to know the following:

- how to listen for many sounds in words
- that letters make specific sounds
- that what you write needs to be readable by others and therefore needs to follow rules of the language
- how to keep track of what they're writing to know what to write next

Since they're all starting with a different set of experiences and understandings about letters, sounds, and words, they need to know that the way they write a word may look different from the way another person writes the same word. We need to show them that as we learn together, we allow room for differences.

One of the many places we address these topics is in the mini-lesson. Some we address based on having looked at students' work, some we address based on what we know about young children and writing, and others come from what we observe during writing conferences, as the following lesson does.

 ## Lesson Listening for Sounds in Words: Writing a Whole Sentence

What's going on in the classroom	• Children work independently in their Drawing & Writing Books. • They have seen a model lesson where the teacher labeled parts of her illustration, each part with one letter, to represent the beginning sound. • They have seen that other children have done the same thing—labeling with one letter to represent the beginning sound.
What's next	• They need to see this strategy illustrated again, and extended.
Materials needed	• a piece of writing in which a child has written a one-letter-per-word "sentence" • a piece of writing from a child in the class who has some parts of the illustration labeled
This is what I noticed . . .	"Boys and girls, remember the other day when Janaya shared her story about when her mom dropped her off at her friend's house to play and then went to work, and then later her dad came to pick her up in his car and took her to McDonald's? Well, when Janaya went back to work yesterday, she did something else to help readers understand her story, kind of like what Jazmine did the other day."

Talking, Drawing, Writing

Let me show you what I mean . . .

I hold up her book so they can see. (See Figure 5.2.) "She put some letters on her page to help readers like us understand her story. Right here there's a *J*."

"For *Janaya*!" someone calls out.

"Why don't you come up here and read this to us, Janaya?" She stands next to me and I point to the *J* and say, "Tell us what you wrote."

"This is me and that's *J* for *Janaya*, and this is *D* and that's my dad."

"And look, you crossed out this *D*. Tell us about that."

"Because it was that way and it 'sposed to be that way," she says, pointing.

"So first you made the *D* going this way." I turn to look at the children on the rug. "Boys and girls, when I was talking with Janaya yesterday, she had written this *D*"—I point to the backward *D*—"and I told her that those are the parts of the letter *D*, but that it had to be going the other way, right, Janaya?"

She nods.

FIGURE 5.2 Janaya: *My dad picked me up.*

"So she just crossed it out and wrote it the way it goes. And that's what writers do. When they write something and it's not the way they want it, they cross out and try again.

"Janaya, you did some other writing right here," I point to the letters *g, R,* and *B.* She hesitates, rubs her finger over the letters, and says, "I forget."

"You crossed them out. You decided you just didn't want those letters?"

She nods.

"That happens sometimes. But then, you wrote some other letters over here," I say as I turn the book sideways and point to the letters *M, D, P, M,* and *I.* "Would you tell the boys and girls what you wrote here?"

She studies the writing and puts her finger on the letters as though she's trying to remember. I turn the book vertically and point to the picture.

"Remember what's happening in the picture?"

"When my dad picked me up and brang me to McDonald's."

I turn the book sideways again, point to the *M,* and say, "So does this say, 'My . . .'" Then I point to the *D* and wait. She reads, touching a letter for each word, "'. . . dad picked me up.'"

"'My dad picked me up,'" I repeat, touching each letter. "Look at that! Janaya thought about the words she wanted to write, she listened to the sound she heard at the beginning of each word, and she wrote the letters for those sounds. And now Janaya can read what she wrote on this page. Would you touch those letters and read it to us one more time, Janaya?"

So, today as you write . . .	"Boys and girls, when you sit down to work today, you might want to try what Janaya did today, or what Jazmine did yesterday. They thought about what they wanted to write, they listened for the sounds at the beginning of the words, and they wrote the letters for the sounds they heard. Maybe you'll decide to label parts of your illustration, or maybe you'll want to write a whole sentence."

Asking Janaya to share her writing during the mini-lesson was a way to honor—and extend—what was beginning to take hold in the classroom. As children draw and talk about their illustrations freely, more and more of our writing conferences focus on how to help them bring text to the page. Little by little they begin to see that they can write anything they want—and that they can read what they've written. But sometimes they have difficulty rereading what they've written. In the mini-lesson with Janaya there was that point when I asked her what the letters *M, D, P, M,* and *I* said, and she studied the writing and put her finger on the letters as though she were trying to remember. I then turned the book vertically and pointed to the illustration, thinking that would help her remember. It did. In the following lesson, I try to teach children how to use that strategy themselves.

Follow-up Lesson Looking at the Illustration When You Can't Read the Text

This is what I noticed . . .

"When Janaya was telling her story yesterday, I noticed something. I noticed how going back to look at the picture helped her remember her words."

Let me show you what I mean . . .

"At first when I pointed to these letters over here, I asked her, 'What does this part say?' I noticed how she looked at those letters carefully, like she was studying them, trying to remember. I thought maybe she had forgotten what she had written. That can happen. Sometimes when you come back and look at the letters you wrote the day before, you don't remember what they say. So here's what I did. I turned the book this way"—I turn it back vertically—"and I got Janaya remembering and telling us what she had drawn in this picture. Looking at the picture helped her remember the story. Then when she looked at these letters again, she was thinking, Oh yeah, I wrote words to go with that story, let's see . . ., and that's when she said, 'My dad picked me up.' Going back to the illustration like that is something that might help you, too."

So, today as you write . . .

"So when you look at your words and just can't remember what you wrote, go back and look at your illustration. Tell yourself the story you drew, and I'll bet that will help you remember what your letters and words say."

What the children didn't get to see in this lesson is *how* Janaya actually wrote the sentence that she read aloud. The truth is, she did not write it independently; she wrote it with the support of the teacher during the conference. We rewind now to the previous day and relay the actual conference with Janaya, a kindergartner in her eighth week of school, as a way to illustrate what goes on and to show how what we learn as we work with one student can inform us about what to address with all our students.

Writing Conference with Janaya

Janaya is working on the page she started the previous day as I sit down next to her. I notice she has added more to the illustration. I also notice the letters g, R, and B written in black crayon. I'm delighted that she is experimenting with letters on her own and curious about the intended meaning, so after acknowledging what her story is about by asking her about the illustration, I point to the g, R, B and say, "Tell me about this." She hesitates, looks confused, then says, "I don't know." It had already been smudged over.

"What do you think you wanted it to say?" I ask again, wanting her to know it's okay if it's "wrong" in case that's why she's hesitant, but again, she shrugs. I know it is possible that those letters represent the sounds she heard when she wrote them, and I know it is also possible that they don't represent specific sounds and that she was just being playful with letters. In either case, the "writing" seems to say that she knows something about a place for letters on these pages, and I want to find out what else she knows. So I push on.

"Janaya, when people look at this picture, how will they know this is you and this is your dad?" I ask, pointing to each figure.

She takes a black crayon and makes a *J* next to the picture of herself. Next to her dad, she makes a backward *D*.

"That *is* the shape of a *D*," I tell her, "but it has to go this way. Watch . . ." I make a capital *D* on my clipboard. She watches, then crosses hers out and writes the *D* correctly.

In those few seconds I learn about Janaya as a writer. She knows

- that you can use letters as well as pictures to tell a story;
- that you use letters to label parts of a picture;
- that you put the label next to the object it represents;
- how to write some letters (*g, R, B, D, J*);
- how to make lowercase *g*, which means she probably knows how to make other lowercase letters;
- the letter her name begins with;
- the letter that the word *dad* begins with;
- that you cross out when you make a mistake;
- and she seems to use letters with ease.

Based on that quick assessment, I decide to push even further. "So, Janaya, if there were words here to tell about this story, what would they say?" I pick up her pencil and hold it poised, looking as though I'm ready to write. I do this because I know that when children are just beginning to learn about how to use letters, they're not convinced they can write whole texts themselves. If I appear as though I'm going to do the writing, it frees them from worrying about having to write it and allows them to think about the message. Really, I have no intention of doing the writing. Janaya will do it; she just hasn't yet discovered that she can.

"My dad picked me up," she says confidently, and I hold up the hand without the pencil, raising one finger for each word.

"'My-dad-picked-me-up.' How many words is that?" I ask.

Janaya counts my fingers with her eyes and says, "Five!"

Five words seems like a reasonable amount, and I notice that each word begins with letters that are commonly recognizable, letters she may know, so I continue. "Let's see, what's the first word?"

"*My*," we say together.

"Watch my mouth," I say.

I wait until her eyes are actually watching my mouth before I speak. Getting her to fix her eyes on my mouth as I say the word slowly is critical, because it slows her down enough to pay attention and gets her to connect the formation of my mouth with the sound she hears as I say the word slowly.

"/M/y," I say, once I see she is watching my mouth. Immediately, I ask her to say it herself. "Now you say it."

Asking her to say the word herself is necessary because it requires her to hear her own voice say her word while feeling the formation of the letter in her mouth. This sensory experience provides children with a strategy for writing words. Sowers tells us that as children are learning to write words, they "determine the spelling of a sound by the position of their lips and tongue when they say the word or sound, that is, the place of articulation in the mouth . . . as well as their ears and eyes" (1991, 176). ⊠ Saying the word slowly and listening to what they hear when they speak is what we are teaching in many of these early conferences. We don't want them to rely on us to hear the sounds for them, but to know how to do it independently. We are teaching a strategy for writing words.

"What do you hear when you say, /m/y?"

"/mmm/ M!" she says before even saying the whole word.

"Let's see, where should we write the M?" I ask, pencil poised, and she points to a space along the side of the page.

"M," I say, thinking. "How do you make M?" She reaches for the pencil as if to show me, and I hand it to her, saying, "You do it."

She makes a capital M.

"My," I say, raising one finger, then raising a second finger. "Dad. What do you hear when you say, /d/ad? You say it."

"D," she says right away, and I say, "Write it!" I didn't insist that she say the word and listen to the sound because she knows *dad* starts with D. She writes D and I say, "Okay, now let's go back and touch the words you've written so far so you'll know what to write next." I show her how to use the end of her pencil to touch each letter as she says the word: *M (My), D (dad)*.

"What comes next?" I ask, starting to lift a third finger and shaping my mouth in the form of a /p/.

"Picked," she says quickly, and I say the word slowly, emphasizing the /p/ but not overemphasizing it. I ask her to watch my mouth as I say it, ask her to say it, then ask, "What do you hear when you say, /p/icked?"

"/p/ P!" she says and she writes P next.

Janaya does the same for the word *me*, quickly hearing the /m/ and writing M. Then, going back and touching she rereads, "'My dad picked me'" (*MDPM*) and arrives at the word *up*. She repeats the /u/ over and over again, then says, "I!" At first I'm surprised, yet the way she says it actually sounds like the letter name I, so I tell her, "Write it!"

Teachers who were observing this lesson asked, "Why did you say, 'Write it' when I was obviously incorrect?" Our answer: because her response made sense for the sound she was saying, and right now our goal is for her to learn that this is something she can do with the information she has at this point. She didn't know that U is

⊠ Note to the Teacher

We're not suggesting, and we don't think Sowers was, that there should be an overemphasis on what children are doing with their tongues and their lips. We just want teachers of young children to understand that, although adults rely "on sound, visual memory or knowledge of word meanings to spell an unfamiliar word" (176), beginning writers rely on a physical component as well.

the letter for /u/, and if we told it to her then, we'd be turning the focus on the correct answer, rather than the strategy we were trying to teach. What she showed she could do, however, was listen closely to the sound she was saying and connect it to a letter that made sense. The /u/ sound is a lot closer to the letter name *I* than it is to the letter name *U*. The letter she named made sense for the sound she made. It's also interesting that she chose a vowel for the /u/ sound and not a consonant.

Children will make many sounds without knowing the correct letters to represent those sounds. Right now, our goal is to help them take control of writing and to give them a systematic, sensible way to apply what they know. Over time and throughout the day, there will be more instruction about words (during interactive writing and word work), and as they learn more letters and sounds, their words will come closer to being correctly spelled.

Teachers also noticed that I kept moving Janaya on to the next word, and they wondered why I didn't ask her what other sounds she heard in each of these words. I could have, certainly, and if I had, she probably would have heard the long *i* sound in *my* and the /k/ sound in *picked* and been able to write more letters for most words. I chose not to, however, because my goal at that moment was for her to feel successful at writing words. By moving her on to the next word, and then the next, she learned that she could write many words, (albeit only the first letters). In fact, she could tell her whole story with words. Once children know this, filling in the letters in individual words is a natural next step.

The most important thing that happened here is that, in a conference that lasted less than five minutes from start to finish, Janaya learned that she could write a whole story with ease. Most likely, she'll want to do it again.

In the lessons that follow, we make explicit for the whole class the strategies we showed Janaya that day, strategies that we show others during the many conferences we have early on: how to listen for sounds in words, how to write the letters for the sounds you hear, and how to reread so that the text makes sense. In the following lesson, we invite a child to model, publicly, what we showed Janaya in the conference. This way, children see a peer, and therefore a writer they can align themselves with, in the act of putting words on the page. We thought carefully about who we might ask to participate in such a lesson because we wanted someone who knew enough about how letters and sounds work and would be comfortable writing in front of the others, possibly someone on the brink of being ready to write independently. We asked Jonathan because he knew most letters and sounds but wasn't writing them on his own. By asking him to share his illustration with us and then posing the question, If there were words to go with this story, what do you think they would say? we could support him as a writer of text while also providing a model for the others.

Lesson Listening for Sounds: Going Back and Touching

What's going on in the classroom

- Children are beginning to label illustrations in their Drawing & Writing Books.

What's next

- They need to know that they (most likely) have the information they need to write whole thoughts.
- They need to know how to write so they can read it back.
- They need to learn the strategy for going back and touching as they write.

Materials needed

- a child who knows many letters and sounds but doesn't write them independently, and his Drawing & Writing Book with an illustration that is almost completed
- felt-tip pen

This is what I noticed . . .

I ask Jonathan if he would like to tell us his story. Standing next to me, he points to the parts of the illustration and says, "This is my dad's car, and he's taking me to the park." I ask him where his dad is, and where he is, and he points to his dad, then says he's going to draw himself in the backseat. Then he points to the tall rectangle on the left-hand side of the page and tells us, "It's the thing for the night" to which I respond, "Oh, the streetlight! The tall post with the light on top that helps you see at night?" He nods and explains that he's going to make another one on the opposite side of the page. (See Figure 5.3.)

FIGURE 5.3 Jonathan: *My dad was driving me to the park.*

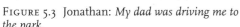

I say, "So it seems you plan to add more to this illustration. You have this streetlight here, you're going to put another one here—it seems you want your readers to understand that when you and your dad were in the car going to the park, there were streetlights on the side of the road," and he nods. It takes about one minute for him to fill us in on the illustration. Then I move into the focus of the lesson: listening for sounds in words and going back and touching as you read your work.

"So Jonathan, if there were words to tell about this part of your story, what do you think they would say?"

He thinks for a few seconds, then says assuredly, "My dad was driving me to the park."

"My-dad-was-driving-me-to-the-park," I repeat, raising one finger as I say each word. "Look, it takes two hands! How many words?"

He uses his finger to count my fingers. "Eight!" he says.

"Eight words, wow! Do you think we can write eight words?"

"Let's think of how it starts. /M/y," I say, putting my finger on my chin and pointing to my lips as I say the word slowly. "/M/y. Watch my mouth: /m/y." I repeat the word slowly, making sure his eyes stay watching my mouth. "Now you say it."

"/M/y, /m/," he says, and his eyes seem to have a look of knowing.

The children on the rug are watching and I've asked them, if they know a letter or a word, to say it softly so that Jonathan can't hear it, because this is his turn to think about the letters for his story.

"*M*!" he says.

I take the pen in my hand, looking as if I am going to do the writing. "How do you make *M*?" I ask. He traces one in the air and I hand him the pen. "Here, you write it!" (If he hadn't known how, I would have made one on the chart paper, then let him copy it.) He writes *M* at the top left of the page.

Drawing on conversations they have had in the classroom during interactive writing lessons, I say to the children, "And look where he's starting, boys and girls, here on the left, because he knows that when we write, we go from left to right." I then place my hand over his, saying, "Now let's go back and touch as you read, like this . . ." I show him how to point the end of the pen under the letter *M* as we read "My."

Then, I raise a second finger and say, "*Dad*. What do you hear when you say /d/ad?" Again I point to my mouth and say, "/d/ad" slowly. "Now you say it."

"Dad," he says.

"Say it slowly, like this: /d/ad," I remind him.

"/d/ *D*!" he exclaims.

"Write it!" I say and he writes *D* next to the *M*.

"Now let's go back and touch." I take his hand again, starting him off as he uses the back of the pen to point as he reads, "'My dad . . .'" Then still holding his hand I slide the end of the pen along the space after *dad* as I say, "/w/as. My dad was . . ." I repeat, raising a finger for each word. "What do you hear when you say, /w/as?"

"/W/as," he says, then, "/w/ /w/ /w/."

I can see in his eyes that he's really thinking, so I offer support. "Like *William* and *window* and . . ." I pause between each word, thinking of other words that make that sound, which gives him (and the others) time to think and contribute. It is too hard for them to stay silent.

"*Winter*!" one student calls out.

Another exclaims, "*Workboard*!"

"*W*!" Jonathan says confidently, and he writes *W*.

I note that he is writing uppercase letters, but I don't say anything about it. There will be plenty of time to address upper- and lowercase. For now, I want him to see how he can write, and fluent writing comes with forming letters he is most comfortable making.

"Now go back and touch."

He reads, "'My dad was driving'" and this time I don't put my hand over his to guide him.

I am surprised when he says, "*D*" for *driving* because usually children say /j/ for the *dr* sound. But, independently he said, "*D*" and wrote a *D*. If he had said /j/ /j/ and then, "*J*," or "*G*," I would have said, "Put it down!" because both of those letters make a /j/ sound, and again, it's the strategy for listening for the sounds in words and writing an appropriate letter for the sound you hear that we are teaching. The message I'd be giving isn't, "That's right" but rather, "The letter you're associating with the sound you hear makes sense, based on what you know right now."

"Look at what Jonathan is doing," I say to the children on the rug. "He's thinking what he wants to write, saying the word slowly, and writing the letters for the sounds in each word. Then, he's remembering to go back and touch. And do you know why we go back and touch? Because it helps us not to get mixed up and lose our place, it helps us remember what word we need to write next, and it helps us learn to read. Right now Jonathan is reading his work!"

Jonathan goes back, touches, and reads, "'My dad was driving me' . . . /m/ *M*!" He writes *M*, then touches and reads, "'My dad was driving me to' . . . /t/ /t/ *T*!" He keeps going. "My dad was driving me to the . . . That's easy: *t-h-e*," he says, and writes it. Then going back and touching each letter, he reads, "'My dad was driving me to the,'" (*MDWDMT the*) and putting his hand on the empty space next to *the*, he says, "park /p/ *P*!" and he writes the letter *P*.

"Now, why don't you read it one more time and make sure it's just the way you want it," I suggest.

He goes back and touches each letter as he reads each word. Someone calls out, "Period!" and he puts a period at the end.

"Now look at what you did, Jonathan. When you wrote 'My dad was driving me to the park,' you told exactly what happened in this one part of your story. By writing the words to go along with the picture, you help readers understand your story."

So, today as you write . . .

"Boys and girls, what Jonathan showed us today is something you can do, too. You can write words to go along with your drawing because you know how to

- "think of what you want to write,
- "figure out what word comes first,
- "say the word slowly,
- "listen to the sounds in the word,
- "write the letters for the sounds you hear,
- "then go back and touch before reading the next word.
- "And if you forget what you're wanting to write, go back and look at the picture to help you remember.

"Going back and touching helps you make sure you have all the words you need and helps you not to get mixed up. And, it helps you to know how to read what you wrote!"

We have said all along that modeling our own writing of text is powerful because it allows us to make explicit how listening and speaking are connected with reading and writing. But when a child writes his text in front of the other students, it is even more powerful. Maybe it's because when they see a peer doing the writing, it no longer feels like such a far reach for them. The message they get is *"One of us* just wrote all that! I could do that, too!" Or maybe, as in this lesson, the power comes from seeing success happening right in front of their eyes. This was a breakthrough for Jonathan and they knew it. Standing there, in front of his friends, he was "getting it," and his pride in himself was palpable. Their pride in him was evident, too.

When a Child Doesn't Know the Letter for the Sound

Jonathan wrote the correct letters for the sounds he was saying in each of the words. We figured he probably would, which is why we asked him to model writing his words in this lesson. The goal was not only to show him and the other children how to actually go about writing the letters for the sounds you hear but also to help a child who was on the brink of being able to write independently to see all that he knows. We all have students, however, who don't know the letters for the sounds they say and who wouldn't have been able to do what Jonathan did, and we wouldn't put them in that situation. We support them during conferences, during interactive writing lessons, and in any possible way throughout the day.

For example, let's take a conference with Nate, who points to the picture on the page and tells me it's a mountain. I repeat to him, "/M/ountain. What sound do you hear when you say, */m/ountain?* Watch my mouth: /m/ountain."

"*B!*" he says enthusiastically, if questioningly.

Given that this is a typical response for this child, and it is in keeping with what I know about his ability to hear and record sounds, I make a split-second decision about how to proceed—and there are different directions to take. I opt to use this as an opportunity to teach Nate the letter *M.* I think he'll be able to learn it quickly because it's one of the early sounds children learn, we can make many associations in the room, and it has come up many times during interactive writing lessons.

"Mountain," I say. "Like *Marvens*—look!" I turn the cover of Marvens's Drawing & Writing Book over to where it says his name. "And *Marie,*" I say, pointing toward a girl sitting across the room.

"And *Mrs. McGinnis,*" another child at the table calls out.

"Let's look over here," I say, taking Nate's hand and walking to the name chart and finding *Marvens* and *Marie* and *Mrs. McGinnis.*

"And look—right here, here's a /m/ouse. That starts just like /M/arvens and /M/arie and /M/rs. McGinnis and /m/ountain, too. And here's the letter," I say, pointing. "Do you know what letter that is?"

Nate shakes his head, so I tell him, "It's *M*. Look." I trace the *M* on the enlarged alphabet chart with my finger. "You try it." Nate traces the *M*, and as we walk back to the table, I say, "*M* is the letter at the beginning of /M/arvens and /M/arie and /m/ilk, and . . ."

At this point other children at the table are jumping in with suggestions: "*Moon!*" "*Monday!*" "*Me!*"

"*Mom!*" Nate says.

Sometimes it takes many associations for children to begin to hear the connection among all of these sounds, but when they do, it's a breakthrough that we want to celebrate.

I show him how to make the letter *M* on my clipboard, then say, "Now you can make *M* for *mountain* on your page. I wonder where you'll put it. Up here, near the mountain? Down here? What do you think?"

One letter to represent an entire story is all we do. That's another at-the-moment decision I make. It is based on my belief that if I focus only on this one letter and give him lots of opportunities to use it, he'll be more likely to remember *M* when he hears the /m/ sound again.

If by some chance, Nate had been in the position Jonathan was, being asked in front of the class, "What do you hear when you say, *mountain*?" and we realized he didn't know that letter, we'd approach it very similarly to the way we have here: as a collective exploration in which the whole class participates, which lends itself nicely to a mini-lesson on making room for difference.

Maybe the most important message we can give our students as they embark on this lifetime endeavor of recording their words on paper is that there is room enough for all learners. This is a particularly important lesson as we work to establish communities of writers.

 Lesson Valuing Differences in How We Write Words

What's going on in the classroom	• Children write daily. • Throughout the day the teacher supports students' attempts to write independently, using sound spellings. • Children are beginning to represent their stories with text.
What's next	• They also need to see that as they are learning to write words, members of the class might represent the same word differently, and that we value differences in the way children hear and represent sounds. • They need continued support in representing their words the best they can.
Materials needed	• Chart paper and marker, dry-erase board, or chalkboard
This is what I noticed . . .	"We've been talking a lot lately about writing words. We said that when you want to write words that you think you won't be able to write, you

- "say the word slowly;
- "listen to the sounds in the word;
- "think, What letter makes that sound?
- "think about how to make that letter; and
- "write it down.

"And boys and girls in this class are writing letters and words to help readers understand their stories.

"We also said, 'If you can say a word, you can write it.' I was looking in your folders last night and I saw how boys and girls are writing big words. Joseph was writing about a bungee cord and he wrote BG for bungee." I write the letters *BG* on chart paper. "He said the word slowly, listened for the sounds, and wrote the letters for the sounds he heard. And because he could say that big word, he knew he could write it. Christian was writing about playing the musical instruments and he wrote, *insnumtes*." I write these letters on the chart paper. "He knew if he could say it, he could write it, so he said it slowly and wrote the letters for the sounds he heard.

"As I was looking through the folders, I noticed something else: Lots of people have written stories about their cousins.

"Jason wrote about being at the park and seeing his cousin,
"Demari wrote about going for a sleepover at her cousin's house,
"Cynthia wrote that story about her cousin's birthday party,
"Frank has a story about going to the beach with his cousin, and
"Jarren wrote about playing at his cousin's house.

"And do you know what else I noticed? Each one of those writers wrote the word *cousin* in their story—but they didn't use all the same letters!"

Let me show you what I mean . . .

- "Jason wrote that story about his cousin a long time ago, and he wrote this, for cousin: *k*." I write it on chart paper.
- "Demari wrote *ksn*.
- "Cynthia wrote cousin this way: *kz*.
- "Frank wrote cousin this way: *cz*.
- "Jarren, you wrote it like this: *csin*.

"Each one of the writers said the word slowly, listened to the sounds, and wrote the letters for the sounds they heard. Sometimes they heard different sounds. That's what happens when you're learning to write words. Their words look different because each one of these writers knows different things about how letters and sounds work.

"Look, all of these writers heard the /k/ sound at the beginning of *cousin*. Some of them wrote *K* and some of them wrote *C* for that sound. Jason wrote his word so long ago that /k/ was the only sound he heard! Cynthia and Demari heard a /z/ sound in the middle, and Cynthia wrote *Z* and Demari wrote *S* for that sound. Jarren was listening to the end and heard the /n/ sound and put the letter *N* for that sound. And you know what? The more slowly you say the words, the more sounds you will hear and the more letters you will be able to write. You writers write words differently for the sounds you hear, but what is important is that everyone is trying hard and doing their best."

So, today as you write . . .

"So here's what I want you to think about today and every day as you write. When you're learning to write words, you can't possibly know how to spell every word correctly. But if you can say the word, you can write it. And when you're just learning about letters and sounds, you'll write the letters for the sounds you hear. Someone else at your table might write the same word. They may hear different sounds, and the way they write the word might look different from the way you write it. And that's okay when we're just learning to write words. So remember, say the word you want to write, listen to the sounds in the word, and write the letters for the sounds you hear even if your word looks different from the way your friend wrote it. That way, you'll be doing your best."

Why we chose these books

We chose these particular books written by the children in the class because as we looked at their writing, we noticed two things: many of them were writing about their cousins, and when they did, they wrote the word *cousin* in a variety of ways. Each spelling revealed what that writer knows and is doing as he or she writes the words.

Suggested other books

It makes sense to look at your students' work and see how they're going about writing words. Are there words that many of them use, and each child writes them differently? Looking closely at the way children write the same word can help us see similarities and differences and tell us about how to move them further as writers.

When You *Do* Know How to Spell Some Words

In this next lesson we present another situation where children learn from a classmate about writing the words they know how to spell. John came to kindergarten knowing very few letters. During assessments at the beginning of the school year, any time he didn't know a letter, he'd respond, "A." When his teacher asked him to tell her a sound that a letter made, he didn't seem to know that letters made sounds. Now, three months into school, he had some letters in his repertoire but wrote them randomly on his pages. Despite the many interactive writing lessons he'd participated in and the continued modeling of how to listen for sounds in words, he wasn't using the strategy independently. As I conferred with him, I wanted to find out if he even understood what to do to write letters down—and the timing was perfect. With support, he became more independent with each "word" he wrote. He shared his story at the end of writing time that day, which provided the substance for the mini-lesson the following day.

Lesson Some Words You Don't Have to Sound Out

What's going on in the classroom
- Children work independently in their Drawing & Writing Books.
- They have seen the teacher model how to listen for sounds in words.
- They have seen other children listen for sounds in words in order to label a picture, as well as write a whole thought.

What's next
- They need to be reminded that when they know how to spell a word, they should spell it correctly.

Materials needed
- a piece of writing from a child who has used sound spelling as well as written a word he knows how to write correctly

This is what I noticed . . .
"I noticed something John did in his writing. It's something that writers do and something that the writers in this class can do, too. John, may I share your story with the boys and girls? Why don't you come up." John comes and stands beside me.

Let me show you what I mean . . .
"I'm going to read your picture from yesterday," I say, and I point as I recall the parts. "This is you and you're playing your game cube—here are the controls in your hand. And over here, behind you, your dad is packing the boxes—these brown boxes—because you're moving to a new house. Is that right?" He nods. "And you wrote some words here. Would you read what you wrote?" (See Figure 5.4 in the color insert.)

John touches each letter—*I m P w my g k*—as he reads, "'I am playing with my game cube.'"

"Look at that. He said the words he wanted to write, he listened to the sounds he heard at the beginning, and he wrote the letters for those sounds. And right here," I point to the word *my*, "he remembered how to write the word *my*, so he wrote the whole word! How did you remember that word, John?"

"Up there," he says, pointing to a chart with text that the children had written during an interactive writing lesson.

"So you remembered that the word *my* is one we've been using a lot when we write and you remembered how to write it."

So, today as you write . . .
"Boys and girls, when you're working on your stories and writing a word that we have all been using a lot, make sure you do what John did: write it the way you know how. Maybe you'll remember seeing that word in the classroom, the way John looked up on this chart to help him. And maybe you won't even need to look at our shared writing or the word wall—maybe you'll just remember how to write it. What are some other words that we've been using a lot that we all might know how to spell?"

Children call out and I write the words on the whiteboard:

the   my   we   me   I

"Those are words we use a lot, so you'll probably know how to write them all by yourself. So don't forget, listen for the sounds and write the letters for the sounds you hear, but if you know how to spell the word, write it the way you know."

Most of the lessons thus far illustrate how to help children gain fluency with writing words. They write whole sentences with ease, even though they may represent each word with only one or two letters. Along the way, of course, we model how to say words slowly and listen for more sounds in words. For example, within days after having done the lesson where I labeled parts of my story about the playground, each with one initial letter, I'd go back and show how I say the words slowly and listen for more than just the initial sounds. I would then write letters for those easy-to-hear middle and ending sounds (*plagrwnd, pla hws, slid*), showing children that when you hear more sounds in the words, you write them. Children need us to model how to slow words down as we say them, to hear more and more sounds.

Once children are including more sounds in their writing, however, other needs surface: they want to know how to spell it "right" or they're fearful of using big words, so we address this in a lesson.

 Lesson Writing Big Words We Use in Telling Our Stories

What's going on in the classroom	• Daily interactive writing sessions are in place in the classroom.
	• Children are representing their illustrations with text.
	• Throughout the day the teacher supports students' attempts to write independently, using sound spellings.
	• In attempting to write words
	◦ some children are writing only words that they know how to spell correctly,
	◦ some are writing words freely,
	◦ some ask, "Is it right?" and
	◦ some won't try at all for fear of being wrong.
What's next	• They need more information about saying words slowly and listening for as many sounds in the words as they can, as well as trusting their attempts to try hard words.
Materials needed	• chart paper and marker, dry-erase board, or chalkboard
This is what I noticed . . .	"I've noticed that you've been working really hard on your stories, putting information in your pictures so that readers can understand them, writing letters and words to go with your pictures the way writers do. But lately some boys and girls have been asking me, 'How do you spell . . .?' or when they're writing words, they say, 'Is this right?'
	"I know that when you're writing a story, you want it to be your best, so you care about how you write the words. But you can't possibly know

how to spell all the words when you're just learning to write! You're telling such interesting stories and you use the exact words you need to tell your story—like Osvaldo did when he told us that story about the mall where he saw the fountain and rode on the escalator. He used big words, and he needed to use those words so we could understand the story he told. And he did the same thing when he wrote his story. Now, if Osvaldo had thought he had to write all those words correctly, he might not have used those big words when he wrote his story.

"So I want to show you what he could do if he wanted to write one of those big words, and what you can do when you want to write a big word and you're worried about how to spell it."

Let me show you what I mean . . . "Yesterday, when Osvaldo drew his story, he wanted to write *fountain* but he didn't know how to spell that big word. Instead of asking me, 'How do you spell *fountain*?' or instead of looking in a book to find that word, Osvaldo did a smart thing. He said the word slowly, and he listened to the sounds, like this: /f/ /ou/ /n/ /t/ /n/. Try it with me."

The children repeat the word and I ask them to close their eyes and try it with me again, slowly.

"Osvaldo said it again and again, slowly, '/f/ /ou/ /n/ /t/ /n/' and then he listened really carefully to the beginning part of the word. He said, '/f/ /f/' and he thought, I know what letter makes /f/, it's *F*! Like /*F*/rank! And he wrote *F* on his page. I'm going to write an *F* right here on the chart paper, for the beginning of the word *fountain*.

"Then he said the word again: '/f/ /ou/ /n/ /t/ /n/.'" I slide my finger under the *F* and beyond as I continue saying the word, emphasizing the sounds, but not overemphasizing any one sound in particular. Some children call out *W*, some call out *A*, some call out *N*.

"People are hearing lots of different sounds," I say, "but let me show you what Osvaldo did. He said fountain like this: '/f/ /ou/ /n/ /n/ /n/ /n/, /f/ /ou/ /n/ /n/ /n/ /n/.' This time he was listening carefully to the middle part of the word." I move my hand slowly under the space next to the *F* as I say, "/ou/ /nnn/. He said, '/n/ /n/. Hey, I hear *N*!' and he wrote *N*, just like this, next to the *F*. Then he went back and touched the letters he wrote, /f/ /ou/ /nnn/."

As I read, I move my finger along under the *F N* and to the empty space beyond as I say, "/t/." I repeat it. Children call out letters. I pick up on what someone says. "You hear *T*? Well, you know what? Osvaldo heard *T*, too. And he wrote *T* right here, after the *N*. Then he went back and read, *fountain*." I move my finger along under the letters *F, N, T* as I read, slowing at the empty space after *T* as I say "/n/."

"Now I'm noticing something, boys and girls. As you're saying the word *fountain* slowly, and listening for the sounds in that word, some of you are suggesting letters different from the ones Osvaldo wrote. Like over here, Jazmine, you said, '*W*.'" I point to the spot after the *F* and before the *N*. "That's because you're hearing some different sounds, so if you were writing this word, you probably would have put a *W* for the /w/ sound in *fountain*. When you're learning how to write words, people may hear different things, and that's because everybody is trying their

Talking, Drawing, Writing

best. So you need to remember, always write the letters for the sounds you hear."

I go back and read *fountain*, moving my finger under the *F, N, T,* then sliding it to the blank space beyond, as I say, "/n/."

"*N!*" someone calls out.

"You hear *N* at the end? Well, Osvaldo did, too. He wrote *N* right here, and then he read the whole word." I move my finger under the letters *F, N, T, N* as I say, "Fountain."

"Now, *that* is a pretty big word for a five- or six-year-old to write, don't you think? But you know what, boys and girls? It doesn't matter how big the word is, because any word you can say, you can write. So if Osvaldo could say *fountain*, he could write *fountain*. He might not write it exactly the way we would find it in a book, but that's okay for now, because he is just beginning to learn about sounds and letters and how to use them when he writes words."

So, today as you write . . .   "Here's what I want you to think about today and every day as you write. When you're learning to write words, you can't possibly know how to spell every word correctly. But what you can do is try your best:

- "First, you think of what you want to say.
- "Say the word slowly.
- "Listen to the sounds in the word.
- "Think about what letters makes those sounds.
- "Think about how to make those letters.
- "Write the letters for the sounds you hear.

"And remember, if you can say the word, you can write it."

Revisiting the Environment

The lessons in this chapter give the impression that children are working hard on their writing and that the classroom is operating smoothly. Most of the time, that is the case. But even well into the school year, when children understand how the classroom operates and know what their responsibilities are during writing time, things can sometimes feel like they are falling apart. One day in Bebhinn O'Connell's kindergarten just after they had all returned from Christmas vacation, that's exactly what was happening. The children were loud during writing, and the recent pages in their Drawing & Writing Books lacked the quality that had been there weeks earlier. They seemed to be imitating each other's new style—dashing something down on the page and then covering it with what looked like a swirl of crayon. When we asked them to tell us about their work, they didn't seem to have a story to tell. It's natural to feel critical toward students when we know that they know what is expected and are not doing it. On the other hand, when we see children having difficulty attending as they supposedly know how to attend, there is usually a reason. We need to give some thought about why that is occurring. Do they need a reminder of how a community of learners works together independently? Is the work still meaningful? Are they invested?

Bebhinn wanted to address this issue right away, so she presented her version of a lesson she had seen us do a year earlier, when we were in a similar predicament.

Lesson How to Do Good Work During Writing Time

What's going on in the classroom

- Children are working independently in their Drawing & Writing Books.
- Lately, though, the noise level is raised during writing time and children seem to be rushing through their work. They seem to have forgotten what they have learned about how to attend carefully to their work.

What's next

- They need to know what it looks like to do good work on their writing.

Materials needed

- teacher's Drawing & Writing Book
- caddie

This is what I noticed . . .

"Boys and girls, yesterday during writing time it was really noisy in here. It got so loud that I couldn't even hear Simone when I was talking with her about her writing. And not only was it noisy, but I've noticed that some boys and girls seem to be rushing through the pages in their Drawing & Writing Books. Sometimes it looks like scribbles on the pages! It's almost like you forgot how writers do their good work. So today I want to help you remember.

"I'm going to pretend I'm five years old and I'm in kindergarten and I'm working at my table during writing—and I want all of you to watch me. While I work, I'm going to think out loud instead of thinking in my head, because I want you to understand how a writer thinks hard about how to do their best work. Then, when I'm finished, I'll ask you what you noticed. I'm not going to talk to you, and I don't want you to talk to me. Just watch me." She turns toward her Drawing & Writing Book, which is standing at the easel, and begins thinking out loud.

Let me show you what I mean . . .

"Let's see, I'm going to tell about when I visited my grandmother in the hospital. I remember there was a purple curtain next to her bed so no one would see her." She starts to draw the curtain, then stops. "Oh, no, if I draw the curtain first, I won't be able to draw the bed in front of it because it will be hard to draw on top of crayon, so I think I need to draw the bed first, then put the curtain behind it.

"How will I make that hospital bed? Well, it's the shape of a rectangle"—she draws a 3-D rectangle—"but the back of the bed was up because she was kind of sitting up." She makes the top third of the bed raised. "It had railings on the sides, but"—she looks in the caddie—"the railings were silver and there's no silver in here."

A voice from the rug says, "You can use the black!"

She ignores the comment and continues thinking aloud. "I think if I outline them with this black, I can shade it in lightly and maybe make it look kind of grayish silver."

Some children start to offer advice—"You could . . ."—but Bebhinn speaks out, not looking at them.

"Sometimes it is hard to do your work when everyone is talking. I really need quiet so I can figure it out myself." Her eyes stay focused on her work as she speaks. The children get quiet. They are engaged as she works.

"I'm going to make my grandmother's head right here, and I'll make the pillow around it." She draws. Once in a while a child contributes an idea, but she ignores it.

"Now I'm going to put the green blanket over the bed because that's what color it was." She colors; the children watch. "Now I can draw the purple curtain. I'll make it over here, on this side of the bed." She begins drawing the purple curtain and coloring it in. Then she says, "Sometimes when I'm telling my story, I get tired, so I stop drawing and I write some words. Let's see, what do I want to write?" She pauses, then says, "I think I'll say, 'I went to the hospital to visit my grandmother.'" She says it again, holding up one finger for each word, looks at her fingers, and says, "Nine words! Let's see, the first word is *I*. I know how to write that word. Just *I*! I know it's a capital *I* and I know I need to write it over here, because words start at the left and go this way, to the right."

She writes *I*. "Now let's see, I went /w/ /w/."

Kids call out, "*W*!"

Continuing to work and looking at her page, she says, "I really don't like it when other kids at the table say the letter for me. I know they're trying to help me, but it doesn't really help me, because I'm trying to hear the sounds myself. Let's see, *W* says, /w/, so I'll leave a space and write *W*." She says the word again: "*went*, /w/ /e/ /n/ /n/ /n/."

Kids call out, "*N*!"

Exasperated, Bebhinn stands up, gathers her Drawing & Writing Book and caddie, and says indignantly, "I just have to find a spot where people won't be telling me things! It just isn't quiet enough here!" She storms away from the rug to a nearby table, spouting, "I need a quiet place to work!" She places her things on the table, sits, and continues.

The children on the rug aren't sure what to make of what has just happened. They follow her with their heads, some get up on their knees to watch her, and no one says a word. Bebhinn continues with her work, saying the words slowly and writing the letters for the sounds she hears. The children don't interject. After a minute or so of work, she says, "Ah, it is much better here. I can really do my work when people aren't always talking and telling me what to write." She says, "to" and writes *t-o*, adding, "because I know that word!" She says, "the" and writes *t-h-e*, adding, "I know how to write that one, too!" She writes *hsbtl* for *hospital*, articulating each sound, naming and writing the letter, and going back and touching after each. Then she says to herself, "It's really easy when you know a word and you can just write it—like *to*."

The children watch in silence. She stops working, puts her head up as though listening in the direction of the children, then says, "Hmm, it seems quiet back there. I think I'll go back to my spot." She packs up her Drawing & Writing Book and caddie, walks back, and places the book on the easel, careful not to make eye contact. She rereads what she has written, touching each word as she says it.

"'I went to the hospital to . . .'" She points to the space after *to* and says, "visit" slowly, repeats it again, and writes *vst*. The children don't speak out. She goes back and rereads, and writes *my*, saying, "There's another one I know," and adds *my*. "This is nice," she says to no one in particular. "Nobody is telling me what to write. This is how I like it when I'm doing my work."

She rereads from the beginning: "'I went to the hospital to visit my . . .'" then slowly says, "grandmother" as she slides her finger along the blank space. She writes *grmr*, going back and touching each letter as she adds the next. No one calls out. She adds one little item to the picture, then says, "I think I'm finished for now."

She turns to the boys and girls and says, "It's okay for you to talk to me now. I want to find out what you learned when you watched me. When I was working, what did you notice?"

Kids are eager to comment, saying, "You wrote a sentence."

"I did. I wanted readers to read my picture and my words so they would understand this part of my story."

"You sketched the bed before you colored it in."

"I did that because I wasn't sure how to make a bed and I wanted it to look like one of those beds in the hospital."

"You wrote lightly to make the bed."

"Yeah, in case I messed up. I figured I could color over it more easily if I did it lightly first."

"You didn't like it when people were talking."

"No, I didn't. It is so hard to think when you are surrounded by lots of noise. I need quiet to do good work. I think you do, too."

"You worked hard."

"I did work hard."

So, today as you write . . .   "And just like I worked hard and did my best, you want to always do your best, too. To do your best work you need to

- "think about what you want to draw,
- "think about how you'll draw it,
- "try to draw it the best you can,
- "think about the words you want to put with your drawing,
- "say the words slowly and go back and touch,
- "and always, always make sure you are working in a good spot, doing your good work. If you are, you'll be helping others do their good work, too."

What happened that day, and the days that followed, was what Bebhinn had hoped would happen: the children remembered. It seemed that they had needed to see again how writers think about their work and what it takes to put it carefully on the page. We know that writing is a social act for children, that they need to speak as they write, and that conversation is often necessary since they discover so much of what they're thinking by saying it. At the same time, they need to experience a calm setting, one that is conducive to thinking, writing, reading, and doing good work.

What may be most significant here is that Bebhinn's lesson was successful, not only because she was explicit about what writers need to work hard, but because she had a topic that mattered deeply to her. The children knew about her grandmother getting sick and being in the hospital, and they knew that Bebhinn was worried about her. Therefore, they could understand why she wanted to do good work on this story. Often, when children lose interest in writing or their work lacks the quality we know they are capable of, it is nothing more than not having a topic they care enough about. No demonstration will elicit high-quality work unless the children are writing about things that are personally meaningful. Although it is implicit in the work we have presented so far, we address the notion of topic choice explicitly in Chapter 8, as it is an aspect of craft that we need to revisit again and again.

What is true of the lessons presented here, and the many others that are not included on these pages, is that most of them came about based on having observed, talked with, and listened to our students during conferences and from having studied their work and observed their ways of working. In the next section, we offer a system for documenting those observations that allows us to see at a glance what they know and need to learn.

CHAPTER 6

Assessment

ON A NOVEMBER MORNING, eighteen kindergarten teachers from across Boston sandwich themselves around four tables in the tiny basement library of the Mason School in Roxbury. The space is so small that if one person wants to leave the room, everyone has to stand so they can pass by. Teachers who arrive early stake out the seats farthest from the door so that when they sit, they're fixed in place.

Yet, we like it here. There's an intimacy and a cozy feeling as we study writing together, surrounded by shelves of children's books. In this space, the twenty of us are close enough to see a page of a child's writing without the use of an overhead projector, and that is exactly what we're doing on this particular morning.

Holding Janaya's Drawing & Writing Book open to the page she worked on minutes earlier, I point to the parts of the illustration and remind the teachers of how Janaya had told her story to me (see Figure 6.1 in the color insert). "'My mom drove me to my friend's house [tiny house on right] and she had to go to work, so I stayed there and played with my friends [mom's car at top of page driving off]. Then my daddy came to pick me up [his car near bottom] and then we went to McDonald's.'"

"So what can Janaya do as a writer?" I say to the teachers, and together we talk about what we see. Later we'll decide how to record it, as shown in Figure 6.6.

Janaya does the following:

- writes about what she knows
- draws the story with detailed information
  - distinguishes people by size, clothing, hairstyle
  - lets reader know that the story is taking place outside: house in background, sun, flower, sidewalk
- rereads and makes changes, indicated by the cross-out on the backward D and the smeared crayon across the letters g, R, and B
- tells a two-part story (at the upper part of the page is her mother's car driving away—takes place early in the day; at the bottom is her father's car when he came to pick her up—takes place later in the day)
- labels parts of the drawing to give readers information
- labels people using first letters of their names, independently (J, D)
- adds information to the drawing after getting response from audience
  - Janaya had gone back and added information—the sidewalk, her father's car—after I queried at the end of the share meeting the previous day, "Janaya, you've just told us so much more about this part of the story. I'm wondering which of those things that you just told us you'll put in so other readers will know that, too." Even though her "going back" is not evident just by looking at the page, we document it because the teacher knows it happened. This documentation is for the teacher, as it gives us important information about Janaya as a writer.
- composes a five-word sentence that captures the story on this page
- writes the first letter for each word in the sentence, with help
- knows these uppercase letters and the sounds they make: M, D, P, J
- knows lowercase g, so possibly she knows other lowercase letters

Since Janaya wrote the sentence with support from the teacher, we have written *WH* at the bottom of the page, meaning she wrote these words "with help." Over time, as we look back at earlier writing, it will let us know that the writing wasn't done independently.

In this chapter we share three ways of collecting data about our students as writers: looking in depth at the work of an individual student, looking at the work of a group of five students at a time on a regular basis, and taking a quick look at the whole class. By sharing the work of a few kindergartners and explaining how we look at, assess, and document what we see, we hope to illustrate for teachers why looking at children's work regularly is essential to our teaching.

Why Look at Children's Writing

Every time we meet with the teachers for a workshop session, we spend some time looking together at the work of one or two children, listing our observations about what they know and can do as writers, thinking about what would make sense to teach next, and considering how we might teach it. We do this for a few reasons.

First, we believe that looking closely at students' writing at a time separate from our work directly with them allows us to see each child clearly and think more deeply about him or her.

Second, by naming what we see, we begin to generate a common language for what craft means in five-, six-, and seven-year-olds' writing. At first teachers grope for words, telling us it is difficult to know what to look for and to put into words what children are doing in their writing. That level of discomfort could have something to do with the fact that we're not used to doing it. Historically, in our profession, we haven't been expected to look at children's writing and name what we see, because for a long time, there wasn't any young children's writing to look at. When there was, we'd focus on the mechanics. Or, more recently, we'd have a list of descriptors in front of us and try to fit the children's writing to the rubric. The unease with this exercise may also be a sign that we need more information about the craft of writing ourselves. "What do you mean by craft?" teachers often ask. Because most of us didn't learn about crafting writing in our own schooling and didn't learn about it during teacher education programs, we aren't sure what craft means. For those who did learn about craft, the focus was probably not on what it looks like in young children's writing. This exercise can point us toward what we need to learn.

Third, by collectively looking at and recording our observations and considering how this information will guide our teaching of this individual as well as inform our instruction of the whole class, we believe teachers will become more comfortable studying their students' writing on their own.

On this November morning as the teachers named what Janaya could do, we added that information in the appropriate columns on her Cumulative Writing Record (see Figure 6.6). The Cumulative Writing Record, or CWR, is an accumulative list of what an individual child knows about craft and conventions of writing at any given point, as well as documentation of what we plan to teach as a result. (See Appendix D for a copy of the form.)

The CWR came about in response to the teachers' question, How do you come up with mini-lessons? The simple answer is, we draw on what we know about our students, what we know about writing, and taking the time to look at their work. But teachers wanted something more substantive. We knew we couldn't give them a day-by-day, week-by-week plan for what to teach and how to teach it, but we could provide them with a way of looking that has helped us: a simple system in which they could document what they see children doing, what children need to learn, and when to teach it to them.

We'd already begun a CWR for Janaya based on the sampling of early pages in her Drawing & Writing Book seen in Figures 6.2, 6.3, 6.4, and 6.5 in the color insert, and recorded it on her CWR on October 31.

Now we add our observations based on the work she's done from that first looking until today (see Figure 6.6).

Recording on the Cumulative Writing Record

In the left-hand column we record the date that we looked at the work and what we looked at. We use D/W to mean the samples came from her Drawing & Writing Book, and we write the page numbers if the pages are numbered (for example, pp. 1–7). If the pages aren't numbered, we write the collective number of pages we looked at (for example, first 7 pages). When children move into booklets, this is where we'll write the number of the book(s) and the title(s) of the piece(s).

In the column titled Knows About Craft, we list those things that children show us they know how to do when expressing their thoughts on paper in both drawing and words (organization, information, voice, and so on).

In the column titled Knows About Conventions, we list what the child shows us he or she knows about how the written language works (spacing, letter formation, punctuation, capitalization, and so on). In these two columns we are creating a portrait of each individual child as a writer. Rather than beginning with a preconceived scope and sequence of what children need to learn and the order in which they need to learn it, the CWR, built from the ground up, becomes a record of what each individual has actually learned.

In the next column, Needs to Learn, we generate the lessons we will teach. In any piece of writing, there will be many things that a student needs to learn, but instead of listing many, we choose one or two that we could work on with that child. We try to choose one aspect of craft and one convention. We know that if we point out many things that the student hasn't done "correctly" and expect her to "fix" all of them, she won't remember all of it the next time. But, if we carefully select one aspect of writing that would be useful to her in future pieces of writing that we think she'll be able to do, explain it clearly, and then allow her to apply it to her writing, she'll have a far greater chance of internalizing that new information.

In choosing what to address we sometimes ask ourselves, What one thing seems most pertinent at this point, based on what I know about this writer? Another way we think about it is, What do I see this writer doing (or not doing) that I also see other writers doing (or not doing)? This question guides us toward mini-lessons for the whole class.

Cumulative Writing Record for Janaya—2005–2006

Date D/W Book or Booklet Topic/Title	Knows About Craft (sense of story, organization . . .)	Knows About Conventions (spelling, punctuation, etc.)	Needs to Learn	When to Teach

10/31/05
D/W Book pp. 1–8
• playing with friends
• apple picking
• church
• washing dishes
	• writes about what she knows
	
	• tells story in pictures
	
	• knows that letters have a place in the telling of a story (although sometimes random)
	
	• includes information in picture
	  - skin color (sometimes)
	  - water flowing from spigot
	  - water flowing down pipe
	  - brackets/balls on chair legs
	  - stained-glass shapes
		• writes these letters to go with pictures:
		m c b t a s d (doesn't always remember what words they stand for)
		
		• writes numbers in reverse: 2, 3, 4 calls them "decorations at the church"
		
		• uses mostly uppercase letters: *S T R M C*
			• color skin so it looks real
			
			• listen to sounds in words, independently
				• ML: Using my story, go back and include skin color (shade w/side of pencil tip)
				
				• IW: focus on initial sounds

11/16
D/W Book pp. 9–15
• playing with my friends
• dancing with my sister
• me and my friends playing
• designs
	• includes small, specific details
	  - size of people
	  - clothing
	  - different hairdos
	  - antennae on car
	  - lines in sidewalk
	
	• depicts setting (outdoors)
	  - outside of house
	  - car
	  - flowers
	
	• rereads her work and makes changes (reversed *D → D*)
	
	• adds words to pictures (WH) [WH = with help]
		• listens to sounds in words (WH)
		
		• knowledge of beginning consonant sounds:
		M P D (WH)
		
		• label independently
		  - *J* for *Janaya*; *D* for *dad*
		
		• writes left → right
			• work on drawing people to make them look more real
			
			• how to write words independently
				• ML: Using my story: "One way illustrators help readers understand the story is to include detailed information in the pictures." Refer to: *My Dog Rosie, My Cats Nick and Nora, Our New Puppy.*
				
				• ML: how to listen for sounds in words
				  - using my story
				  - using a child's story

ML= mini-lesson   IW = interactive writing   Conf = conference   RA = read-aloud   Conv = conversation   MM = morning meeting   WS = word study

FIGURE 6.6 Janaya's Cumulative Writing Record, 2005–2006.

Often, we see something that we could best address with students at a time other than the writing mini-lesson—such as during read-aloud, interactive writing, or an informal conversation, say, when children arrive in the morning. We record that information in the final column: our Plan for Teaching. The information we list in these last two columns guides us toward our next teaching.

As we look at Janaya's CWR (Figure 6.6), we see that she has stories that matter to her, that she includes information as she draws those stories, and that she knows some letters and sounds and forms letters with ease. What we notice is that she includes people on many pages and depicts the girls with long, black, curled-out hair and "triangle" dresses, and that on the first page she's colored their skin using the multicultural pencils. After that, however, she has left the skin uncolored. We consider the skin tones a way for children to include specific information about the people in their stories, and we wonder if she remembers that she has access to the tools that will allow her to do that. In terms of the conventions of language, we want to teach her a strategy for writing words independently. She needs to

- think about what she wants to write,
- say one word at a time, slowly,
- listen for the sounds in the word,
- think about what letter makes that sound, and
- write the letters for the sounds she hears.

We know she can do this with help; now we want to teach her to do it on her own.

The goal in looking at children's writing is for us to be informed and instructed by our students: who they are as writers, what they know, and what they need to learn. Looking at one child in depth not only allows us to learn more specifically about him or her, but also gives us the opportunity to learn something about our teaching. We see what information students have made sense of and are applying to their writing, and we wonder why they haven't incorporated other things. We see what we've overlooked and need to go back to, what we need to address that we haven't, and what individual students are doing without any instruction from us.

It seems that this careful looking informs our teaching best when we look at the work of each student in the class on a weekly basis, perhaps looking at a few students' work each day. But teachers tell us that it's time-consuming, and it becomes especially so when we don't keep up with it regularly. As weeks and weeks pass without having looked at each child's work and documented what we see, the task becomes daunting. At the same time, we know that unless we look at students' work regularly, our teaching won't be effective.

Talking, Drawing, Writing

After we listened to teachers' laments, we came up with a more doable system. One that seems to work for many teachers is to look at a small group of children's writing in a given week. We may choose to look at the Drawing & Writing Books of the children who keep their work in the red bin, or we may choose to look at the books of four or five of the children we haven't conferred with in a while, or we may just randomly select a quarter of the class. However we make the choice, we know that looking carefully at the work of a small group of children at a time gives us a glimpse of what the whole class is doing. From that looking, we can make informed decisions about what to address in mini-lessons with the whole class as well as what we want to address with individual children.

Assessing the Work of a Small Group of Writers

We present the work of five kindergartners as a way to model this small-group assessment. In the section on each child, we show four samples that represent the work they did between late September when they began working in their Drawing & Writing Books✉ and this day in mid-November. We explain how we looked at the work and what we documented as a result of that looking. Although this is only a quarter of the class, we know that by looking closely at five students, we'll get a sense of what's happening in the larger class. If we look at five next week and five more during each of the following weeks, we'll have documented the work of the whole class by the end of the month.

You will notice that this chart is similar to, yet different from, the individual CWR.

Figure 6.7 shows the Small-Group Writing Record, which is in Appendix E. The second column, titled What I Notice Before Reading, is not on the individual CWR and we find it incredibly instructive, particularly in terms of what it reveals about the culture of the classroom. Immediately, before we even begin looking at individual pages of their work, we see how the students are interpreting the procedures for the workshop and the expectations for the care of materials. For example, if, when we take the Drawing & Writing Books out of the files to look at, we notice that the books have been placed every which way—spirals on the bottom with open pages facing up and someone else's Drawing & Writing Book stuck down into its pages—or we can't figure out what page the child worked on most recently because the clip is missing and he or she has used random pages and none have been dated, it tells us there is a discrepancy between what we think we've explained to our students and their ability to carry out those expectations. It probably means we need to show them, more explicitly, how to use and care for tools and materials, and to build in respectful ways that help them stay accountable to themselves and to each other.

> ✉ **Note to the Teacher**
>
> We say "late September" because kindergarten children in Boston start the school year later than the rest of the grades. It was nearing the middle of September by the time they began school, and they spent the first weeks telling stories orally, sketching, learning how to use and take care of materials, and being introduced to the Drawing & Writing Book. By the time they were working in the Drawing & Writing Books independently, it was late September.

Small-Group Writing Record: Assessing and Documenting
Date: _____

Child/ Writing	What I Notice Before Reading	What Writers Are Doing Craft/Conventions	Information Writers Need to Learn	When to Teach
Child's name If looking at pages in the Drawing & Writing Book, write *D/W* and indicate the pages being assessed. If looking at a booklet, write title of story or topic.	Assessing student writing can be time-consuming, particularly if the teacher has to sort through the writing to figure out where the child is and what he or she has done. In naming what we notice about how the child cares for and uses materials, teachers learn what the writer understands and still needs to learn about how to acquire an important study habit: being organized. Also, teachers can see what they need to attend to in terms of their own record-keeping.	Name elements of *craft* the child is using in his or her writing. • • • • • *Then, separated only by a space,* list elements of *convention* the child is using in his or her writing. • • •	Building upon what the writer already knows how to do, choose: • one new element of *craft* that the writer can begin to consider as he or she moves forward in understanding effective writing. • one *convention* that the writer can begin to consider as he or she moves forward in understanding how to make writing conventional.	Next to each element of *craft* and *convention*, we note when we plan to teach it. For example, we might address it during a mini-lesson (ML), during a conference (Conf), or during read-aloud (RA) The variety of teaching and learning opportunities listed in this column is a reminder that the teaching happens throughout the day and not just during a writing time.

ML= mini-lesson   IW = interactive writing   Conf = conference   RA = read-aloud   Conv = conversation   MM = morning meeting   WS = word study   RI= reading instruction

FIGURE 6.7 Explanation of Small-Group Writing Record.

In the middle columns we document What Writers Are Doing and include both the elements of craft and conventions, separating them only by a space. In the column called Information Writers Need to Learn, we list one aspect of craft and one convention for each child, even though there are many we could address. As with the individual CWR, it is the information in these two columns that points us toward the final column, where we record when to teach what children need to learn.

We invite readers to look with us at the work of five children who represent various places across a spectrum that we see in many kindergarten classrooms as we model how we notice, collect, and record what we see.

Looking at and Documenting the Work of Five Children

Janaya

See Janaya's Small-Group Writing Record in Figure 6.8.

Small-Group Writing Record: Assessing and Documenting
Date: _____

Child/ Writing	What I Notice Before Reading	What Writers Are Doing Craft/Conventions	Information Writers Need to Learn	When to Teach
Janaya D/W Book 1st 8 pages	• page clipped randomly • lots of pages skipped • clip ends left sticking out • no date recorded • pages done in random order—had to figure out what came 1st, 2nd, 3rd . . . . • transcriptions would help	• writes about what she knows • tells stories in pictures • puts detail in (don't know what it is unless I talk to her—then it's obvious) • includes clothing, hairstyles, background • puts letters on page—usually random	• color skin so it looks real • strategy: listen to sounds in words	• ML: use multicultural pencils to color the skin of people in my story accurately • ML: listen for more than one sound in each word

ML = mini-lesson IW = interactive writing Conf = conference RA = read-aloud Conv = conversation MM = morning meeting WS = word study RI = reading instruction

FIGURE 6.8 Small-Group Writing Record with just Janaya's assessment.

The information we've recorded next to Janaya's name on this small-group writing record is based on the same samples we presented earlier, in Figures 6.2, 6.3, 6.4, and 6.5 (see color insert). As we look at what we've written here and compare it with what we've documented on her individual CWR, we see that on this form we have more information about how she works, yet less specific information about what she can do as a writer. By presenting one child's work on two different forms, we illustrate that there is no one way to document students' work and that both ways have their strengths and drawbacks. From each system we glean information that helps us plan teaching that is appropriate, based on what our students show us they need to learn.

John

Looking at pieces of John's writing in Figures 6.9, 6.10, 6.11, and 6.12 in the color insert, we see that he tells stories about what he knows. He writes about his dad having a meeting with the people at work (Figure 6.9 in the color insert), and going to his cousin's pool, not having a bathing suit, and borrowing army shorts from his cousin Elijah so he can swim (Figure 6.10 in the color insert). When they swam, they "played with these long sticks," which I imagine are foam noodles. He draws the pool and the people around it and tells me that this is when they were swimming. The green crayon that goes up and down the right-hand side of the page is the grass next to the pool, and next to it is a flower.

A few pages later is the drawing of the circus (Figure 6.11 in the color insert). "She's climbing up a pole," he told me in a conference, pointing to the horizontal line across the center of the page. When I asked who was climbing, he said, "The girl."

"Is it the person on the tightrope—you know, that rope that they walk across with their arms straight out, like this?" I asked.

"I forgot what you call it," he said, but he knew that surrounding the pole is the audience, or "the people watching the circus." It's an aerial view that we will learn is John's trademark.

It is always humbling when I look at a page like this and see it from my teacher-as-evaluator perspective as inexperienced drawing, and then allow the child to instruct me. When I sat with John and asked him about these pages he had drawn, I looked from his perspective and was reminded of the brilliance of this five-year-old. As he pointed to the different parts of the drawing and spoke with such authority about what was happening, the page became alive with story . . . and so did he. His words and how he spoke them revealed his investment and his ability to engage in meaningful work. I could see the intention behind the marks he had put on the page and acknowledged his hard work and all that he knows how to do.

In his story of going to the beach (Figure 6.12), he pointed out the water (blue) and the sand (yellow), and I asked him to listen to

Small-Group Writing Record: Assessing and Documenting
Date: _____

Child/ Writing	What I Notice Before Reading	What Writers Are Doing Craft/Conventions	Information Writers Need to Learn	When to Teach
Janaya D/W Book 1st 8 pages	• page clipped randomly • lots of pages skipped • clip ends left sticking out • no date recorded • pages done in random order—had to figure out what came 1st, 2nd, 3rd . . . • transcriptions would help	• writes about what she knows • tells stories in pictures • puts detail in (don't know what it is unless I talk to her—then it's obvious) • includes clothing, hairstyles, background • puts letters on page—usually random	• color skin so it looks real • strategy: listen to sounds in words	• ML: use multicultural pencils to color the skin of people in my story accurately • ML: listen for more than one sound in each word
John D/W Book 1st 10 pages	• clip on next blank page • clip ends sticking out • no date recorded • transcriptions would help	• writes about what he knows • tells story in picture • includes details (pool, audience, buildings) • most illustrations are aerial views • writes *B* for beach, with help	• drawing people to look real • listening for initial sounds	• ML: refer to sketchbook; reminder—ovals • IW: labels in room • Conference

ML= mini-lesson   IW = interactive writing   Conf = conference   RA = read-aloud   Conv = conversation   MM = morning meeting   WS = word study   RI= reading instruction

FIGURE 6.13 Small-Group Writing Record with John added.

the beginning of the word /b/each to see if he could associate that sound with the letter. He needed me to help him hear the sound and to show him how to make a *B*, so I wrote *WH* at the bottom for "with help."

On the Small-Group Writing Record in Figure 6.13 with John added, we celebrate this writer while noting elements of craft we want to work on with him over the next days and weeks: how to draw people with heads, necks, torsos, arms, legs, and hands. In terms of conventions, we'll continue to work on the strategy for listening to sounds in words and writing a letter to represent an initial sound. We'll address it during interactive writing, because many children need support with this strategy, and we'll be sure to engage John's participation during the lessons. We'll continue to support him with this strategy during writing conferences as well.

Aisha

Aisha, whose work is shown in Figures 6.14, 6.15, 6.16, and 6.17 in the color insert, came to school knowing letters and sounds and how to write some words, and feeling comfortable doing it. Right on the first page of her Drawing & Writing Book she began by showing what she knows: how to draw a house, draw a person, give specific information in the story (the birthday cake on the table and her sister sitting at it), write her name, number the page, and write words even if she doesn't know how to spell them. She knows how to listen to the sounds in words and write the letters for the sounds she hears. During these first weeks, she wrote a sentence, labeled, and was comfortable crossing out when she made a mistake (the *R* for a *D*). What isn't evident by looking at her work is that Aisha would return to the page she started for many days, putting in more details and working slowly and methodically. She would also wait for the teacher to come and say, "If there were words to go with this story, what do you think they would say?" We want her to learn to do this on her own.

So in the Information Writers Need to Learn column we listed two strategies that have to do with craft and conventions that we want Aisha to learn to use on her own. The first is to ask herself, What words will I put on this page to go with my illustration? The second is to go back and touch each word as she rereads to make sure her writing makes sense. Both strategies will help her become a more independent writer. (See Figure 6.18 for a Small-Group Writing Record with Aisha added.)

Jarren

Right from the first day we learn that Jarren, whose work is shown in Figure 6.19, 6.20, 6.21, and 6.22 in the color insert, has a passion for race cars. We'd continue to be reminded of it throughout the year, especially as he chose "Making My Pinewood Derby Car" as his

Small-Group Writing Record: Assessing and Documenting
Date: _____

Child/ Writing	What I Notice Before Reading	What Writers Are Doing Craft/Conventions	Information Writers Need to Learn	When to Teach
Janaya D/W Book 1st 8 pages	• page clipped randomly • lots of pages skipped • clip ends left sticking out • no date recorded • pages done in random order—had to figure out what came 1st, 2nd, 3rd . . . • transcriptions would help	• writes about what she knows • tells stories in pictures • puts detail in (don't know what it is unless I talk to her—then it's obvious) • includes clothing, hairstyles, background • puts letters on page—usually random	• color skin so it looks real • strategy: listen to sounds in words	• ML: use multicultural pencils to color the skin of people in my story accurately • ML: listen for more than one sound in each word
John D/W Book 1st 10 pages	• clip on next blank page • clip ends sticking out • no date recorded • transcriptions would help	• writes about what he knows • tells story in picture • includes details (pool, audience, buildings) • most illustrations are aerial views • writes *B* for beach, with help	• drawing people to look real • listening for initial sounds	• ML: refer to sketchbook; reminder—ovals • IW: labels in room • Conference
Aisha D/W Book 1st 9 pages	• does pages in order • clip on next blank page • has a way of organizing her work so it's easy to access • no date recorded	• writes about what she knows • tells story in picture and words • includes detailed information (cake, plates, present on table, legs on table) • hears/records sounds in words (brsday, cand str) • writes independently: I weah TV (watch)	• add text independently • go back and touch as you write to make sure it makes sense	• Conf: Ask yourself, And what words will I write to go with my picture? • ML: go back and touch in my own story

ML= mini-lesson   IW = interactive writing   Conf = conference   RA = read-aloud   Conv = conversation   MM = morning meeting   WS = word study   RI= reading instruction

FIGURE 6.18 Small-Group Writing Record with Aisha added.

first book to be published. Jarren tells stories in pictures and begins labeling and writing words fairly early on. Although he writes about what he knows, he doesn't always attend to the detail that gives readers specific information, so we want to work with him on that. One way to do it is by pointing out how the illustrators of the books we love give readers specific, detailed information. "I'm noticing how on this page of *Bigmama's*, Donald Crews shows just what the Cottondale station looked like. Here, he's put . . . and over here . . . and look, we know the kind of town that station is in because . . . And that's what you do in your writing, too, isn't it? You put that information in the picture, information that isn't in the words but needs to be there to help the reader understand the story." Another thing we want to address with Jarren is to write text independently and to extend the thought on each page, because we know that he can do that.

Attending to the detail in the illustrations is something we want children know how to do because it is our belief that if they attend to the tiny, specific details in their illustrated stories, they're more likely to understand the place for specific detail in their texts. Figure 6.23 shows the Small-Group Writing Record with Jarren added.)

Marisol

The four samples in Figures 6.24, 6.25, 6.26, and 6.27 in the color insert reflect the type of entries Marisol made in her Drawing & Writing Book during late September, October, and the beginning of November. She came to kindergarten knowing her letters and sounds, spelling a handful of words, and reading. Yet at first, she didn't write letters or words on her illustrations. The illustrations were stories in and of themselves, and she worked carefully on them. But once she saw her teacher put letters down to label parts of her own illustration, Marisol did the same in her book (Figure 6.25), and in those labels, she reveals what she knows about how words work. As time went on, she'd say whole thoughts and we'd repeat them to her, saying, "That information you just told me, Marisol— where are you going to put that so readers will understand it, too?" Eventually she didn't need us to ask; she wrote whole thoughts independently.

See Figure 6.28, where Marisol's information has been added to the SGWR.

When we look at the work of prolific writers such as Marisol, we sometimes think we have to get her right into a booklet because that is, after all, what we're working toward. She's writing with ease, she has a lot to say, and she knows a lot about how written language works. Certainly she's got the tools she needs to write books. Yet she was happy working in her Drawing & Writing Book during those first weeks of school, and there was still more that she could learn as she worked in the Drawing & Writing Book. We were pushing her to include more specific information in the drawings and fill out her

Small-Group Writing Record: Assessing and Documenting
Date: _____

Child/ Writing	What I Notice Before Reading	What Writers Are Doing Craft/Conventions	Information Writers Need to Learn	When to Teach
Janaya D/W Book 1st 8 pages	• page clipped randomly • lots of pages skipped • clip ends left sticking out • no date recorded • pages done in random order—had to figure out what came 1st, 2nd, 3rd . . . • transcriptions would help	• writes about what she knows • tells stories in pictures • puts detail in (don't know what it is unless I talk to her—then it's obvious) • includes clothing, hairstyles, background • puts letters on page—usually random	• color skin so it looks real • strategy: listen to sounds in words	• ML: use multicultural pencils to color the skin of people in my story accurately • ML: listen for more than one sound in each word
John D/W Book 1st 10 pages	• clip on next blank page • clip ends sticking out • no date recorded • transcriptions would help	• writes about what he knows • tells story in picture • includes details (pool, audience, buildings) • most illustrations are aerial views • writes *B* for beach, with help	• drawing people to look real • listening for initial sounds	• ML: refer to sketchbook; reminder—ovals • IW: labels in room • Conference
Aisha D/W Book 1st 9 pages	• does pages in order • clip on next blank page • has a way of organizing her work so it's easy to access • no date recorded	• writes about what she knows • tells story in picture and words • includes detailed information (cake, plates, present on table, legs on table) • hears/records sounds in words (brsday, cand str) • writes independently: I weah TV (watch)	• add text independently • go back and touch as you write to make sure it makes sense	• Conf: Ask yourself, And what words will I write to go with my picture? • ML: go back and touch in my own story
Jarren D/W Book 1st 12 pages	• does pages in order • clip on next blank page • no date recorded	• writes about what he knows • tells story in picture • sometimes sacrifices accuracy/detail for speed • writes letters to represent sounds he hears • knows about leaving spaces between words	• include detail in all stories • extend thoughts on each page; get him talking, telling more	• RA: *Bigmama's*—point out specific details that give readers information • Conf: And where will you write that so readers will know that, too?

ML= mini-lesson   IW = interactive writing   Conf = conference   RA = read-aloud   Conv = conversation   MM = morning meeting   WS = word study   RI= reading instruction

FIGURE 6.23 Small-Group Writing Record with Jarren added.

Small-Group Writing Record: Assessing and Documenting

Date: _____

Child/ Writing	What I Notice Before Reading	What Writers Are Doing Craft/Conventions	Information Writers Need to Learn	When to Teach
Janaya D/W Book 1st 8 pages	• page clipped randomly • lots of pages skipped • clip ends left sticking out • no date recorded • pages done in random order—had to figure out what came 1st, 2nd, 3rd . . . • transcriptions would help	• writes about what she knows • tells stories in pictures • puts detail in (don't know what it is unless I talk to her—then it's obvious) • includes clothing, hairstyles, background • puts letters on page—usually random	• color skin so it looks real • strategy: listen to sounds in words	• ML: use multicultural pencils to color the skin of people in my story accurately • ML: listen for more than one sound in each word
John D/W Book 1st 10 pages	• clip on next blank page • clip ends sticking out • no date recorded • transcriptions would help	• writes about what he knows • tells story in picture • includes details (pool, audience, buildings) • most illustrations are aerial views • writes *B* for beach, with help	• drawing people to look real • listening for initial sounds	• ML: refer to sketchbook; reminder—ovals • IW: labels in room • Conference
Aisha D/W Book 1st 9 pages	• does pages in order • clip on next blank page • has a way of organizing her work so it's easy to access • no date recorded	• writes about what she knows • tells story in picture and words • includes detailed information (cake, plates, present on table, legs on table) • hears/records sounds in words (brsday, cand str) • writes independently: I weah TV (watch)	• add text independently • go back and touch as you write to make sure it makes sense	• Conf: Ask yourself, And what words will I write to go with my picture? • ML: go back and touch in my own story
Jarren D/W Book 1st 12 pages	• does pages in order • clip on next blank page • no date recorded	• writes about what he knows • tells story in picture • sometimes sacrifices accuracy/detail for speed • writes letters to represent sounds he hears • knows about leaving spaces between words	• include detail in all stories • extend thoughts on each page; get him talking, telling more	• RA: *Bigmama's*—point out specific details that give readers information • Conf: And where will you write that so readers will know that, too?
Marisol D/W Book 1st 10 pages	• does pages in order • clip on next blank page • has a way of organizing her writing so it's easy to access • no date recorded • can read easily	• tells about what she knows • gives detailed info in illustrations (color, size of people, hairstyles, expressions . . .) • labels parts of illustration • represents sounds w/appropriate letters • extends thought on the page • uses exclamation mark appropriately	• tell more parts of the story • use mostly lowercase letters	• Conf: introduce booklets (within two weeks) • IW: emphasize lowercase letters • Conf: show pages in a book—mostly lowercase

ML= mini-lesson IW = interactive writing Conf = conference RA = read-aloud Conv = conversation MM = morning meeting WS = word study RI= reading instruction

FIGURE 6.28 Small-Group Writing Record with Marisol added.

story with words and she was, so as of this point in November we hadn't introduced booklets to Marisol and it would probably be another couple of weeks before we did. Thanksgiving was right around the corner, which meant a shortened week, and then there would be getting back into the routine when the students returned from a four-day weekend. We'd continue to address aspects of craft and conventions that would push her forward as a writer while allowing her the time to feel grounded with her peers. And we'd watch for the signs: Is she continuing a story on subsequent pages? Does she have a lot to say about this part? Is she writing a lot and with ease? When children naturally extend their stories in this way, they are moving their way into booklets.

How This Looking Informs Our Teaching

Just from looking at the work of these five children we've collected weeks worth of mini-lessons that will address the needs of many if not all of our students. At first it can feel overwhelming. Next to each student's name we've listed specific things that he or she needs to learn, and they're different from what the others need to learn. It's easy to feel pulled in five different directions (and if we had looked at the whole class, twenty different directions!). How, we wonder, will we be able to address the needs of each individual when the needs are so varied? As we look more closely, however, we begin to see how these different needs fall under some broad topics, and organize them accordingly:

Including specific information. Drawing people so they look real; including detailed features (size, skin color, hairstyles) that will help the reader understand the story; making sure words and illustrations go together; making sure illustrations and the words work together to give readers a fuller understanding of the story but don't always give the same information; writing about what you know so you can write with information; and so on. We can address these in mini-lessons, and they pertain to children working in Drawing & Writing Books as well as booklets.

How writers work. Writers ask themselves questions as they work. For example, What else do I need to include? What do I need to take out? What words will I write to go with my picture? What else will readers need to know? No matter the level of sophistication of the writing, all children need to know to look at the work they've done and ask themselves questions that will help them think further about the work.

Writing words. Strategy for listening for sounds in words and listening for initial sounds; listening for many sounds in a word; going back and touching as you reread; using what you know about words to write other words; using mostly lowercase if you know how; and so on. Some of this we'll address in mini-lessons, some we'll address in interactive writing, some in morning meeting, some in individual conferences.

Procedures for care of materials. For example, how to put books away so everyone has easy access to them; how to check that the materials in the caddies are put away carefully; and how to move on to the next page. These won't be just mini-lessons but something to address throughout the day, especially if they'll be using these materials throughout the day.

What I need to do better as the teacher. For example, transcribe as often as I can in small print in an inconspicuous spot on the page (or on the back of the previous page) so we'll have a record of earlier works; teach the children how to use the date stamp or to write the date so there is a record of when pieces were done; more role playing on how to return the Drawing & Writing Books to the files; and watching as they put materials away at the end of writing time and guiding them, and giving helpful reminders.

Writers use the materials that will help them tell the story as best they can. When the Drawing & Writing Book is appropriate, when to choose a booklet (which means, for us teachers, when to introduce booklets if we haven't already), and so on.

Categorizing the lessons makes the work feel less fractured, more whole. It helps us make decisions about what will become lessons for the whole class, what things we'll mention in passing as we work on our own writing, what we'll address during other parts of the day, and what we want to set in place right away in terms of helping our students—and ourselves—take on behaviors that will help make the culture of the classroom work better.

Looking at student work is essential in that it forces us to look, to name, and to write down what children can do. Always, always we are surprised at how much there is to say. It is essential because it reminds us of how much children are capable of doing and how much more they can learn.

Looking at the Work of the Whole Class

We realize that these two systems for documenting what we see when we look at children's work can still feel overwhelming, so we offer a third option—a quick look at the writing of the whole class at once. It involves taking the whole class set of Drawing & Writing Books, looking through the most recent work, and writing down what we see. This "quick read" is what teachers tend to do most easily; the part they often leave out is writing down what they see—

and that is so important. Naming, listing, and then looking at the data makes clear, and sometimes makes obvious, what we need to address.

Figure 6.29 shows part of a handwritten record of the whole class in late October. You'll notice that we didn't write it on a form. We looked closely, noted what students needed to know about in terms of craft, conventions, and strategies, and compiled a list of possible lessons. This quick assessment gives different information than that of the individual CWR, yet it seems that having had experience looking in depth and recording on the CWR would help teachers name and gather helpful information quickly, as we do here. Clearly, the three systems we've presented serve different purposes. What they have in common is that they all keep us looking, noticing, naming what we see, and turning us back to our students so that they might inform how we teach. Because looking at students' work and documenting what we see is something we do throughout the year, we have included a sample assessment of one child's work as he moved into booklets (see Figure 6.30).

In the next two chapters, we draw on what we have learned by looking at student work as we present lessons on craft and conventions. We begin by introducing booklets.

A Look at The Whole Class - Late October

Name	Medium	What I see	Possible Topics for Mini Lesson
TaShayla	D/W	stick people, lots of color, hearts & designs	→ drawing people so they look real
Yulexy	D/W	tells one part of a larger story, some labeling, arms & legs coming out of people's heads	→ drawing people so they look real
Sumiko	D/W	Lots of designs (is there a story?)	→ more opportunities to tell stories
Jerrod	D/W	Lots of colorful designs, not many people (is he comfortable drawing people? Is there a story?)	→ drawing people
Simone	D/W	tells 1 part of a story, lots of people - all look the same	→ how to distinguish people by clothing, hairstyles, skin color.
Imani	D/W	Draws story then colors over it	→ making sure readers can "read" picture
John	D/W	Includes specific detail in illustration, most stories have people - arms & legs coming out of head	→ drawing people so they look real
Flerov	D/W	Tells/draws w/ detail, sometimes stick people, sometimes filled out & in action!	→ Can he show others how he draws people?
Marisol	D/W	Lots of information in illustration, Reveals "plot" through background, people dressed in different clothes, labeling w/ words & letters, people look real - filled out	→ Show others how she draws people so they look real

FIGURE 6.29 Handwritten whole-class writing record in late October. (Only half the class is shown here.)

Cumulative Writing Record for Ezedequias—2002–2003

Date D/W Book or Booklet Topic/Title	Knows About Craft (sense of story, organization . . .)	Knows About Conventions (spelling, punctuation, etc.)	Needs to Learn	When to Teach

9/12–11/7
10 pages
D&W Book
 	
• action Figures
 	
• Sponge Bob
 	
• McDonald's
	• mostly random drawings of objects
	  - action figures
	  - Sponge Bob
	  - cats, dogs
	
	• drawings represent things from his life
	
	• includes information in picture
	  - tires and windows on car
	  - divider line on road
	  - pointy ears on cat
		• labels McDonald's (midons)
		
		• draws an *M* for golden arches
		
		• copied the word *car*
		
		• starts to write his name using a capital *E* and then all lowercase
			• tell a story with more than one part
			
			• tell a story through pictures
				• throughout the day encourage lots of talk
				
				• RA: include wordless books

11/8–12/22
22 pages
D&W Book
 	
• Free Willy
 	
• Scooby Doo
 	
• the woods
 	
• Stop & Shop
	• picture and text go together
	
	• draws people realistically:
	  - all the body parts
	  - different hairdos
	
	• includes information in picture
	  - store and its logo
	  - shoelaces
	  - Shaggy with blue pants and green shirt
	
	• shows back views of people
	
	• shows perspective in drawing
	  - screen in relationship to the people at the movies
	  - mom taller than he is
	
	• uses colors to make things look real
		• writes words in columns or wherever there is space
		
		• experiments with writing left → right and top → bottom
		
		• writes words independently: says words slowly, listens for sounds and writes the letters
		
		• uses some sight words:
		  and it my stop
		  fun me see the
		  I mom shop to
		
		• uses & in Stop & Shop
		
		• randomly uses both upper- and lowercase letters
			• extend story by drawing/writing more than one part
			
			• write words left → right and top to bottom
				• Conf: introduce booklets (lined pages to help with directionality?)
				
				• IW: focus on writing words left → right

ML= mini-lesson   IW = interactive writing   Conf = conference   RA = read-aloud   Conv = conversation   MM = morning meeting   WS = word study

FIGURE 6.30 CWR for Ezedequias.

| 1/5–1/10
1 booklet

• Christmas (no title) | • writes about what he knows and cares about

• writes what happened next on each page (B-M-M-M-E)
  B = beginning
  M = middle
  E = end

• includes details specific to Christmas
  - red nose on Rudolph, sleigh
  - fireplace with Santa
  - ornaments and star on tree
  - presents with bows

• expressions on faces match the feelings expressed in text | • writes words left → right and top → bottom

• experiments with periods—sometimes puts one at the end of the page

• uses new sight word: was

(Some confusion in story making sense—more because he is a second language user than a writing issue) | • write a title for his story

• leave spaces between words | • RA: point out that each book has a title

• ML: look at the titles of several books written by children in the class

• ML: use a piece of student writing that has spaces between words and show how spaces make writing easier to read

• IW: let Zeddy be the "spacer" |
| 1/11–3/15
15 pages
D&W Book

• walking dog

• aquarium

• skiing

• birthday party

-AND-

2 booklets

• video store

• going to school | • writes a title on each story

• depicts settings (outside)
  - buildings - ski slopes
  - sun   - cars

• depicts setting (inside)
  - a car
  - the Aquarium, water and fish
  - easels in the classroom

• draws people in different positions
  - side view of people and animals walking (man has one leg up)
  - people sitting

• rereads page as evidenced by crossing out unwanted words

• added a page to include another part (B-M-M-M-E-M)

• took a page out because he had too many (B-M-M-E)

• knows something about how stories begin— mostly about going to a place.

• knows something about how stories end—mostly about going home | • leaves a tiny bit of space between words

• copied February

• uses new sight words: in, we, went

• uses ing

• uses mostly lowercase letters

(In previous drawings as well as in these, he always makes his car look real by coloring it green.) | • when adding a page, (a new part) reread whole story to figure out where new page belongs so story makes sense

• dates his writing

• begin recording titles of stories on page in folder called My Finished Writing | • ML: reread my story to show how I decide where to put a new page for a new part

• remind whole class to remember to date their writing

• ML: using a folder of child who is already recording titles on My Finished Writing page |

ML= mini-lesson   IW = interactive writing   Conf = conference   RA = read-aloud   Conv = conversation   MM = morning meeting   WS = word study

FIGURE 6.30 CWR for Ezedequias (continued).

Talking, Drawing, Writing

| 3/13–5/1
10 pages
D&W Book

• the beach

• playing marbles

• Arthur

-AND-

3 booklets

• cousin's house

• the circus

• apple orchard | • decides and chooses whether to write in the D&W Book or in a booklet

• one statement per page

• most sentences begin with "I" or "We"

• adds more to each part by telling who he's with in story

• decides when to abandon a story | • has strategies for writing words independently
 - hears many sounds and writes the letter(s) for the sounds:
 rolkostr = roller coaster
 srcis = circus
 stashun = station
 - uses a known word to help write an unknown word:
 plays = place
 - continues to use new sight words

• writes date on his writing

• records titles of writing on the My Finished Writing page in the writing folder | • when appropriate, to tell more about what the people are doing in his story

• put a period where he wants readers to stop

• proofread for items on his proofreading list | • ML: use *My Big Brother* and *My Best Friend Moved Away* to see how writers tell about what the people are doing when they are together

• While reading books, he stops at periods. Point out how periods tell him when to stop and how he, as the writer, needs to help his readers know when to stop.

• ML: check the proof-reading list and do each item on the list |
| 5/2–6/12
5 pages
D&W Book

• watching TV

• the piñata

-AND-

3 booklets

• aquarium

• cousin

• McDonald's | • abandoned story: "I don't have much to say about my cousin."

• begins most pieces with "I went . . ." or "We went . . ."

• ends most pieces with "Then we went home." | • uses periods more consistently (story nine has all of them)

• does all five items on proofreading list | • give readers more information by filling out story on each page

• other ways to begin stories | • Share his writing with class to see what else his readers want to know about his story. Let him actually add some info at the share.

• ML: Read some different ways writers in class have begun stories |
| ML= mini-lesson   IW = interactive writing   Conf = conference   RA = read-aloud   Conv = conversation   MM = morning meeting   WS = word study |

FIGURE 6.30 CWR for Ezedequias (continued).

CHAPTER 7

Introducing Booklets

GIVING CAREFUL ATTENTION to our students' work and observing them at work lets us know when they're ready to move beyond a single-page story. The signs are there: on the pages of their Drawing & Writing Books, in their flowing talk during conferences, in the confidence they exude as they make decisions about what to write and how to write it. They show us when they're heading toward more complex, fuller writing, and when we see the signs, we respond by inviting them to write whole stories with many parts in a booklet.

By *booklet* we mean pages of copy paper stapled together with a color cover. It's a format that makes sense for young writers for the following reasons:

It is familiar. It has a cover on which to write a title and their name, and pages inside on which to draw pictures and write words; thus it looks like the picture books they've been reading at school if not well before.

It invites playfulness. If we were to put a group of five-year-olds, some paper, a container of colored pencils, and a stapler in a room together, it wouldn't be long before we'd see pages stapled together and covered in exquisite, colorful markings, and the children who made them eager to read their stories. Children naturally, playfully, put pages together when given the chance and the tools, so it seems logical to use this affinity for homegrown books to usher them into the world of reading and writing. In *About the Authors: Writing Workshop with Our Youngest Writers* (2004), Katie Wood Ray and Lisa Cleveland suggest that it is this developmentally appropriate act of creating books that gives the work meaning. "Over time and with experience," they tell us, "we have come to believe that it is the energy of making stuff in a daily writing workshop that drives all our teaching with our youngest writers" (6).

It has a built-in expectation that you have a lot to say on this topic. Booklets are made up of many pages and therefore show children that stories build, one part upon the next. When we introduce booklets, we begin with five pages, for good reason: fewer than three just isn't booklike; three gives the message stories have a beginning, a middle, and an end, and although that is true, we want children to see that the middle is much fuller than either of the ends and therefore needs to be filled out; and four pages is too symmetrical. Two end parts with two middle parts just doesn't have the right rhythm. So we start out with a beginning page, an ending page, and three pages for the middle, which gives the story room to build.

Some teachers are concerned at first that five is too many, that some students will be overwhelmed by the number of pages, but we don't find that. Maybe it's because we expect that they have a lot to say and then show them that they do. We get some students telling their stories so all the others can see, and we turn one page for each part as they tell it, just as we do during storytelling sessions. They see that they do have one part to tell on each page, and when they sit down to write, they have a plan for what to do. Some children may not use all five pages, whereas others may choose to add a few more. Either way is okay. Over time, they will decide how many pages they need and staple the booklets together themselves. What is most important is that the format of the booklet says, You have a lot to say about this. Built into the structure of the booklet is an expectation for fullness of information.

It offers a logical structure for teaching elements of craft. The booklet provides a concrete way to address story structure (beginning, middle, middle, middle, end, for example), telling one part on each page, making sure the illustrations and the text go together, and other aspects of craft that have to do with organizing and ordering a cohesive story. They learn that writers make decisions about what to include, what to leave out, and how to put the information on each page so readers will understand and want to keep reading. The booklet allows us to address more sophisticated elements of craft as well. By looking closely at and imitating what other writers and illustrators do, these young writers use elements of foreshadowing, suspense, and integrity before they ever learn the literary terms. When they use these elements in their writing, we show them what they have done and explain why it makes the piece of writing effective. Having that information will allow them to use it intentionally in another piece of work at another time.

It makes revision easy. Part of crafting a piece of writing means rereading what you've done and making changes so it makes sense. For five- and six-year-olds, revision means adding to or reshaping the picture, crossing out unwanted or indecipherable letters or words, using a caret to insert a missing word, drawing arrows to redirect the reader, or changing whole parts: adding a page or taking a page out. These young writers remove staples when they need to rearrange pages and staple their booklets back together in the order they want them, sometimes with new pages added or pages removed. Moving parts of a story around would be difficult for them if the entire story was written on one single page, but the booklet allows them to manipulate the parts without having to actually "cut" or "rewrite." The format makes revision doable, logical, and playful.

It lends itself to writing sentences and paragraphs. This may be a by-product of working in booklets, but when children tell one part of a story on each page, they almost always write a complete thought. Teachers often worry about how to teach young children to write in full sentences, yet in these booklets, most children naturally write one sentence per page. Eventually, as they extend the thinking on each page, their simple sentences become elaborated thoughts about one particular idea, and instead of a sentence per page, they're writing a paragraph per page.

As with the Drawing & Writing Book, we have information that we want our students to know about using booklets: where they're kept, how to get them and return them to their places when writing time is finished, how to take them apart and put them together when necessary, and how to do high-quality work on the pages. Since they already do most of these things in their Drawing & Writing Books, we just work this new medium—booklets—into the system that's in place. It is our hope that as children move into booklets, they use what they've acquired through telling one part well to tell many parts of a single story well.

Different Ways to Introduce Booklets

In the following three lessons we model different approaches for introducing booklets to children. In the first, we introduce booklets to the whole class at once. In the second, we model how we might introduce booklets to children individually. Third, we model introducing booklets using our own writing, which will be familiar because it parallels the way we introduced storytelling using our own stories first.

Lesson Introducing Booklets to the Whole Class: Telling Many Parts of a Story

What's going on in the classroom

- Children are working in their Drawing & Writing Books.
- Some write fluidly and with ease, using drawings and sound spellings.
- Some children are continuing to tell other parts of their stories on subsequent pages, indicating that they have more to say on the topic.

What's next

- They need to know that they have a choice of forms for writing: the Drawing & Writing Book, where they work in depth on one part, or a booklet, where they extend one story, telling many parts.

Materials needed

- sample Drawing & Writing Book with a detailed illustration
- sample booklets, one with unlined pages and one with two lines per page
- *My Dog Rosie*, by Isabelle Harper, illustrated by Barry Moser

This is what I noticed . . .

"Boys and girls, remember the other day when Osvaldo told us that story about how he and his mom drove in her black van to pick up his brother at the mall? He told us that his brother was working at a sports store where they sell sneakers, basketball shirts, footballs, and things, and he and his mom went into his brother's store and got to see him work for a while. Then, while they were waiting for his brother to finish work, they walked around the mall, they shopped in the stores, and that's when they saw the big fountain with a lot of pennies on the bottom from people making wishes. Remember that? Then, when his brother finished work, they went food shopping on the way home.

"And here, in your Drawing & Writing Book, Osvaldo, we see you drew and wrote about that story. Here you are at the big fountain and we can see the water coming down the wall—part of the fountain—and then over here, the pool, with all those pennies on the bottom! You even wrote something here. Will you read it to us?" (See Figure 7.1.)

Osvaldo touches each letter—*I T T P P M B*—and reads, "'I went to pick up my brother.'"

"In the illustration, you show the escalator. Remember that big word Osvaldo used for the moving stairs they have at the mall?"

"And these are the lights," he says, pointing to the colorful spheres hanging from the ceiling.

"And this is . . ." I point to the larger person and wait for him to finish.

"My mom," he says, then points to the smaller person. "And this is me."

"Is this when you're throwing the pennies into the fountain?"

Talking, Drawing, Writing

FIGURE 7.1 Osvaldo: *I went to pick up my brother.*

Osvaldo nods.

"Usually, boys and girls, when you work in your Drawing & Writing Book, you do what Osvaldo did—you tell about one part of a story. And when you tell one part of a story, you can tell a lot about that part. Look at what Osvaldo told about this part of his story where he threw pennies into the fountain. But when you work in your Drawing & Writing Book and tell one part, that means you have to leave parts out. In this picture we don't see Osvaldo in the sports store watching his brother work. We don't see Osvaldo and his mom shopping in the stores. We don't see them at the grocery store and finally at home. There are many parts to that story, but because he had only one page, he told about only one part.

"Sometimes, though, authors want to tell more than just one part. The story is so special, they want to tell many parts. It's like what Isabelle Harper and Barry Moser do in their book *My Dog Rosie*."

Let me show you what I mean . . . "They could have told just about one part, like giving Rosie a bath. But no, they wanted to tell a lot of parts. So they wrote the story in a book with lots of pages, and they put one part on each page: on this page they told the part about feeding Rosie his breakfast, on this page they told the part about giving him a bath, on this page, the part about playing catch, on this page, the part about reading him a story . . . One part on each page, and they tell the whole story.

"Now here's what I'm wondering. Who thinks they have a story and might want to tell many parts, like Isabelle Harper did—in a book like this?"

I show a booklet. Children raise their hands. Osvaldo is one of them, as I was hoping he would be. (Actually, I was pretty sure he'd volunteer because he was so proud of his story.) I ask him to come up.

"Osvaldo, I'm wondering if you're going to tell that story about going to the mall to get your brother, or if you have another story in mind."

I ask him because I am hoping he will want to write about the mall. I want to model how to go from telling about one part in the Drawing & Writing Book to telling all the parts of that same story in a booklet. Since he already told that story and the children are familiar with it, we won't have to take the time to hear a new story first. However, if he says he wants to write a different story, I am prepared to have him tell it to us. Then I will model how it might sound in a booklet as I turn one page at a time, telling back each part. But I don't have to do that.

"The mall," he says.

"Now, I have another question for you. Do you think you'll want to tell this story on paper with no lines so you can decide where to put the pictures and the words, like this?" I show a sample of blank paper. "Or do you think you'll want to tell your story on paper that has a space for a picture and space for words, like this?" I show a sample of paper with a few lines.

Osvaldo chooses no lines, and I take one page at a time from the pile as I say each part of the story as he previously told it:

"This first page will be about when you and your mom drove to the mall in your black van to pick up your brother from work. This next page will be about when you went into the sports store where he sells sneakers and footballs and sports stuff and you watched him work. Then the part where you walked around the mall and shopped in the stores while you were waiting for him—and that's when you saw the fountain. Then this page, the one you wrote about in your Drawing & Writing Book when you threw pennies into the fountain. Then you went back and got your brother, and you stopped at the grocery store on your way home."

I ask him to select a cover from the three color choices (I want him to have choice but I keep them few so as not to overwhelm him) and, together, we staple the five pages into a book, just three staples, one in the middle and one near either end. I talk about how not to slam the stapler down, but to press down hard and listen for the *buum-buum*-like sound of the stapler fastening. The children are enchanted as they watch the making of a book and listen closely for the *buum-buum*. I retell his story once more, using his words as I turn each blank page.

"It seems like you're ready to write that whole story, Osvaldo," I say. "I know you probably will get started on only one page today; it takes a while to write a whole story in a book like that, especially when you work hard to make your illustrations the best they can be and think hard about what you write. If you don't want to put the title on yet, that's okay, because sometimes writers just don't know the title until they're finished. But remember to write your name on the cover. Okay, you may get started."

Osvaldo takes his booklet and goes to a table to work.

"Who else thinks they will need one of these booklets today?" I ask. I walk one more child through the telling of his story as I did with Osvaldo.

So, today, as you write . . .

"Boys and girls, today during writing time you have a choice. You can continue in your Drawing & Writing Books telling a part of your story on one page, or you may tell your story in a booklet like this, where you tell many parts. And as you think about your story, remember what Isabelle Harper and Barry Moser did: on each page, they drew and wrote about a different part.

"Who thinks they're going to work in their Drawing & Writing Book today?"

Some children raise their hands.

"Okay, you may get started," I say, and about half of them go off to work.

"So it seems like you boys and girls are planning to write in a booklet," I say to those remaining at the rug.

Because I don't plan to staple a booklet for every child the way I did for Osvaldo, I ask them to turn toward the writing center. "Okay, let me show you where we'll keep the booklets."

Procedure for Getting Booklets

I walk past them to the shelves that house the writing materials, to where the booklets are already made, five pages in each with two different choices of paper—lined and unlined—and three color choices of covers. They are stacked neatly on plastic trays, two high and two wide. (See Figure 7.2.) I ask a child who plans to write a booklet to come up.

"What kind of paper do you want in your booklet, Liliana?" I ask, pointing to the loose paper on the trays. "This kind, with no lines, or this kind, with some lines for writing and some space for drawing?"

She points to the stack of unlined paper on top of one row of trays.

"So Liliana wants a booklet with this kind of paper," I say, taking a piece of unlined paper from the tray so they all can see, then putting it back. "That means she'll choose a booklet from this pile." I point to the stack tray right next to the pile of unlined paper. "Since the paper in this

FIGURE 7.2 The writing center has premade booklets of two kinds of paper.

pile is unlined, that means the booklets in this tray right next to it will have unlined pages. So now," I say in an I'll-bet-you-can-figure-this-one-out voice while taking a piece of paper from the tray below, "since the paper in this pile looks like this"—I hold up the piece—"with two lines for writing and most of the space for drawing, what kind of paper do you think will be in these booklets right next to it?"

"That kind!" they say, pointing to the paper I'm holding.

"This kind of paper. All you have to do is look at the paper in the trays on *this* side"—I point to the stack trays on the right—"and that will help you know what kind of paper is inside the booklets in the trays on *this* side."

By now, most of the children who went back to work at their tables have stopped working and are watching—and that is a good thing. They'll know the procedure when they make the decision to write in a booklet.

"So Liliana, what color cover do you want on your booklet?"

"Red," she says.

"Now, boys and girls, Liliana wants a red cover for her booklet, but when we look at this pile of booklets with unlined pages, green is on top. Do you see one with a red cover, Liliana?"

She nods and points to one, way down in the pile.

"Now, I know that if I was about to start a story in a booklet today and I really wanted a red cover, I would want to take the one way down there with the red cover, so here's what you need to remember. You may take the color cover you want, but you have a responsibility to make sure that you leave the pile nice and neat for the next person." I look at Liliana. "Do you think you can do that?"

She reaches right in to get the red-covered booklet, and as she does, I say what I see, just as I did when I introduced the Drawing & Writing Books:

"Look at how carefully she's sliding that booklet out and holding the other books with her other hand so they don't fall on the floor," and "Do you see how she put her booklet down on the shelf and she's straightening the pile for the next person?"

"So, boys and girls, when I call your name, you may come over and get a booklet. I know you'll do just what Liliana did, take the booklet out carefully and make sure the pile is nice and neat for the next person.

"Don't forget, as soon as you get to your place to work, put your name on the cover of your book, because all authors' names are on the covers of the books they write."

Why we chose this book   *My Dog Rosie* illustrates the idea of one part on each page simply and clearly. Also, the children know the book well, so we didn't have to read it during the lesson.

Suggested other books
- *Ginger*, by Charlotte Voake
- *Matthew and Tilly*, by Rebecca C. Jones, illustrated by Beth Peck
- *My Cats Nick and Nora*, by Isabelle Harper, illustrated by Barry Moser

When we decided to introduce this lesson, all the children were working (happily) in their Drawing & Writing Books. Because one of our goals is to help children move from telling one part to writing full stories with many parts, and because we noticed that some children were doing this naturally, we decided to introduce the option of telling their stories in booklets. This lesson worked fine.

What we prefer, however, is to introduce booklets to individual children when we see they're ready. By *ready* we mean a combination of these things: they're beginning to tell multipart stories in their Drawing & Writing Books, they have a lot to say about a particular topic during a conference, and they write and draw independently and with confidence. Introducing booklets gradually makes sense because it allows us to meet children where they are and helps them see the purpose for this format.

Typically, when we introduce booklets to the whole class, many children want one. They want to try the new booklet whether or not they have a story that needs to be told on many pages, and why wouldn't they—the booklets are beautiful! But when individual children ease their way into booklets because their writing would be best told in that medium soon, the whole class learns that the booklets are yet another choice they'll make as writers. We offer the option of a booklet to another child, and to another, and another, and by the time we talk about them to the whole class, they're already familiar with what the booklet is and why they might want to use one. We have also found that when we introduce booklets this way, children tend to move back and forth freely between the two options—the Drawing & Writing Book and the booklet—choosing the medium that best suits the work they plan to do that day. For the most part, we don't see a frenzied whipping their way through booklets and competing to see who has the most.

Introducing a Booklet to an Individual Student During a Conference

We said earlier that we prefer to introduce booklets gradually, when a child's energy for the topic is so overflowing during a conference that it causes us to say something like, "Boy, you sure have a lot to say about ——. It seems you could write a whole book about that." At those moments I get up and go to the writing center to get some paper, a color cover, and the stapler and bring them back to the child's table:

"I'm just imagining this story as a book, where, instead of telling one part as you're doing here in your Drawing & Writing Book, you could tell all the parts," I say, laying the colored paper cover on top of the pages, unstapled. "It would sound something like this."

I clasp my hand around the edge of the pages where the staples would go, and as I turn each page, I retell the child's story, one page for each part, the way the child has told it to me. Kids nearby look up and pay attention.

"You know, all the boys and girls are going to have a chance to write stories in books like these," I say, "but I'm thinking that if you wanted to try writing your story in a booklet now, you could. Actually you could use this plain paper just like the Drawing & Writing Book, or you could tell it on paper like this, that has a space for drawing and some lines for the words. And we could staple it here so it would open like this. What do you think?"

Sometimes children are so eager, they can't wait to get their hands on the booklet and get started; other times they're unsure about this new idea. In that case I place the pages off to the side and say, "I'm going to leave these pages here in case you decide you want to write a booklet."

Other times, a child who is totally happy in her Drawing & Writing Book might dig her heels in when you try to move her on to a new place. Cynthia did that. She was a confident writer, drawing pictures that had full stories around them and writing letters and words with ease. So after she told me her story, I said, "Now, I understand this part about the birthday party when you're singing 'Happy Birthday' to your cousin, and I also understand that you have many other parts to that story. It seems like you could write a book about your cousin's party!" She looked at me, determined. I knew that her teacher had suggested that she write a story in a booklet a couple of times, but Cynthia wasn't interested. I got up and went to the writing center and got a booklet—one without lines to keep the pages similar to the type of page she is used to working on (even though I thought she could and, I believe, *should* have been writing on lines!) because I didn't want to overwhelm her by introducing too many different things at once.

Sitting down next to her I placed the booklet between us and started right in. "I can imagine there would be a title here—something about the birthday party or your cousin or this special day," I said, and I quickly turned the cover to the first page. "Then let's see, what did you tell me first? Oh yes, it was about how you drove to your cousin's house." I turned the page. "Then you all went outside to play—all the cousins were there." I turned the page. "Then you came in and opened the presents"—I turned the page—she was watching me with trepidation—"and then you sang 'Happy Birthday' and she blew out the candles and you had cake." I gave back her words so she could see how her whole story might look, but I had no intention of pushing this. I just wanted to make it sound so good that she'd find it irresistible. "What a story!" I said. "That may be one you decide to write someday." Then I took the book and said, "I'm going to put this booklet back on the shelf in the writing center. That way, you'll know just where they are if you need one."

It was important not to push Cynthia into putting her Drawing & Writing Book aside and writing a booklet. She wasn't willing to give it up right then, and I sensed that. There may come a time where a child is so reluctant or adamant that we have to say, "Today I want you to try this," but that wasn't the case here. I know that, as long as I keep modeling how a story might look in this extended format, and as long as their classmates are writing in booklets, they'll eventually make that choice themselves. Cynthia did the following day!

On the other hand, Christopher was one who was eager to get started. It was December when he began his first story in a booklet, and he returned to it with gusto when school resumed after the break. In early January, I used Christopher's booklet-in-process to talk to the others about writing booklets.

Lesson Introducing Booklets to the Whole Class After They've Gradually Been Introduced

What's going on in the classroom
- Children are writing in Drawing & Writing Books.
- Some children have begun to tell stories in booklets.

What's next
- All the children need to know that they can tell their stories in the Drawing & Writing Books or in booklets.

Materials needed
- one child's Drawing & Writing Book opened to a page where the child has drawn a detailed picture and written some words to tell about the picture
- one child's booklet where he has told many parts, one part on each page
- visible access to the Writing Center where materials are kept

This is what I noticed . . .
"Boys and girls, I noticed, when I was looking at Taleaha's Drawing & Writing Book, that she has this story about when she first met Ms. McArdle."

I hold up her book, open to the page. (See Figure 7.3.)

"Here I see Ms. McArdle and Taleaha sitting at the kidney-shaped table, that table right there in this classroom. It looks so real in this picture. And here I see the pillow in the listening center. And over here I see Ms. McArdle's chair on wheels. All that information in the picture helps readers know just what it looked like in this classroom when you were sitting down with your teacher, Taleaha. It does look like this classroom, doesn't it?

"And here she wrote some words," I say, pointing to the text. "Taleaha, would you read those to us?"

Taleaha comes up and touches the words she wrote as she reads her story: "'Me and Ms. McArdle was reading together.'" (*Me Nad Ms. McArdle WaZ Red togather.*)

"So you and Ms. McArdle were reading together! And here you are, Taleaha," I say, pointing to the figure I'm guessing is Taleaha, "and here's Ms. McArdle. I can tell you apart by your hair!

FIGURE 7.3 Taleaha: *Me and Ms. McArdle was reading together.*

"Boys and girls, Taleaha told about that one part about coming to kindergarten and about meeting Ms. McArdle, and I'll bet it was because that was special to her. Was it, Taleaha?"

She nods.

"That's what you've been doing all year in your Drawing & Writing Books. You think of your story and you choose one part to write about on the page in your book. Now, sometimes boys and girls have longer stories to write, so they write in booklets."

Let me show you what I mean . . . "You know that Christopher has been working in a booklet," I say as I hold his booklet up. "He's writing this book about playing with his brother, and look . . . On the cover he has written his name. When we look at books, we usually see the author's name on the cover, don't we?" I point to books right there in the library as a way to align the writers in this class with published writers. "Christopher put his name on the cover of the book he's writing. He also stamped the date on the cover. That way he will always know when he wrote this book.

"Inside, Christopher tells many things he and his brother did: On this page he tells about . . . On this page he tells about . . . On this page he tells about . . . I imagine Christopher decided to write in a booklet because he had so many parts of the story—he didn't want to tell just one, he wanted to tell many. I also notice that each page is about one important part. He does just what authors do when they write a book: he tells many parts, but he puts only one part on each page. Then, when we read the story, we understand the whole thing because it has all the parts. Well, not all the parts, because Christopher decides which parts he wants to put in and he gets to decide which parts to leave out, too.

"Also, Christopher knows that when an author writes a book, he doesn't do it in one day. Not even in two days. Look at this: Christopher started this story on January 4. Today is January 7, so that means he's been working on it for . . . let's see," I say, holding up one finger for each day, "January fourth, fifth, sixth, and now, today is the seventh—three days. Today will be the fourth! And he's probably not going to finish today because there are still a few pages left. He is taking his time, working hard on the illustrations, and thinking carefully about what to write on each page, because he wants to make it the best it can be so that readers can understand and enjoy his story."

So, today as you write . . .

"So, boys and girls, you might be thinking that you have a story with many parts and you don't want to tell about just one part, you want to tell it all. Now you can. From now on, you have two ways you can tell your story during writing time: you can tell it in a booklet, with many parts, or you can tell it in your Drawing & Writing Book, choosing one part.

"I wonder what Taleaha will decide to do today. Maybe she'll work on this page again today, putting in other things. Maybe she is finished with this page and she'll turn to the next page and tell a part of a new story. Maybe she'll say, 'I have a story with many parts and I want to tell it in a booklet.' And maybe sometime, Taleaha will decide she wants to tell the whole story about coming to kindergarten. Instead of telling this one part about sitting with Ms. McArdle like she did here, she may want to write a whole book about it where she tells all the parts. My goodness, there are so many choices.

"Taleaha, what do you plan to do today?" I ask, holding up the page in her Drawing & Writing Book. "Continue on this page, go on to the next page, or start a booklet?"

Taleaha says she wants to start a booklet. I am prepared with single sheets of the two choices of paper I plan to offer—one with two lines and one with no lines—and three different colors of paper for covers. I ask her to come up.

What will your story will be about?" I ask.

"Ballet," she says without hesitation.

"Tell us about ballet," I say eagerly, and she recounts going to ballet lessons and doing exercises with the teacher and with her friends. I tell it back, raising five fingers, one at a time for each part. She agrees that I understand the story, and I ask her which kind of paper she'd like, lined or unlined, and count out five pages. Then I ask her what color she'd like for a cover and employ her help as I model for the boys and girls how to staple the pages together (as described in the previous lesson). ✉ I then "read" the blank pages of her story, turning one page as I retell each part. She's itching to get her hands on it, and I remind her as she heads off, "Don't forget to put your name on the cover!"

I look at the children on the rug. "Christopher, I'll bet I know what you plan to do today!" I say next, and he comes up, takes his booklet from my hand, and goes off to a table.

"Today, boys and girls, as you start writing, here's what I want you to ask yourself:

✉ **Note to the Teacher**

Although we showed Taleaha how to staple her booklet, we didn't put the stapler out so the children could staple their own books that day. Some children, of course, know how to use the stapler already, so we will most likely enlist their help as we model for all of them: how to use the stapler so it won't jam, how to put only three staples in and where to put them, and where in the room they may do the stapling (these will be mini-lessons of their own). These "little things" are actually "big" things in the working of a classroom. *Nothing is too small to mention* has become our motto, and modeling and talking through how to use the stapler before we put it out for them to use independently is one of those small but big lessons that we don't want to rush.

- "Do I have a story that is so important that I want to tell all the parts? If you do, you will probably decide to write a book, like Taleaha and Christopher.
- "Do I have a story where I want to work on one part? If so, then you will probably work in your Drawing & Writing Book.
- "Do I want to go back to a page in my Drawing & Writing Book that I was working on yesterday because I have more to do and I want to make it better?
- "Do I want plan to continue in the booklet that I started?"

I then show them the procedure for getting booklets as described in the previous lesson, and dismiss them.

Again, as when we introduced the Drawing & Writing Books, this lesson seems long—and it is. The children barely have a chance to get started in their booklets because of all the procedural things we want to set in place, but that, we believe, is a good thing. It gives them a chance to just begin a story that they will continue, thus setting the stage for conversation about how to continue in a booklet.

 Lesson Rereading Your Work: Helping Readers Understand Your Story

What's going on in the classroom
- The option of using a booklet has been introduced to the whole class.
- Some children continue to use the Drawing & Writing Book.
- Most children who chose booklets wrote one or two pages. One child filled all the pages. Some began working on the cover.

What's next
- Children need to know how to continue in the booklet, since the format is different from the Drawing & Writing Book. They need to be shown how to reread what they've done and consider what else they could do to help the reader understand, and then what to do as they go to the next page.

Materials needed
- student Drawing & Writing Book with a page carefully done, where the child may still have more to add
- student booklet, preferably one where the child has worked on only one page and has more to do on that page

This is what I noticed . . .
"Boys and girls, yesterday we talked about different ways you might choose to tell your story during writing time: in your Drawing & Writing Book, or in a booklet. Today, I want to talk about how you continue to work in a booklet if you started one yesterday."

Let me show you what I mean . . .
"You already know how to continue in the Drawing & Writing Book. When you leave the rug and get your Drawing & Writing Book, you open to the page you were working on yesterday, look at that page, and ask yourself some questions:

- "What other information do I need to include so readers will understand my story?
- "What do I need to add to the picture?"
- "What words do I want to write?

"Then you put that information in the picture or you add words, so your story is the best it can be. When you've made it your best, you start a new page in your Drawing & Writing Book.

"Yesterday, Jazmine worked in her Drawing & Writing Book." I show Jazmine's page and ask her to come up. She points to the parts of the drawing and tells about going with her mom to Target.

"Now, Jazmine," I say, "one thing a writer asks herself is, What else do I need on this page so readers will understand my story? So can you look at your page and read it and ask yourself, What else can I put on this page so that readers will understand my story?"

Jazmine looks at the page. "Put more in the picture?" she asks, as if searching for the answer she thinks I want.

"Yes, a writer might add some more to the picture. What else will you add to the picture?" I press, and she says she will draw the lunch boxes and the boxes of pencils and the backpack with sparkles, the one she actually bought.

"And then a writer asks herself, What words might I add to the page? I say. What words will you write on this page?"

"Me and my mom went to Target," she says moving her finger across the top of the page.

"So here, you will add some more things to the shelves so we know what you were looking at," I say, giving back what she has just told us, "and up here, you'll put the words?"

She nods.

"You know how to do that, don't you, boys and girls?" I say, turning to the children on the rug. "You know how to go back and look at what you worked on yesterday and ask yourself those questions that writers ask. And you know what? If you are working in a booklet, you do the same thing. If you started a booklet yesterday, this is what you do when you sit down to write.

"Open your booklet to the first page of the story and ask yourself, What other information do I need to include so readers will understand my story?

"Look at your picture and ask, What do I need to add to the picture?

"If you wrote words, look at the words and ask, What other words do I want to write?

"Then add that information to your picture or write words so your story makes sense and it's your best. Or maybe you want to change something in your picture or change the words you wrote. Then you turn the page. If there is anything on that page, you do the same thing: What do I need to add to the picture or what do I need to change? What words do I want to write or change?

"If there's nothing on that next page, ask yourself, And then what happened? and tell what happened in the next part of your story.

"For example, Taleaha started her booklet yesterday. Remember the story she told us she was going to write—about ballet? Taleaha, why don't you come up here." Taleaha comes and stands next to me.

"When Taleaha goes to her place to work today, she'll first look at the cover of her booklet to make sure her name is on it." I point to her name on the cover. "Then, she'll open it and look at what she did yesterday. She'll look at the picture"—I point—"and she'll read the words she wrote, 'Me and Tai was exercising,' [*menadTAiwazaciZ*] and she'll ask herself, What do I need to do so readers will understand my story?

"She'll look at that picture carefully and ask herself, Do I have all the information I need in this picture? What do you need to do to this picture, Taleaha, so readers will understand your story?"

"The floor," she says, pointing to the space underneath the ballerina.

"Then she'll read the words and ask, What else do I need to add to the words, or what words do I need to change so readers will understand? What do you need to do to the words, Taleaha?"

Taleaha looks carefully at the words. I sense she may be confused, maybe thinking about what she should add because she thinks I want her to add something. I don't, necessarily. My goal is to teach her to ask that question of herself as she rereads her words from the previous day. I try to put her at ease.

"Why don't you read what you wrote," I say.

"'Me and Tai was exercising,'" she says, pointing to the words.

"Do you want to change any of that?"

She shakes her head.

"So once Taleaha has added the floor and anything else she decides to put in this picture," I say to the children sitting on the rug, "she'll turn the page and do the same thing."

I turn the page. "There's nothing on the next page, so she'll ask herself, And then what happened? and she'll draw and write the next part."

So, today as you write . . .

"So, today, boys and girls, whether you are working in your Drawing & Writing Book or a booklet, you do the same thing. When you sit down to write, open your book, read the page or pages you worked on yesterday, and think about those questions that writers ask: What other information do I need to include so readers will understand my story? What do I need to add to the pictures so readers will understand? What words do I need to add so readers will understand? And when you've made them your best, you move on to the next page."

Introducing Booklets Using Our Own Writing

Another way we've introduced booklets is to use our own writing as a model. We start by telling a story, "one we like so much that we want to tell many parts," then begin to draw in an enlarged booklet as we think out loud, right there at the easel. Just as we modeled putting our story down on the first page of the Drawing & Writing Book, our students hear our idea for a booklet, listen as we tell the story, watch as we plan out the parts we'll put on each page, and see us get started with the drawing on the first page. Even though we didn't include this entire lesson here, we mention it for two reasons: one, because we think it is an important lesson to present during the early days of booklet introductions (if not the first day), as it provides yet another opportunity for our students to see us as writers, and two, when we refer to our booklet later in this chapter, it is based on having presented this lesson.

When presenting our own story, we use an enlarged booklet so they all can see, keep the topic ordinary and everyday, and keep the information on each page simple. "Alexandra and Jessica came to my house for an overnight / We played on the hammock / We played hide-and-go seek / We made cookies / We read stories in bed . . ." is a topic that they can all relate to and one for which the illustrations and words can be simple on each page.

Over time, we've introduced booklets in each of the ways presented here (and then some) with different groups of children, and each one worked. In other words, there is no one right way. We expect that the decisions teachers make about how and when to introduce booklets are based on what they know and see and understand about their students at that point.

Then, once the booklets are presented, we need to think about where they will be kept and how children will get them. At first, as children began working in booklets, they'd slip the booklet inside their Drawing & Writing Book at the end of writing time. This was a choice Caitlin McArdle and Megan Sinclair made because they didn't want to create a division among the writers—those with folders, those without folders—during this transition into booklets. But we knew that as they finished a second and then a third booklet, slipping them inside the Drawing & Writing Book wasn't going to work. They would need an official place to keep them, and the folders were prepared and ready to go. In four colors—red, blue, green, and yellow—the folders matched the color of the name strip on each child's Drawing & Writing Book as well as the plastic file that housed them. It was a matter of adding the folders to a system that was already in place.

As we've noted throughout this book, we give students messages all the time about how we value them and their work. The systems we set up for where children will keep their work is a consistent message. They know that we care about their writing when we provide beautiful folders where the writing will stay neat and organized and containers in which to place those folders so that they are easily accessible to both student and teacher.

Lesson Writing Folder: A Place to Keep Your Writing

What's going on in the classroom

- Some children have begun writing stories in booklets, and until now, they've slipped their booklet inside their Drawing & Writing Book at the end of writing time.

What's next

- They need a specific place to hold the stories they write in booklets.

Materials needed

- two-pocket folders with gusset (fasteners in the center), in four colors, the colors divided evenly among the students
- folder inserts (samples of these are in Figures 7.4a–7.4d and Appendix G)

This is what I noticed . . .

"Writers have places where they keep their work so they'll always know where it is. You writers in this classroom have a place where we keep your Drawing & Writing Books, right here on these shelves, in these colorful files. And you know that if your Drawing & Writing Book has a red label with your name, you keep it in the red file, and if your Drawing & Writing Book has a blue label, you keep it in the blue file, and the same for green and yellow. We do that so when it is time to write, you know where to get your book quickly and can get to work.

My Finished Writing	
1	2
3	4
5	6

FIGURE 7.4A Using pictures and/or words, children record the titles of their finished pieces of writing in the boxes.

My Ideas for Writing	
1	2
3	4
5	6

FIGURE 7.4B Using pictures and/or words, children record their ideas for writing.

"Also, some of you have been telling your stories in booklets, and you've been keeping your booklets inside your Drawing & Writing Book. That has been a good idea so far, but as you write more and more, your booklets will be spilling out of that Drawing & Writing Book—it will be a mess! So you'll need a special place to put your booklets where they'll be nice and neat and in order so you'll be able to find them easily. Today I'm going to give you a writing folder and show you some things about this special place for your stories."

Let me show you what I mean . . .

I show the folder. "Your folder will be the same color as your Drawing & Writing Book. So if your name is in yellow on your Drawing & Writing Book, you'll have a yellow folder, and if your name is in green, your folder will be green. The same for blue and red."

I open the folder and explain:

- "The folder has two pockets and some pages in the center, which we'll talk about at another time.
- "In this front pocket you'll keep the story you're working on.
- "When you finish, you'll put your story in the back pocket.
- "Then, what do you think you'll do?"

The children respond, "Get another book!"

FIGURE 7.4c When a piece of writing is finished, children read each item on the list and check to make sure they have done each item.

FIGURE 7.4d Children use this alphabet linking chart as a resource when writing words independently. They learn how to use it during interactive writing lessons.

So, today as you write . . .

"Yes, you get another book and begin your next story. And that new book you're working on will go right here, in the front pocket.

"Let me tell you one thing about these pages in the center. These are to help you keep track of your stories and all of the things you know how to do as a writer. As you keep writing and doing new things, I will show you why these pages are in the folder. For now, don't worry about them, and don't write on them yet. ⊠

"So now, when it's writing time, you will come to the writing center just as you usually do and get your Drawing & Writing Book. Your new folder will be here, too, but if you're working in your Drawing & Writing Book, you won't need the folder yet. Just take the Drawing & Writing Book to your workplace, as you usually do, and get started.

"Boys and girls who are working in a booklet will do something different. When you go to the writing center, you are going to take your Drawing & Writing Book *and* your new folder. This is where you'll be keeping your booklets from now on. When you get to your workplace, open your Drawing & Writing Book and take the booklets out. If you have finished a story, put it in the back pocket of the writing folder. Then close the folder and put it on your table, next to where you're working. Then put your Drawing & Writing Book back in the proper file. When you get back to your seat, just continue work in your booklet and do your best. When you hear the music that lets you know writing time is over, you'll put the booklet you're working on in the *front* pocket, put your folder in the container that matches the color of your folder, then come to the rug."

I ask a child who has begun writing in booklets to come up and model how to take her stories out, return the Drawing & Writing Book to the file, put her finished story (or stories) in the back pocket, and leave out the one she is working on.

"Now you will always know where your writing is, which pieces you have finished, and which one you are working on. And, in this beautiful, new folder, they will stay nice and neat."

"So if you are working in a booklet and you keep your writing in a red file, get your Drawing & Writing Book and take your new folder—it's right in the file—and when you get to your workplace, organize your booklets the way we just talked about and then continue with your work. If you keep your work in a blue file . . . green . . . yellow . . . you may go. If you're working in your Drawing & Writing Book, you know what to do."

Teaching the procedure for keeping booklets in folders and how to get and return the folders is crucial, and is made much easier because students already have a system in place for getting and returning their Drawing & Writing Books.

We've learned as we've watched students use this new medium that they don't always understand how the booklet is different from the Drawing & Writing Book. We did the following lesson because we thought children needed to see that booklets are for telling a lot of information about one thing.

Lesson A Story Is About One Thing

What's going on in the classroom

- About half of the children are working in Drawing & Writing Books.
- The others are working in booklets.
- Some who have chosen a booklet write about something different on each page (which is what they were doing in the Drawing & Writing Book).

What's next

- They need to know that a story is about one thing. They need a vision for what that means.

Materials needed

- teacher's enlarged Drawing & Writing Book
- teacher's enlarged booklet with several pages finished and the last page needing some work
- colored pencils for drawing

This is what I noticed . . .

"You've been making choices about how you want to tell your story, in the Drawing & Writing Book or in a booklet. When you write in your Drawing & Writing Book, you tell about one part, like Luis did yesterday. He's telling the part about jumping on the bed with his brother. Everything on that page is about that one thing: here's the bed, he's jumping on it with his brother next to him, and since it's in his bedroom, here's his nightstand and a picture on the wall.

"If you write in a booklet, the way Samantha did yesterday, you tell a part of the story on each page but the whole story is about one thing. Each page in Samantha's story tells something about when she and her mom went to the store.

"Remember yesterday, how I started to write my book about taking care of my nieces? Well, yesterday when I went home I worked on it."

Let me show you what I mean . . .

I read my story to them, page by page, pointing out things in the drawing that I want them to notice and touching the words as I read them. When I get to the fourth page, I add something little to the drawing, then say the words slowly, modeling how I'm listening for the sounds as I write the last three words of the sentence I had begun.

"Now, I ask myself as I turn the page, And then what happened?"

I explain what I plan to do next, using my hand to show them where different parts of the drawing will go, and begin drawing. I don't do the whole drawing—I don't even do most of it—and I don't write the words, although I tell them what I think the words will be. I leave my thoughts tentative, modeling that there is always room for rethinking when I'm in the process of getting my story down. I'm also letting them know that this isn't something I do quickly.

"You know, boys and girls, it takes a long time to write a story like this and to make sure that it's about just one thing. I sure didn't do it quickly. I worked on it after school and again after supper, then right before I went to bed, and again this morning when I was eating breakfast. Each time I went back to it, I had to make sure I kept telling all about taking care of my nieces. And it's not even finished. Now, you won't be working on your story after school and at home because you don't take your stories home; you work on them here at school. So each day you'll have to go back and look carefully to be sure your whole story is about one thing."

So, today in your writing . . .

"Today, you'll be making a choice about what you're going to do. If you're working in a booklet, like Samantha, you will go back and read what you wrote, like I did with my story, and ask yourself, Now, what else do I need to put in here so readers will understand this one story I'm trying to tell? And as you're working in a booklet, you want to make sure that all the pages tell parts of the same story."

Booklets were introduced to the class in the belief that children had stories with many parts and that they had strategies for drawing pictures with details and writing words using sound spellings so readers could understand their stories. But not all children choose booklets for our reasons. With all those pages and the beautiful color covers, booklets can be enticing, and children can get caught up in that, as Hector helped us to see.

Moving Freely Between the Booklets and the Drawing & Writing Books

In the early days of our work with kindergarten teachers in Boston, Hector (and others) taught us that it is through the Drawing & Writing Book that children gain confidence and acquire the tools they need to write stories in books. In January 2000 when we began, we had no such thing as a Drawing & Writing Book. We moved from oral storytelling right into five-page booklets and quickly found that the booklet wasn't working for some children.

Hector was one of them. He chose a booklet on the day we introduced them, and two weeks later he was putting finishing touches on his story that looked like Figure 7.5.

It's not uncommon to see this type of thing once children have begun work in booklets, and Hector had a folder full of them. There was the book called "Fish," and on every page was the same sketch of the same tiny fish with the word *fish* underneath, everything done in the same color crayon. There was the book called "Car" and the book called "Truck." On this particular day it was book number ten: "Bear."

"Done!" he exclaimed as he scratched his last *baer* onto the page and closed the booklet. He stuffed it in the back pocket of his folder and announced to everyone at his table, "I'm on eleven!"

What Hector was doing was delightfully five-year-old: modeling each story after the previous one, whipping through one story after the next, and acquiring as many books as he could. But he was also instructing us in what we needed to pay attention to. Did he lack a

FIGURE 7.5 Hector: *Bear, bear, bear, bear, bear.*

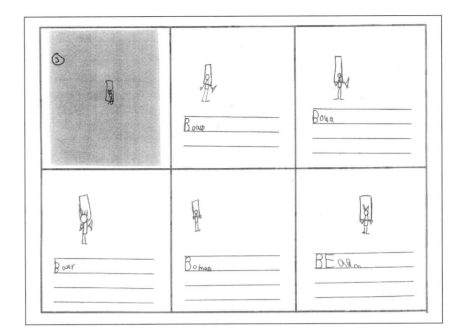

sense of story? Did he not have an understanding of how to tell his story so that it continued on each page? Was the idea of drawing *and* writing just too overwhelming? In thinking about how to give him the support he needed, we named what he could do as a writer. Hector

- could draw about what he knows (he had done it previously);
- knew a handful of letters and the sounds they represented; and
- was attempting some sound spelling on his own.

What he needed, we thought, was to know how to draw stories with detailed information and include letters and words independently.

So we conferred with him, trying to find out what he knew—about fish, about bears—and we watched to see what influence our conferences had on his writing. We conferred with children working near him, knowing that sometimes the information that children overhear from another conference makes a difference in their work. And we watched to see if his writing was at all changed after he had listened to stories that other children shared. These attempts didn't seem to have much influence. Yes, he was being playful with the booklets, and we let him be that way for a while, yet at the same time, we wanted to be sure he knew how to find and represent his own stories in ways that revealed him, his interests, his expertise. We wanted him, and others who listened to his stories, to hear his voice and take his writing seriously.

So the day after Hector put his name on the cover of booklet number eleven, we presented a mini-lesson about how "writers need to use the kind of paper that will help them tell the best stories they can; for some it is a booklet, for others it might be something like this . . . ," and we showed them the spiral-bound book that we would come to call the Drawing & Writing Book. Hector (and four or five other children) seized the opportunity to work in one of those beautiful new spiral-bound books with pages of unlined paper where you

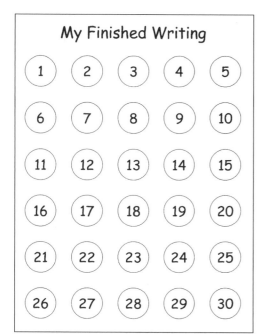

My Finished Writing

① ② ③ ④ ⑤

⑥ ⑦ ⑧ ⑨ ⑩

⑪ ⑫ ⑬ ⑭ ⑮

⑯ ⑰ ⑱ ⑲ ⑳

㉑ ㉒ ㉓ ㉔ ㉕

㉖ ㉗ ㉘ ㉙ ㉚

FIGURE 7.10 My Finished Writing: This page is attached to the inside cover of the Drawing & Writing Book. When the student finishes a page of the Drawing & Writing book, he or she colors in the numbered circle for that page. This requires that the pages in the Drawing & Writing Book are numbered.

Kindergarten Class List

Albana

David   Marciana
Devianna   Marisol
                      Michael
Ezedequias   Mohammed

Gus   Niyara

Imani   Osvaldo

Jahaan   Samantha
Jazmine   Shammala
Jelyia   Taleaha
John   Tyriq

Lynasia   Yanniel

FIGURE 7.11 List of student names. The children use this list of classmates' names as a resource when writing words independently. They learn how to use it during interactive writing lessons.

draw part of a story on one page. Hector worked independently for the entire writing time that day and shared his page with the class during the share session. (See Figure 7.6 in the color insert.)

Through this illustration and the story he told around it, Hector showed us that he did, in fact, have an understanding of story and the ability to tell it with specific information. What he put on one page was very different from what he put on each page of his booklets. Most likely, it was because he had the chance to focus on one aspect—drawing—and the whole thing was contained on one page. Chances are, he didn't feel pressure to get to the next page and the next and the next. We noted that he didn't include any text as he worked independently, which seemed to indicate that he didn't have the same ease with text that he had with drawing. Over time as we continued to support him as a writer by acknowledging his oral stories and drawings along with helping him acquire strategies for hearing and recording sounds, he gained fluency in representing his story with letters, words, and sentences. This added instruction—aimed at meeting his particular needs—paid off. (See Figures 7.7, 7.8, and 7.9 in the color insert.)

Although once we introduce booklets, we allow the children to choose the medium they want to work in, we find there are times when we need to usher some children away from them, to a medium in which they can do better-quality work.

For example, as we looked at Crystal's work, we saw random letters, and each time she told us the story, it had changed a bit. She didn't know letters and sounds in a way that she could represent them with ease, yet she wanted to write letters because she saw her peers writing letters on their pages. We knew she would be better off working in the Drawing & Writing Book, and we found the right moment to tell her so. "I want you to work in your Drawing & Writing Book for now because I think that on a page like this, you can do your best work" can be a relief to a child who is not clear about how letters and words and booklets work. In the language of Alfie Kohn (1998), we give a "working with" message, *I'm with you here and I want to make it possible for you to be successful,* rather than a "doing to" message, *I'm sending you back to the Drawing & Writing Book because you aren't able to work in a booklet.* They're not going *back;* they're using the medium that will allow them to do their best work as we help them build the foundation for fluid, crafted writing.

Teachers show their students that they continue to value the Drawing & Writing Book even as more and more children spend more and more time working in booklets by occasionally giving children a brand-new one, or changing some physical feature so it feels different. They may include a recording sheet on which to keep track of pages completed (see Figure 7.10); attach an alphabet linking chart (as in Figure 7.4d); or a list of classmates' names inside the back cover as references (see Figure 7.11); or provide a new clip to mark the page. These features make the second Drawing & Writing Book inviting, "grown-up," and compelling enough for them to want to continue to do good work on the pages inside.

With the time and space to strengthen what they know about letters, sounds, and words, and with the support to help them integrate that knowledge with their detailed drawings, we make it possible for children to be writers of stories that are personally meaningful and filled with voice as Hector's was, when, at the end of that kindergarten year, he found his way back into a booklets and eventually published (see Figure 7.12).

FIGURE 7.12 The published piece: "The Park," by Hector.

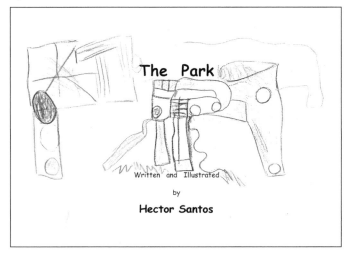

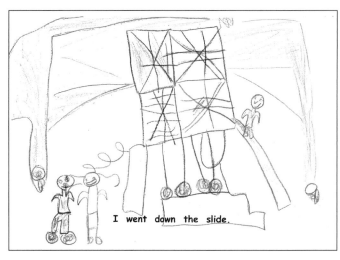

CHAPTER 8

Moving Writers Forward

ONCE CHILDREN HAVE BEGUN working in booklets, they need information that will push them forward as writers: they need to know more about craft, and they need more information about the mechanical aspects of writing.

In this chapter we offer a collection of lessons that aim to address those things. We've divided the chapter into ten small sections around topics we consider important for young writers. In each section we provide background on that topic, offer a sample lesson or two, and end with suggestions of other possible lessons. These are not the only topics we address over the course of a school year, but we find ourselves returning to them over and over again:

- Making Sure the Story Makes Sense
- Writing About What's Important
- Time and Place
- Being Specific
- Revision
- Topics
- Proofreading
- Conventions: Attending to the Mechanics of Writing
- Beginnings, Endings, and Titles
- Making the Characters Come Alive

Once again, it is not our intention to provide teachers with all the possible mini-lessons we can think of, but rather to offer a look at *why* and *how* we addressed certain topics with the children we were working with at a particular point. We hope you will find this way of looking helpful as you observe your own students and their work in order to decide what you will teach.

Making Sure the Story Makes Sense

As children write books and tell stories that continue from page to page, they need information about how to ensure that their multi-page stories make sense. Some of this information we address during mini-lessons and some we address at other times of the day, such as during a read-aloud, as the following interaction illustrates. The teacher is reading *Roller Coaster* by Marla Frazee, and the children are interacting the way kindergartners do:

"Hey, that's the same as the one on the other page!" a child calls out, raising himself up from his spot on the rug to point out a character he recognizes. The teacher responds by flipping back to a previous page. The child points to a man's shirt and says, "Look, red," then, flipping forward to the page the teacher had just read, he points to the same character's shirt and says, "and red!"

"So, you knew *this* person on *this* page was the same as *this* one on *this* page, didn't you!" the teacher says, delighting with him in his discovery.

"Yeah, because *he* has a red shirt and *he* has a red shirt," he says, pointing out the character on both pages. "And the things," he adds, sweeping his thumb and forefinger across his eyes, alluding to the sunglasses as he sits back down on the rug.

"You knew that this person standing in line for the roller coaster is the same as this one who's calling to his friend, because on both pages he's wearing the same shirt"—"And the same pants!" someone calls out—"and the same pants, and the same sunglasses. We can even tell because his hair is the same, his skin color is the same, and he's the same size on both pages, too, isn't he? You know, I'm sure Marla Frazee did that on purpose. I'm sure she wanted us to know that . . ."

Conversations like this happen naturally. When they do, we give language to what children are noticing. This interaction has to do with *consistency*. We're helping children see that being consistent in drawings helps readers understand the story. At this moment, they're noticing consistency in information from the perspective of the reader; we want them to see that it has a place in their repertoire as writers, too. While working in their Drawing & Writing Books, they didn't need to think about being consistent on each page, because, for the most part, each page was about something different. But once they move into booklets where they tell stories that continue from page to page, being consistent with the information becomes important. One way we help them understand this concept is to point out how writers and illustrators of the books we read are consistent with their information.

In the following lesson (one of the many, many we do on this topic), we illustrate how writers and drawers keep certain things consistent and make decisions about what to include and what to leave out because they want their stories to make sense so readers will understand. In these lessons, we're teaching them about integrity in a piece of writing.

Lesson Consistency in Clothing

What's going on in the classroom
- Children draw their stories in detail, but they sometimes dress people differently on each page, even if the events of the story take place on the same day.

What's next
- They need to know that writers and illustrators want their stories to make sense, and that one way they do that is by being consistent with the information.

Materials needed
- *Matthew and Tilly*, by Rebecca C. Jones, illustrated by Beth Peck
- *Roller Coaster*, by Marla Frazee

This is what I noticed . . .
"Remember the other day when we read *Roller Coaster*, by Marla Frazee, and you were noticing the characters standing in line, and you could recognize the same characters from page to page? Well, that's because writers and illustrators work hard to tell their stories so that readers will understand. And Marla Frazee isn't the only one who pays attention to how she makes the people in her story. Lots of writers and illustrators do that. I was noticing how Beth Peck did that in her illustrations of *Matthew and Tilly*.

"In these first pages, we see Matthew and Tilly doing things together:

- "Here they're riding bikes.
- "Here they're playing hopscotch.
- "Here they're having an ice cream at the soda fountain.
- "Here they're helping the lady get her cat out of the tree.

"We recognize Matthew and Tilly on each page, because they always look the same: they're about the same size on the first page, and they stay about the same size all through the story. Matthew has light brown skin and Tilly has dark brown skin, and that skin color stays the same. And they each have a certain kind of hair. Sometimes Tilly has bows or bands in her hair, but usually it's all done in those beautiful braids, and Matthew's hair is brown and straight and usually looks pretty much the same.

"Another thing that helps us understand the story is their clothes. Beth Peck helps us know if Matthew and Tilly did these things on the same day or on different days just by the clothes they're wearing."

Let me show you what I mean . . "In these first pages, we can tell that they did these things on different days because they're wearing different clothes in each picture:

"Notice that when they're playing hopscotch, Matthew has on a short-sleeve, blue shirt with an orange stripe across the middle and brown knickers, and Tilly is wearing a peach-colored shirt with blue pants rolled up.

"Here, when they're at the soda fountain, Tilly is dressed in her white shorts and shirt, and Matthew is wearing an aqua shirt with brown shorts. Those outfits are very different from what they were wearing on the page before, aren't they?" I flip the page back so they can see.

"And then, on this page, when they're helping the lady get her cat out of the tree, Matthew is wearing a long-sleeve, blue shirt with gray pants, and Tilly is wearing a yellow shirt with a red turtleneck underneath and blue pants. It must have been chilly that day!

"You know, we can be pretty sure that Beth Peck had Matthew and Tilly wearing different clothes on those pages because she wanted us to know that they did those things on different days.

"But, in this part of the story"—I flip to the second half of the book—"when they get mad at each other, Beth Peck lets us know that the argument happened in one day:

"Here, where they are coloring and the crayon got broken, Matthew is wearing his white shirt and blue pants.

"Here, where they are arguing, Matthew is in his same white shirt and blue pants, and Tilly is wearing her orange top and blue pants.

"Here is Matthew, feeling sad on his stairs, still in his white shirt and blue pants.

"Tilly is playing hopscotch by herself, still in her same shirt and pants."

I show the next few pages as I say, "We know that in this part of the story, the argument happened on one day because both Matthew and Tilly are in the same clothes, page after page."

So, today, as you write . . . "Writers and illustrators want their stories to make sense to readers, and you need to do that in your stories, too. So if you are writing about a person, dress them so that your story makes sense. If the events of the story happened all in one day, the people will be wearing the same clothes from page to page. If the events of the story happened on different days, they will probably be wearing different clothes."

Why we chose this book This one story shows both situations: events happening on different days with clothes looking different, and events happening on the same day with clothes looking the same. Also, the children know the book well.

Suggested other books
- *My Best Friend Moved Away*, by Nancy Carlson
- *Subway*, by Anastasia Suen, illustrated by Karen Katz

- *The Paperboy*, by Dav Pilkey
- *Bigmama's*, by Donald Crews

Other possible lessons

- Consistency in setting: Children need to know about consistency in the setting, too. Referring to *Matthew and Tilly* we'd show them how, on those first pages, the incidents happen in different places, but that the argument that goes on for pages in the second half of the story happens in one place—at the apartment building. We know this because of the information Beth Peck gives us in the backgrounds. We'd also call attention to children's own work that illustrates this point. For example, Yulexy, a kindergartner, had dressed the people in her story in the same outfits on each page since her whole story was about her mother's wedding, yet she hadn't included background on any of the pages. As she told the story to me during a conference, she explained where each part of the story took place—"at the church" and "at the party"—so I asked her, "What will you draw here so that when people read the story, they'll know that here, you're at the church, and here, you're at the party?" That conference with Yulexy became a mini-lesson for the whole class on how the background helps readers understand the story, and when parts of the story occur at the same place, the backgrounds let readers know that.
- Consistency in characters from book to book: Sometimes children write about the same people or pets from booklet to booklet. We point out how, in the "Rosie" books, illustrator Barry Moser does that, too. We can always recognize Rosie and Woodrow and Isabelle and all the other people and animals from book to book because certain details about them are always the same, and those details are what helps us recognize them. In this lesson we'd pose the question, If you write about a person or animal or place in one book and then in another, what are the details that you'll include so readers will recognize them?
- Consistency in characters' physical features
- Rereading your work to check for consistency

Writing About What's Important

In their Drawing & Writing Books, children work on one page and usually tell about one part of a bigger story. They do this because that is how we presented the Drawing & Writing Book to them: *You've got this one big page and you want to make it your best. What part of the story do you want to tell about, and how can you do it so that readers will understand?* We believe that by focusing on one part they'll be better able to include information that is detailed and specific. When they move into booklets, our hope is that they'll do the same in-depth, high-quality work on each page of their multipart stories.

Very often we find that they tend to tell stories in list fashion—"first we did this, then we did this . . ."—giving equal weight to each part. Although this is perfectly reasonable and age-appropriate, we want to show them how to fill out parts of those all-encompassing stories and that within them are often small parts that could be stories of their own. As we so often do, we turn to the writing of other children to provide a vision for what we mean. In the example that follows, a kindergartner has written a story about a tiny part of something much bigger, and we use that piece to teach.

We also show children that illustrators help readers know what's important and what to pay attention to, just by what they draw and how they draw it. During read-alouds, for example, we point out how on some pages, Barry Moser shows a close-up of one part of a person, animal, or object, whereas the surrounding illustration reveals only parts of other people, animals, or objects, providing readers with the information they need to understand what's going on. During the writing lesson, then, we present this as a technique that this illustrator uses intentionally, one they may choose to use in their drawings.

In the following lessons, both the writer and the illustrator help readers know what is important by highlighting one small part. In these and other such lessons, we're really teaching children about focus.

 ## Lesson Writing a Whole Story About One Little Part

What's going on in the classroom	• Most children are writing stories in booklets. • Most of their stories include the whole day or event, even if the story is really about one part.
What's next	• They need to know that a story can be about one part of the day or event.
Materials needed	• story of one child who has written about one little part • *Roller Coaster*, by Marla Frazee; and *Shortcut*, by Donald Crews.
This is what I noticed . . .	"I have a book here called 'A Day at School' by Taleaha Browne. Taleaha is a girl who used to be in this kindergarten. When I first saw the title of this book, I expected it to be about all the things she does at school. But when I read it, I was surprised. I'm going to read it to you." I read "A Day at School." "In this book I learn how Taleaha feels about school, and I learn about things she does, but what surprises me is that the book isn't about what she does all day at school. Instead, her whole story is about what happens in that few minutes early in the morning when Taleaha comes into the classroom, before most of the boys and girls are even there. Can you believe it? She wrote a whole book about the part of school before the day even begins!"

Talking, Drawing, Writing

Let me show you what I mean . . .	I flip the pages of her book as I retell each part:

- "It starts when she comes into the classroom.
- "Then Brittney comes in.
- "Then they're eating breakfast—and the teachers are drinking coffee!
- "Then a few more kids come in,
- "and then it's time to come to the rug.

"Taleaha's story actually *ends* as the school day is *beginning*!

"I think Taleaha knows what Marla Frazee knows and what Donald Crews knows—that you can write a whole story that happens in just a short bit of time. Imagine, a whole story, with all these pages, just about what she did before the other kids came into the classroom!

"You know, sometimes writers want to tell a story that happens in a whole day, or more than one day, but sometimes they want to tell a whole story that takes place in one little bit of time. Like how Marla Frazee tells the story of that first ride on the roller coaster—that whole story is about something that probably lasted about ten minutes! And Donald Crews wrote about when the kids took the shortcut home. That whole story happened in just that little time of day when it's starting to get dark. These stories show us that you can tell a whole story about something that happens in just a little bit of time, because that thing was the most exciting or the most important or the saddest or the funniest."

So, today as you write . . .	"So as you think about stories you might write, you may discover that you have a long story with lots of different parts but you want to tell just one part of it. You can think about *Roller Coaster* and *Shortcut* and 'A Day at School' to help you remember how these writers tell whole stories that happen in just a short bit of time."
Why we chose these books	The children know them well and they are good examples of what we want them to understand: they focus on a little part.
Suggested other books	• *Dim Sum for Everyone!,* by Grace Lin (It doesn't tell everything they did during the whole day, but rather goes into depth about one aspect of a day.) • *The Paperboy*, by Dav Pilkey
Other possible lessons	• Seeing ideas for stories within a larger story in books we've read (Refer to possible stories depicted in the illustrated memories in *My Best Friend Moved Away*, by Nancy Carlson.) • Recognizing other stories in one story you've told aloud or written • Remembering the stories you tell during the day to your teacher or friends • Choosing a title that reflects what your story is about (Taleaha's title alludes to a much longer span of time.)

Lesson Highlighting the Important Part of the Illustrations

What's going on in the classroom

- Children are good at including detail in their drawings.
- During read-alouds, they've begun to notice that illustrators may draw only a part of a person or an object or a scene.

What's next

- They need to know that one way to emphasize what is important is to make the important part the focal point and show just enough of the other parts so readers have the information they need.

Materials needed

- *The Paperboy*, by Dav Pilkey
- *My Dog Rosie* and *My Cats Nick and Nora*, by Isabelle Harper, illustrated by Barry Moser

This is what I noticed . . .

"Last night I was thinking about how Barry Moser sometimes helps readers pay close attention to a particular part because it gives information that is important."

Let me show you what I mean . . .

"Look at this page in *My Dog Rosie*." I show the page with the girl holding the leash.

"Here we see Isabelle pulling Rosie on the leash, but we see only part of Isabelle and part of Rosie. We see the leash wrapped around Isabelle's arm and her two hands pulling on the leash—and that look on Rosie's face! I get the feeling that Rosie is being stubborn and Isabelle is pulling hard, and you know what? I think that is exactly what Barry Moser wants us to see.

"Then here"—I turn to the illustration two pages later—"she is taking the ball from Rosie, and again we see only part of Isabelle and part of Rosie. We see the top half of Isabelle, how she's really concentrating and using two hands to get the ball out of Rosie's mouth, and we see a close-up of Rosie with the ball in his teeth. I'm sure Barry Moser did that on purpose because that's what he wants us to pay attention to.

"He does it in *My Cats Nick and Nora*, too. On this page"—I show the page with the doll carriage—"we see Isabelle and her cousin taking Nick and Nora for a walk, but we see only part of Isabelle and her cousin. We see enough of them to know they are there, but I think Barry Moser wants us to pay attention to the cats in the carriage. He wants us to see that the girls have dressed them up and put them in their doll carriage, and how the cats are feeling about it!"

So, today as you write . . .

"That's another reason that illustrators show only part of a person or a thing or a scene. They want you to pay close attention to a particular part of the picture because it is giving the information that is most important. If you have something that is very important that you want your readers to pay attention to, you might try that technique."

Talking, Drawing, Writing

Why we chose these books	Barry Moser focuses the reader on exactly the part he wants us to pay attention to while giving us a larger context through partial illustration.

Suggested other books

- *Subway*, by Anastasia Suen, illustrated by Karen Katz
- *Karate Hour*, by Carol Nevius, illustrated by Bill Thomson
- *Sally Goes to the Vet*, by Stephen Huneck

Other possible lessons

- Giving information through partial illustrations: Sometimes illustrators show a whole scene but reveal only part of an object in that scene. For example, in *The Paperboy*, on the page where the boy is in the garage preparing the newspapers, only part of the bicycle wheel is visible. Illustrators use this technique to get readers wondering, predicting, and asking questions. It is really about foreshadowing.
- Illustrations sometimes extend off the page, bringing the reader right into the room or the setting.
- Putting important information in the forefront and making the background less prominent.

Time and Place

Time and place are two elements of craft that are depicted in a variety of ways in children's books, and we explore them with our young writers. By *time*, we mean how writers and illustrators represent the time of day, the time of year, and the passage of time, some rather sophisticated elements of craft to be thinking about with five- and six-year-olds. As we look at children's work, we see that they usually depict daytime with one inch of blue colored across the top of the page and a round, yellow sun in the corner; nighttime is usually a crescent moon and a black strip of night. Yet in the children's books they read, they rarely see that.

By *place*, we mean where the story is happening. When young children draw the outdoors, they often put grass and flowers no matter what the actual environment or time of year (see the lesson called Going Beyond Safe Drawings in Chapter 4). Sometimes they draw the outdoors, even when the part of the story they're writing about takes place indoors. That may be because they're not sure how to draw the inside, or because they're comfortable drawing flowers and houses and sky and the sun.

We want to show them that writers and illustrators want readers to know where the story is happening because that usually gives them information that helps them understand the story. Is it inside or outside or both? If it is outside, is it in a place with buildings and parks and trees? Is it in the springtime with flowers, when it's raining or snowing, or when leaves are falling on the ground? Does it happen in a place like your home in Cape Verde or Guatemala or Beijing, and if it does, what would you put in your drawings that would help readers know that? What do the trees and the buildings look like? Do they look the same or different from what we see here? Without squelching their delightfully five-year-old way of drawing, we think it's important to show them how writers and illustrators attend to the tiniest details to help readers understand when and where the story takes place.

Lesson Sense of Time: Revealing the Daytime

What's going on in the classroom
- Very often, when children draw the outdoors, they put a round yellow sun in one corner to show it is daytime.

What's next
- We want to show children that authors and illustrators reveal daytime in many ways.

Materials needed
- *The Stray Dog*, by Marc Simont
- *Sit, Truman!* by Dan Harper, illustrated by Cara and Barry Moser
- *Bigmama's*, by Donald Crews
- *Sally Goes to the Beach*, by Stephen Huneck
- a child's story, set during the day, where there's no sun or blue sky

This is what I noticed . . .
"I've been noticing how you let readers know what time of day it is in your stories.

"Ana-Marie, here is an illustration you did a long time ago in your Drawing & Writing Book, about when you went to your cousin's house. We can see that you have the sun up in the blue sky. Right away, we know it is daytime.

"And Brittney, you wrote about going to the beach with your mom and your sister. Here you and your sister are, floating in the water, and here's your mom on the lounge chair, and we can read what it says: 'We went to the beach.' We can also tell it's a sunny day because we can see the blue sky and the sun. That's a good way to show readers that it was a sunny day, isn't it?

"But I'm noticing that illustrators in the books we read show daytime in many different ways."

Let me show you what I mean . . .
"I was just noticing the kind of day it is today. Would you say it is a sunny day?"

The children say, "Yes!"

"And if we went over to the window and looked out"—I motion them to follow me—"we can tell it is sunny, can't we?"

"Yes," they say.

"Well, I'm looking out this window and I know it is sunny, but I don't see the sun. Do you?"

They look around the sky and say things like, "It's probably over there," and "It's on top of the school . . ."

"I'm also noticing that the sky isn't blue. There are little patches of blue here and there, but the sky is mostly whitish! And I don't even see clouds."

They talk for a minute or so, saying that the sun is in the sky, we just can't see it from these windows, and we should go outside and look.

"We could go outside and look, and I'll bet we would see the sun up there somewhere, but here's what I'm figuring out: you don't always have to see that round sun or the blue sky to know it is daytime. If I was going to draw that building right there, I wouldn't put blue behind it and a sun in the sky because I don't see the blue sky or yellow sun. Readers would still know it is day even though they wouldn't see the yellow sun or a mostly blue sky, wouldn't they?"

I bring them back to the rug and continue. "I think Marc Simont knew that when he wrote and illustrated *The Stray Dog*. For example, on these pages"—I flip the pages as I speak—"when they go back to the picnic grove to see if they can find the stray dog and the dogcatcher comes, I notice that there is no round sun up in the sky on any of these pages. I also notice that there is no blue to show the sky but still I know it is day. Look at this page where the girl and boy get the dog back and the girl is holding it on the leash they've made from the boy's belt. It almost looks greenish whitish in the background, doesn't it, but we know it is day. So I'm starting to see that one thing illustrators do is make sure the picture looks bright when they want readers to know it's day.

"You know, I think Jason knows about showing daytime this way. Jason, you wrote this book about the guys who were digging up the road in front of our school. The whole story happens outside, but we never see the yellow sun or the blue sky. Yet we know this is happening outside, don't we?

"One way we know is because of these huge machines! We know they'd be outside! Another way we know it's outside is because we can see the street and this pile of dirt over here. Another way we know is because the words help us to understand. Here it says, 'They dig a hole outside school.'

"You tell us what's happening and where it's happening. And your drawings really help us see those big backhoes and payloaders and the jackhammer and the shovels. But, there is no yellow sun or blue sky. And I'm thinking, you didn't really need it!

"It seems like Jason did just what Marc Simont did, or what Donald Crews does on these pages of *Bigmama's*"—I flip open to a page of daylight—"or what Stephen Huneck does in *Sally Goes to the Beach*"—I show a page at the beach—"or what Cara Moser and Barry Moser do in *Sit, Truman!*" I show a page where they're outside. "They use bright colors in the background, or sometimes no color at all so the page is bright and we know it's day."

So, today as you write . . .	"You might keep these different ways of showing daytime in mind as you draw your stories. Maybe you'll think about what these illustrators and writers did and try out different ways of letting readers know what time of day it is in your stories."
Why we chose these books	They are books the children know well, and they don't have the ball of sun in the sky. In most, the sky is not blue. The books offer another way

of thinking about daylight, and that's really what we're trying to do: show them that authors and illustrators depict day in different ways.

Suggested other books

Just about any book will depict daytime without a sun high in the sky. However, in *Sally Goes to the Vet*, Stephen Huneck shows the sun coming up as a yellow ball in the sky with rays shooting out from it. It is important to show this example to the children as well.

Other possible lessons

- Time passing within a day (when illustrations reveal a changing color of the sky and so on)
- Time passing within a short time: *Dim Sum for Everyone!*, by Grace Lin, reveals a change in the plates on the table in the restaurant—they're clean and set neatly at the beginning of the story, and they're used and moved by the end. The change in table settings reveals use and that time has passed.
- Variety of ways to show night (for example, lights on in buildings, car headlights, darkening of sky, stars, and moon)

Being Specific

Typically, when we return from classroom demonstrations with teachers, we open each child's Drawing & Writing Book or booklet to a page they worked on that morning and spread them out across the table. We do this in preparation for our discussion with teachers about what they observed that morning, but it never fails: as the two of us spread the books out, we hear ourselves saying things like, "Look at what Niyara did!" and "Isn't this gorgeous!" and "How could anyone look at these and not be just blown over by what children can do!" Mostly that's because their voices come leaping off the page through the specific details in their drawings and writing.

"The writing becomes beautiful when it becomes specific," Fletcher tells us (1991, 47), and children's writing is both beautiful and specific. On the first page of his story called "My Cousin's Aunt's Wedding," Eldon has drawn the inside of the church: four brown pews with people standing behind them, and flower petals strewn over the center aisle. He has outlined everything in the illustrations with black felt-tip pen, heightening attention to the details. Underneath, the words say, "I am in the church." On the next page we see fourteen round tables covered in yellow tablecloths with chairs at each, and one long, rectangular (head) table with a blue scalloped-edge covering. Every single table is set with plates of food and place settings of knives, forks, and spoons. At one side of the page we see a hatch shell—"for the people to dance," Eldon says, and at the other side are double doors with high windows, exactly the kind that lead from this type of hall into the kitchen. At the bottom, his words say, "Then we went to my cousin's aunt's party."

"Writing becomes beautiful when it becomes specific," and this work is not only beautiful and specific, but stunning.

In some ways, to have a section on being specific feels redundant, because in all of our lessons, from the oral telling of stories to modeling our own stories on paper to helping children think about how to reread their work, we've attended to the importance of including specific information. And once children learn how to pay attention to the tiny details, their stories are filled with specific information. It is evident, first, in their drawings. Next, we help them do it with words.

In the following two lessons we focus on being specific in the texts.

 ## Lesson Writing with Specific Information About a Familiar Topic

What's going on in the classroom
- The children are writing stories in booklets with multiple parts.
- Many of the children are writing in general ways about their topics:

I like my dog.	I take dancing lessons.
My dog is nice.	I like dancing lessons.
My dog is fun.	I have fun.
I love my dog.	Dancing lessons are the best.

What's next
- The children need to tell more specific information about their topics so readers can understand why they like their dog or dancing lessons or anything else they're writing about. One way to do this is to include what the characters in their stories are doing.

Materials needed
- *My Dog Rosie*, by Isabelle Harper, illustrated by Barry Moser, which the children have heard and interacted with many times

This is what I noticed . . .
"Boys and girls, I was noticing something that Isabelle Harper and Barry Moser did as the author and illustrator of *My Dog Rosie* that helped me understand a lot about Rosie and the little girl in the story. They told so much about what the little girl and Rosie do when they're together, that as a reader, I could tell how much they enjoy being together."

Let me show you what I mean . . .
"On the first page they wrote, 'When Grandpa goes into his room to work, it's my job to take care of Rosie.' Then on each page, they wrote and drew a picture of each thing the girl does when she takes care of Rosie:

- "Here she's feeding him breakfast.
- "Here she's giving him a bath.
- "Here she's drying him off, and
- "Here she's reading him his favorite story.

"They go on to let their readers know all the other things she does when she's at Grandpa's taking care of Rosie. As a reader who likes good stories, I'm so happy they didn't just say,

- "'I take care of Rosie.
- "'I do lots of things.
- "'It is fun.
- "'I love Rosie.'

"I wouldn't know about the exact things she had to do when she took care of Rosie. And when Isabelle Harper and Barry Moser let us know all the things the girl did, I can just tell that she loves Rosie."

So, today as you write . . . "So today, think about the things your characters are doing and try to include what they're doing in your stories."

Why we chose this book This book is written with lots of parts, and the one or two lines of text on each page helps beginning writers see that this is something they can do, too.

Suggested other books
- Other books by Isabelle Harper, illustrated by Barry Moser: *My Cats Nick and Nora* and *Our New Puppy*
- The "Sally" books by Stephen Huneck: *Sally Goes to the Beach, Sally Goes to the Mountains, Sally Goes to the Vet, Sally Goes to the Farm*

Other possible lessons
- The actions of the characters match in pictures and words.

 # Lesson Including Feelings

What's going on in the classroom
- Children are writing stories in booklets.
- They include detailed information by being more specific with the facts.

What's next
- We want them to know that there are many ways of being specific in the writing; one way is to include feelings.

Materials needed
- "Eusebio Cardoso," by Liliana Andrade (student in the class)
- writing of other children in the class who include specific examples

This is what I noticed . . . "I've noticed how writers in this classroom are including exactly what the people in their stories are doing.

"For example, . . ." I share examples of what individuals have done.

"Showing the exact things people in your stories are doing really helps readers understand the story, doesn't it? Well, today, I want to talk to you about another way writers help readers understand: sometimes they do it by including feelings."

Let me show you what I mean . . . "That's what Liliana did in this story she wrote about her grandfather. Liliana, will you come up and read your story?"

Liliana reads her book "Eusebio Cardoso." The children have heard it already, because Liliana shared it a few days ago.

"Every time I read this story, I am reminded all over again how special your grandfather was to you," I say to Liliana. Then to the class I say, "Liliana tells the exact things the people in her story are doing—going to the store, buying the flowers, having the party, and going to the cemetery—and by including those things she helps us understand her story, doesn't she? But Liliana does something else in this story that helps readers understand. She lets readers know how she feels.

"On this last page, it says, 'I miss him.' Just those words let us know how Liliana feels and that she's sad that her grandfather isn't here anymore."

So, today as you write . . .	"So today as you work on your writing, think about what you need to include in your story so readers will know not only what happened but also how you felt. When you include those things, they help readers understand your story better."
Why we chose this book	A child in the class wrote it, so it's accessible to the others—and she has included specific information.
Other suggested books	• *Sally Goes to the Vet*, by Stephen Huneck • *My Big Brother*, by Miriam Cohen, illustrated by Ronald Himler
Other possible lessons	• Including thoughts

Revision

Revision in writing grows from a classroom culture that is built on the value of "seeing again," which is what *revision* means. Revision is a natural part of writing, and we want our students to view it that way, but it will be natural to them only if it is natural to us. Therefore, they need to see us revising our writing. If *we* return to *our* writing with creative energy, engagement, and investment, chances are, they'll not only learn to value "reseeing," but learn that it's actually fun. And we can't fool them. Children know whether or not we're being genuine, and if our view of revision is "having to do over," or "not right," those messages will come through. That's why it's so important for us teachers to know, firsthand, the fun of going back and deciding whether or not we've got what we need and if it's where we want it. Revision is just part of what creators and composers do, and writing is about creating and composing. Of course, it always comes back to topic. They won't care to revise, to make it better, if they're not writing about something that matters to them.

One of the first lessons we present when children begin writing stories in booklets is Parts on a Page, meaning that you tell one part of the story on each page (see the lesson called Introducing Booklets to the Whole Class: Telling Many Parts of a Story, in Chapter 7), but it can still happen that parts get mixed up, left out, or put in unnecessarily. We want children to see that they can move the parts of the story around easily, in order to make the story look and sound just the way they want it to.

In the following lesson, we address how to take the booklet apart to add pages.

Lesson Adding Pages to Include More Parts

What's going on in the classroom

- Children are using drawing and words to tell their stories in booklets.

What's next

- Premade booklets of five pages were made available when children began writing stories with more than one part. Because the stories they're writing vary in length, the children need to know that they can add pages to their booklets so they can include all the necessary parts of their stories.

Materials needed

- Joyceline's booklet titled "I Went to the Zoo." Yesterday in a conference she learned how to add pages to her booklet so that she could tell more parts of her story. I removed those three added pages so that she could re-create that lesson for her peers.
- lots of paper in the writing center
- stapler, stapler remover, and small cup for used staples

This is what I noticed . . .

"Boys and girls, remember when Joyceline read her story 'I Went to the Zoo' and showed us how to add more information to each part of her writing? Well, listen to how it sounds now:

"'I Went to the Zoo,' by Joyceline

"'I was going to the zoo on Saturday.

"'I saw a giraffe at the zoo. He was eating the leaves off the tree.

"'I saw a tiger. The tiger was roaring.

"'I saw a chick. The chick was making noise.

"'I saw a hippo. The hippo was in the water.'"

"Wow," and "That's good," and "That was a lot of work, Joyceline," the children comment.

"It sure was a lot of work, and because she was thinking and working like a writer, we now know what Joyceline saw at the zoo and we also know what she noticed about each of the animals she saw. She won't have to be with her readers so they will know all that information. They can read it for themselves.

"But something else happened to Joyceline as a writer. She was thinking about her story and she has even more parts to write in her story."

Let me show you what I mean . . .

"When you started writing in booklets, the booklets were five pages with a cover stapled together. We talked about how sometimes you might have to add pages or take some pages out. Well, yesterday when I was talking with Joyceline about her story 'I Went to the Zoo,' she told me that she didn't have any room to write the part about the pigs. She has so much information to share with her readers, it won't all fit in just five pages. Joyceline, do you remember what you wanted to add?" (I motion to her to join me.)

"Now, let me think . . . oh, yeah, I wanted to tell about seeing a pig and then getting a snack, and then going home."

"And can you show and tell the boys and girls what you did so that it would include these parts about seeing the pig and getting a snack and going home?"

"Sure! I went over to the writing center"—she starts walking over as the others watch—"and I got this same kind of paper that is already in my booklet. I like this kind of paper. I counted out three papers and I put them at the back of my booklet. And then I used this stapler thing," she says as she joins us on the rug.

"The staple remover?" I ask.

"Yeah, that's it, the staple remover. And it has this little silver tip on it, and I put that under the staple like this and"—she holds it up so all the children can see—"and then I put the writing on the table"—she uses the clipboard on my lap—"and hold it down real tight so it doesn't move, and slide the staple remover up and away from me, and look, the staple came right out."

"Wow" "That's neat!" "I want to try that!" "I have one of those at home!" the children are saying.

Joyceline continues, "After you take all the staples out, you take the staples off the tip of it and you place them in this little cup. We don't want garbage all over our room. Then you get all the corners of the pages together and you staple the booklet back together. And you have to listen to the sound of the stapler."

The children are very quiet as she pushes down on the stapler.

"Did you hear it? It went buum-BUUM."

Children respond, "I hear it" and "Do it again" and "Can I try it?"

Joyceline continues to listen carefully to the sound of the stapler as she explains, "You need three staples along the edge—one in the middle and one on each of the sides. And voila, it's all done."

As she holds up the booklet, I say, "Now Joyceline's booklet has the pages that she needs to tell her whole story. And who knows, as she is writing, she may think of even more things that happened and she may want to add even more pages to tell those other parts."

So, today, as you write . . .

"So, boys and girls, when writers begin to write, they're not sure how long their stories will be. In this class we have booklets made of five pages and a cover, and that's a place for us to begin. However, sometimes as you're writing, you'll have more information and ideas for your story, and you'll need to get more paper so that you can include all the information your readers will need to really understand and enjoy your stories. And now you know how to add those pages using the stapler and stapler remover."

Other possible lessons

- Taking pages out (because you have too many pages to begin with)
- Taking pages out (because you no longer want that part in the story)
- Moving pages around so that the order makes sense

Lesson Using a Caret to Insert a Missing Word

What's going on in the classroom

- Children are writing independently in booklets.
- They've been using some revision strategies when they need to change the information in their stories—crossing out, adding more information to each page, taking a page out, adding a page—so that the story makes sense.
- While conferring, we've talked to individual children about how to insert a missing word using a caret.

What's next

- They all need to know how to use a caret to insert a missing word(s).

Materials needed

- a child's piece of writing where he or she has used a caret to show a missing word(s)
- my booklet with at least one page completed, including illustration and text, with a word missing

This is what I noticed . . .

"You know how we've been talking about different ways that writers change the information in their stories? We said they might add more information on a page or they might add pages or take some pages out? Well, today I want to show you what writers do when they discover they've left out a word."

Let me show you what I mean . . .

"Yesterday as I was talking with Cynthia about her story, she read this page to me. She touched each word as she read and this is how it sounded:

"'Me my cousin played hide-and-go-seek.'"

"Me *and* my cousin," a voice calls from the rug.

"That's exactly what Cynthia did. She said, 'Me my cousin! That doesn't sound right!' so I showed her what to do when that happens.

"See this little mark right here? That tells readers, Look up, there's a word that belongs here! Cynthia, would you make that mark here on the chart paper so all the boys and girls can see it?"

Cynthia comes up and makes a caret.

"Do you remember what it's called?" I ask her.

She thinks for a moment. "A caret," she says.

I turn to the children on the rug. "It's called a caret. It's just like the pointy end of an arrow, and it tells your eyes, Look up. There's something that belongs here. It's not like the carrot you eat. You write it this way"—I write *caret* next to the symbol on the chart paper—"which is different from this carrot." I write the word, then make a quick sketch. "Sometimes words sound the same but they're not the same at all."

"When I went back and reread my story"—I open my booklet to the page I'm working on—"I found I had done the same thing." I quickly retell what's happening on the page, pointing to the illustrations, then say, "But when I read the words like this—'It cold but we played anyway'—I thought, Wait a minute: It cold! That doesn't sound right! I wanted that to say it *was* cold. So, I'm going to do what Cynthia did. I'm going to use a caret to put in the word that I left out.

"I make the caret down here, along the line where the words go, and I make it pointing up here, where I'm going to write the word. Now, do you know why we put the word that belongs down here," (I point) "up here" (I point)?

Kids say things like, "Because you forgot it" and "Because it's too crowded to write it down there."

"Yes, we write the missing word up here because there's no room for it down here where it belongs, and there is room up here. That's why we have things like carets—because all writers, kids and grown-ups, leave words out sometimes, and carets let us slip the word in where it goes."

I point to the beginning of the sentence and read: "'It'—now this arrow tells my eyes, 'Look up,' and right up here I'll write the word I left out: '/w/ /a/ /s/.'" I say it slowly, enunciating each sound as I write.

"So now when readers read this arrow, they'll know what to do, too. They'll read, 'It, *Look up*,' and their eyes will go up here and read, 'was,' then they'll come back down and keep reading, 'cold but we played anyway.' Now it sounds right."

So, today as you write . . .   "So if this happens to you—you're writing and you realize you've left out a word—you'll know what to do. You can use a caret to put in that missing word. And that's why it's always a good idea to go back and touch, like we do when we write together, because that helps us know if we left out any words."

Other possible lessons
- Attaching a strip of paper (taping or stapling a 2½-by-8½-inch strip of paper onto the side edge of the page so you can write in the information you want to include but can't fit within the text on the page)
- Covering over a section (of drawing or text) with a piece of paper so you can rework that part
- Different ways writers in this class change the information in their stories

Topics

When children work hard on a piece of writing and, in the end, have something of quality that they're proud of, it's usually because the topic mattered to them. On the other hand, when the work appears to lack care—letters are indecipherable, drawings appear to be quick markings and there's little attention to detail—it usually indicates that something is amiss. Maybe the child wants to acquire lots of books, and quality suffers at the expense of quantity. Maybe the child doesn't see the purpose for writing. Maybe he needs more support to put his ideas on paper. Most often the issue comes down to topic. Over and over again we have seen situations where children lack care about a piece of writing or lose interest in writing itself because they're not writing about what matters to them. Helping students find topics that matter is something we return to repeatedly in our lessons throughout the year.

Not having a topic that matters manifests itself differently for young children than it does for children in intermediate grades and older. Most kindergartners don't sit slumped over the desk complaining that they're empty of ideas. Instead, they get into ruts. They write about the same thing over and over again, or they write about whatever the person next to them is writing about, or they spend many days on the same page, covering over, layer upon layer, their original work. Often, it seems, this happens because they don't know their options or how to access the information they have or possibly how to represent it. What they need from us is not help coming up with a specific topic for this page at this moment but to direct them back to what they know. Murray tells us, "Writers don't write with words, they write with information" (1984, 17). Our students have information; they sometimes need help finding it, discovering all that they have to say about it, and knowing how to put it on paper.

When we see more of the same scrawl that we've seen for pages, we slide the Drawing & Writing Book or booklet to the side, sit face-to-face, and get the child talking. We get them to teach us what they know, and we listen.

In the first lesson on topic choice, we show young writers how to pay attention to their worlds, to their own past writing, to stories they tell and those others tell, to books read aloud, and to how published authors work. Often, they need to see how to move from the ideas in their heads to putting them on the page, so we return to our own writing, thinking aloud as we model how we put our thinking on paper. We also show them how to collect ideas that might someday become stories or pieces of their own. Although some of the lessons we suggest in this section are specific to writing in booklets, most apply to children working in Drawing & Writing Books as well.

In the second lesson, we acknowledge that sometimes writers write about the same topic over and over again, particularly when it's a topic they know well and love.

 ## Lesson Noticing Ideas for Writing

What's going on in the classroom	• Many children are writing stories in booklets during writing time. • They have been introduced to the idea of recording possible topics on the My Ideas for Writing page.
What's next	• They need more information about recognizing and recording possible topics.
Materials needed	• student writing folder with inserts (see Appendix G) • enlarged My Ideas for Writing page on which to model for students • pencil • *Sit, Truman!* by Dan Harper, illustrated by Cara and Barry Moser

This is what I noticed . . .

"Yesterday, I was reminding you how you're always telling stories, to me and to each other, and that those stories you tell might be things you want to write about.

"Today, I want to talk to you about other ways of noticing ideas for stories that you might want to write about sometime."

Let me show you what I mean . . .

"Sometimes when I'm working on one story, it reminds me of something. I get an idea in my head and I think, Now, *that's* a story I want to write! I don't want to start writing about the new idea because I'm already working on a story, but I also don't want to forget the new idea. It's kind of like what happened with Angelica yesterday.

"When that happens, you want to do something with that idea right away, so you won't forget it. So if you're working, and you get an idea for another story, this is what you can do: stop writing and go to the My Ideas for Writing page, and make a quick sketch or write some words so you won't forget the idea.

"Or, sometimes you get ideas when you're listening to other people share their stories. For example, remember the story Angelica shared yesterday, about going to the pet store and getting her cat? As I was listening to her story, it reminded me of my story—not about getting a cat, but about getting a doll. When I was little, we used get these special green stamps at the grocery store when we bought our groceries. You would collect them, and put them in a special stamp book, and when you filled a whole book, you could trade it in for a brand-new toy. The stamps were like money. My mom let my sisters and me lick the stamps and put them in the stamp books after she went grocery shopping, and she told us that when the books were full, we could each get a doll. Finally the day came when all the books were filled. My mom took us to the S&H Green Stamp store—that's what the store was called. We looked at all the dolls on the shelf, and they were so beautiful. It was so hard to decide which one I wanted.

"Listening to Angelica's story yesterday got me thinking about my story and I thought, I might want to write my doll story sometime. Now, I couldn't just get up when Angelica was sharing her story to write down my idea. So I held on to that idea in my mind, and after school yesterday, I went to my My Ideas for Writing page and made a quick sketch of the S&H store and a doll on the shelf, to remind me." I show them my enlarged page.

"And something else happened this morning, boys and girls. When I was reading the book *Sit, Truman!* to you, and I got to this page about Truman playing Frisbee, I was thinking about playing Wiffle ball with my dad and uncles and cousins. Now, I *know* I have a story about that, but I couldn't just stop reading and get up to write my idea down, could I! So right now I'm going to make a sketch here on the My Ideas for Writing page, next to the picture of the doll. And in this box I'm even going to put some words to help me remember."

I draw a bat and a ball, and I write "wfl bl," saying the words slowly, listening to sounds, and going back and touching.

"Sometimes when these ideas come to you, you can go right to your My Ideas for Writing page and write the idea down. And sometimes you have to wait—hold on to the idea like I did, and write it down later."

So, today as you write . . . "So, here's what I want you to do: pay attention to the stories you tell. Pay attention to those ideas you get when you're writing. Pay attention when other people are telling their stories. Pay attention to stories that people read. Very often, something in those stories might remind you of an idea for a story. If that happens, maybe you can turn to your My Ideas for Writing page right away and make a sketch or write some words to remind you of your idea for a story. And maybe you have to hold on to your idea until there is a good time to write it down. The important thing is to get those ideas down. That way, all your good ideas for stories will be waiting for you when you're ready to start a new story."

Why we chose these books We refer to the book we had read aloud most recently. Just as in story-telling sessions, we intentionally did not make a connection to the topic but modeled how some little thing in the book triggered a memory of a totally different topic.

Suggested other books
- any book that will remind you of a story

Other possible lessons
- How to record ideas on the My Ideas for Writing page
- Recognizing ideas for stories in those you've already written

Lesson Writers Return to Topics They Know and Love

What's going on in the classroom
- Most children are moving into booklets; some are writing in Drawing & Writing Books.
- We've been talking about how writers write about what matters to them.

What's next
- They need to see that writers and illustrators often return to the same topics, things they know and love, and write about them in different ways.

Materials needed
- Drawing & Writing Book and booklet where a child has written about the same topic in different ways.
- *Bigmama's, Shortcut,* and *Freight Train,* by Donald Crews
- *My Dog Rosie, My Cats Nick and Nora,* and *Our New Puppy,* by Isabelle Harper, illustrated by Barry Moser
- *I Love My Hair!* and *Bippity Bop Barbershop,* by Natasha Anastasia Tarpley, illustrated by E. B. Lewis

This is what I noticed . . . "Boys and girls, yesterday Albana started a booklet about going to work with her mom at Dunkin' Donuts. Remember she shared it yesterday?" I hold the book and point to the words she has written—*I WT to the*

DgNS DNSg Wa Mom—as I say, "'I went to the Dunkin' Donuts with Mom.'"

"I'm going to tell the story back to you," I say, and I begin with the drawing.

"This is the train and here's Albana and her mom getting on the train—we can see the wheels and the windows—and here is the conductor, and she and her mom were waiting there on the platform. It looks like it must be one of those T stops above ground, because we see the sun."

Albana nods, saying, "It's the one near the church."

"Is it the Orange Line?" I ask, and she nods. I turn the page.

"On this page they are inside Dunkin' Donuts, aren't they? Albana told us that: this is her mom, and here is Albana next to her mom, and her mom has a cup and she's going to pour the coffee. Here's the coffee-pot, and this is the cream machine, and behind them are all the doughnuts. This is the door where the man goes to make the dough-nuts, and all these people are waiting in line, and over here, behind them, we see this stand, and on top are the napkins and straws. Here is the door that they come in and go out. Wow, so much information, and I remembered it all! I think that's because you put so much detail in the drawing, it helped me remember.

"Underneath it says, 'I was waiting for my mom.'" I point to the letters that represent each word as I read, just as she had done the previous day: *I wZ WTG F MY Mom*.

"You know, I'll bet you remember, a long time ago, when Albana shared *this* page in her Drawing & Writing Book." I hold up the page. "Here is CVS. She told us that Dunkin' Donuts is next to CVS, and these are the doughnuts in the window. And here's Albana and her mom. She's going to work at Dunkin' Donuts with her mom. You've written about this before, haven't you, Albana?"

"Yes," she says, "because I go there a lot."

"And you know a lot about it, don't you? That's why I wasn't surprised that your first book is about this topic." I turn to the children on the rug.

"Albana has written more than once about going to work at Dunkin' Donuts with her mom, but what's interesting is, that even though the stories are about the same thing, they're not the same story.

"Authors often go back to a topic they've written about before and write about it again, and sometimes again and again and again, but each time they write about that topic, they write about it differently."

Let me show you what I mean . . .

"Barry Moser and Natasha Anastasia Tarpley and Donald Crews all have done what Albana has done: they've written more than once about something they know well and something, it seems, they care about.

"We know that Barry Moser and Isabelle Harper love those dogs and cats, don't we? They wouldn't keep writing about them over and over again so carefully if they didn't.

"And Natasha Anastasia Tarpley has these two books about hair. We know that *I Love My Hair!* comes from her memories of her mother combing her hair at night, because we read it in the author's note in the book. We know that *Bippity Bop Barbershop* comes from her memories of getting her hair cut in the barbershop and watching the men there and once in a while watching a boy come in with his dad to get a first haircut, because we read that in the author's note, too. We know that Natasha Anastasia Tarpley has special memories about hair and so she keeps coming back to that topic. Who knows, maybe one of these days she'll write another book that has something to do with hair.

"And Donald Crews has trains in many of his stories. In *Bigmama's* he takes the train south for 'three days and two nights,' *Shortcut* is about how he and his cousins and brothers and sisters had a scary experience with a train, and *Freight Train* lets us see what a freight train is and how it travels. We know he watched trains a lot, because in the dedication of *Freight Train*, it tells us that trains were always passing by Bigmama's house in Cottondale.

"These three authors do just what Albana is doing: they wrote more than once about something they did a lot, about something they know well, about something they love. Writers find those topics that they care about, and they don't write about them just once; sometimes they keep coming back to them, over and over again. And each time, the story is different."

So, today in your writing . . .   "As you think about ideas for your books, you might want to go back to your Drawing & Writing Book and look there. You may have written about things you care about that may be good ideas for stories. Or, you may look through your booklets and think, Hmm, I think I have another story about that, the way Albana did, and you might want to write that story."

Why we chose these books   The children know the books and authors and illustrators well. They make the point about how writers keep coming back to a few topics they love.

Suggested other books
- *Elizabeti's Doll, Mama Elizabeti, Elizabeti's School,* by Stephanie Stuve-Bodeen, illustrated by Christy Hale
- *Sally Goes to the Beach, Sally Goes to the Mountains, Sally Goes to the Vet, Sally Goes to the Farm,* by Stephen Huneck
- *Dim Sum for Everyone!, The Ugly Vegetables, Kite Flying,* by Grace Lin (the topic that holds these stories together is childhood memories)

Other possible lessons
- How to look through the Drawing & Writing Book to see if there are topics to revisit
- How to look through the collection of booklets you've written to see if you want to write about any of those topics again
- Writing about the same topic in a different genre (informational text, poem, letter, announcement, etc.)

Proofreading

When writers complete a piece of writing, they usually proofread, which the American Heritage Dictionary defines as "to read (copy or proof) to find and correct errors" (2002, 1116). Although we believe that attending to the mechanical aspects of writing is important and, in many ways, informs future interactive writing and mini-lessons, there is a bigger reason for proofreading: it requires our student writers to become their own readers. Proofreading means going back to this piece of work that they know inside out and have looked at and worked on day after day, and becoming a person who will read it for the first time.

Proofreading matters because it's what writers do when they finish a piece of writing, and we want our writers to engage in all aspects of what writers do when they write. We want them to know that once their ideas are on the page the way they want them, they have a responsibility to make sure the piece of writing is ready for readers' eyes. It also matters because it is here that we make our students accountable for the conventions of writing that we have taught and, we hope, they have learned. It is where teacher and student keep track, together, of what we can expect students to incorporate into their writing.

Besides understanding *why* we proofread, we need to teach them *how* to proofread. From the start, we want them to be successful, so we need to make it doable. One way teachers do that is to give their students a list of things to check for, thinking carefully about the items they put on that list so the students will be successful. Then they teach them how to use the proofreading list.

Early on, the items on the list are few (maybe only one or two things for these young writers) and mostly procedural: write my name, write the date, number my writing, give the story a title (see Appendix G). *We include only things the students can do, because at this point, we're not teaching them the skills to proofread for, we're teaching them the skill of proofreading.* If we want them to be good proofreaders, and to acquire the habit of "checking their writing for errors and making corrections," we need to make it possible for them to be successful at it right from the start.

To begin with things the children already know how to do means that these are things we've already addressed with them. From the time individual children or the whole class begin working in booklets, part of the introduction is to show our writers how an author always puts his name and a title for his story on the cover of his book. During read-alouds and mini-lessons, we point out authors' names and titles on books, and with the help of many reminders, children begin to understand the need for their names and titles to go on their writing. We talk about putting the date on the cover because it helps us know when they started a piece of writing. Numbering the stories helps us know the order in which they wrote them, which is especially helpful if children have forgotten to put the date on a story. We also begin to show them how to do some record keeping themselves: how to write the title of their pieces on a page in the folder called My Finished Writing. These five items are all things that over time most writers can do effectively with a little prompting (and in some cases a lot of prompting) from the teacher.

But our goal is for them to independently complete the procedural items that they know how to do. Although they have nothing to do with finding errors and correcting them (we can hardly call not including a name, title, or date, not numbering stories, or not writing the title on a page in their folder an error), they are necessary for a reader to know who wrote the piece of writing, what it is about, and when it was written. And because they are items that young writers can easily reread and check for, they are ideal for beginning to teach children how to "proofread," thus helping them to acquire the habit of rereading and checking for those things they know how to do.

Although the next lesson is done with the whole class, we have learned through the years that it is best to explain the procedures for proofreading to one or two students at a time when they are ready to take on another part of what writers do. (The items on the proofreading list will not make sense to a writer who is still working in his Drawing & Writing Book.) Some children will already have two, three, or even four booklets completed, but they might not have numbered or dated each story, and they need help organizing their completed work before they begin writing the titles on the My Finished Writing page.

As we help them walk through the procedures, it allows us to see what they do or do not understand. Once some children start proofreading their work, they teach others. By the time we introduce proofreading to the whole class, as in this lesson, the children are familiar with the items on the list and it is more of a reminder, rather than a lot of new information.

 Lesson Proofreading Your Work

What's going on in the classroom	• Children are writing stories in booklets during writing time.
	• They may know how to do some of the things listed on the Proofreading List, but they don't do them consistently. One reason may be that, with some exceptions, they have not been introduced to the list that will help them remember.
	• They need to learn that when they finish a piece of writing, they go to the page in their folder called My Proofreading List and proofread according to the items on that list.
Materials needed	• student writing folder with inserts (Appendix G)
	• enlarged My Proofreading List on which to model for students

This is what I noticed . . .

"Boys and girls, I know that as you write, you ask yourself questions that writers ask:

- "Does my story make sense?
- "Do I need to add more information in the pictures?
- "Do I need to add more information in the words?
- "Do I need to take some information out of my pictures or words?
- "Have I written my words the best that I know how, reading each word carefully and touching each letter and making sure I have a letter for each sound I say and hear?

"These are things you do as a writer so your readers can understand your stories.

"When writers think their stories are finished, that they make sense and they've put all the information in the pictures, and they've put information into words so readers can read their stories easily, they usually do one more thing. We call it *proofreading*. Proofreading means checking for things like putting your name on your story, giving the story a title, putting the date on it, numbering your story, and writing the title on the My Finished Writing page. They're things that can be helpful to you as a writer and to me as your teacher."

Let me show you what I mean . . .

"In your folders you have a page called My Proofreading List. Writers proofread for things like the items on this list." I show the page as I read:

- "'I can write my name on my writing.
- "'I can write a title on my writing.
- "'I can write the date on my writing.
- "'I can number my finished writing.
- "'I can write the title of my writing on the page called My Finished Writing.'

"I want to show you how to use this proofreading list so that you can proofread when you're finished with your work. From now on, when you're finished writing your story and have it just the way you want it, you'll open your folder to this page called My Proofreading List and proofread for the items on this list. What you do is read each item, one at a time, and check to see that you've done that thing.

"Christopher, since you said you were finished with your story yesterday, I thought you might come up and proofread right now, so we can all watch to see just what to do."

He comes and stands next to the easel, where he opens his folder to the page called My Proofreading List.

"Okay, here, next to number one it says, 'I can write my name on my writing.' So Christopher will look at the cover of the story he just finished and check to see if he wrote his name."

Christopher points to his name on the cover.

"He did, didn't he? But if he didn't, what would he do?"

The children offer suggestions.

"Yes, he would just write it. Next, he reads number two."

"Number two says, 'I can write the title on my writing.' Christopher will look at the cover of his writing and see if he has a title. Do you, Christopher?"

He says, "Yes," and I ask him to read it to us.

"If he didn't have a title, what do you think he would do?"

The children suggest, "Write it!" and "Think of one!"

"Yes, he would think of one, write it, then go to number three.

"Number three says, 'I can write the date on my writing,' and look at that! Christopher, you didn't write the date, but you stamped it right on the cover. Pretty soon, I'll bet, he'll be writing the date. On to number four.

"Number four says"—I pause and point to the words, and Christopher and the children read along with me—"'I can number my finished writing.'"

"Did he number the story?" I ask, pointing to the one in the upper left-hand corner. "Yes, he did. This is his first story. I know because he made a one right there. That helps him remember which story he wrote first, second, third, and fourth, and it helps me, too.

"And the last one, number five."

We read together: "'I can write the title of my writing on the page called My Finished Writing.' That means he turns to the very first page, where it says My Finished Writing, and next to the number one it should say, 'When I Broke the Car.' Let's look. Does it say the name of this story?"

Christopher puts his hand against his head and says, "Oh, I forgot!"

"You know, boys and girls, sometimes you do forget. That's why we put this list here—to help you remember." I lay his folder against the easel and say, "Why don't you write the title of story number one right here, next to the number one." He takes the black felt-tip pen and begins.

We all watch as he writes, *Wan i brok the car* (When I Broke the Car).

Since the boys and girls sitting on the rug can't see what he is writing, I say things like, "You should see how he is writing each letter so carefully," and "I think he really wants people who look at the first page in his folder to be able to read the titles of his stories!" and "He's going back and touching so he won't forget what word comes next . . ." When he is finished, he stands aside so we can all see.

"Boys and girls, these are easy things to do, aren't they? You're already doing most of them! But sometimes you forget, so this list will help you remember to do them. Now when you finish a piece of writing, you'll be doing what writers do. You'll check to make sure you've done the items on your proofreading list, just like Christopher did."

So, today as you write . . . "I'm wondering, are any of you boys and girls thinking you might be finishing a story today?" Some children raise their hands.

"Well, before you put your story in the back pocket and begin a new one, open your folder to the page called My Proofreading List and read each one of these reminders on the list, just as Christopher did, and check to see that you have done each one."

Conventions: Attending to the Mechanics of Writing

When we speak of conventions, we are referring to things such as words going left to right and top to bottom, leaving spaces between words, spelling, punctuation, and capitalization. Throughout history, writers have come to an agreement about how these things will look in text. For example, readers' eyes expect to see spaces between words, and when writers leave spaces between words, readers have an easier time reading and thus a greater chance of understanding the writer's intended meaning. A writer not only composes his message, chooses his words, and puts them together to clearly convey his message, but also has to consider which letters and words to write, how to write the letters and words, and how to mark the words with punctuation. Careful attention to all these things helps readers understand his message.

As we have mentioned before, most teaching of the conventions takes place during interactive writing sessions where the class, along with the teacher, composes a text together and the teacher helps the children write the message conventionally. Our goal is for them to begin using these same conventions as they write independently during the writing workshop. However, we have learned that we can't expect children to automatically transfer what they've learned in one setting, in this case during interactive writing, to another setting, the writing workshop. Therefore, in mini-lessons we talk with them about what they are learning during the interactive writing time and how they might try that out as they write independently during the writing workshop.

 Lesson Leaving Spaces Between Words

What's going on in the classroom	• Most children are writing in booklets.
	• They are gaining confidence as writers, fluently writing a sentence per page. For the most part, they spell correctly those words they know how to spell, and they use sound spellings to write words they don't know how to spell.
	• Although we address it during interactive writing, most don't leave spaces between the words.
What's next	• They need to be reminded about leaving spaces so readers will be able to read what they've written.
Materials needed	• Jazmine's two most recent stories, one where she's written words with no spacing, and the second, which she's just begun, where she's left spaces between the words.

This is what I noticed . . . "Boys and girls, today I want to remind you about leaving spaces between words when you write. You know about that, don't you? When we write together, like we did this morning, we always leave spaces between the words.

Let me show you what I mean . . . Let's take a look at this sentence we wrote today to add to our list of What Writers Do. Help me read it." I point to the words as we read together:

"'Writers include important information.'"

"It's easy for us to read that sentence, isn't it? One of the reasons it's easy is that we know it—we just wrote it a little while ago. Another reason it's easy to read is that there are spaces between the words. When there are spaces, we know which letters go with which words.

"Yesterday I was talking to Jazmine as she was finishing a story and about to start a new one. Remember this story about her fish? Well, when Jazmine and I were looking at it, this is what happened. She started reading the words and she stopped, she pointed, and she went slowly, because she was trying hard to figure out which letters went with which words. That's because the letters were all close together.

"Like right here she read, 'Me and my mom' and then she was stuck. I was stuck, too, and I was asking myself, Now which letters go with which words? Then I said, 'Oh, is it "Me and mom had a fishy?"' And it was! That was hard work, wasn't it, Jazmine?

"You don't want your readers to have to work that hard to read your writing—because they won't! They'll say, 'This is too hard to read,' and they'll choose something else that they can read more easily. So one thing writers do is leave spaces between the words so readers will know which letters belong with which words.

"When Jazmine got to the last page of that book yesterday, I asked her to show me where she thought the spaces would go. She put her finger where the spaces should be. She was about to begin her next story, so I told her to try to remember to leave spaces, just like we do when we write together.

"Well, she began her story yesterday, and wait till you see what she did! Here's the first page of the fish story"—I hold up the booklet—"and here's the first page of her new story."

The children say, "She left spaces!" and "She did it!" and someone claps.

"Look at the difference between the first pages of these two books! I think Jazmine really understands about leaving spaces in her writing."

So, today as you write . . . "You want to remember to do that, too. Sometimes when you're just starting to write words, you can't remember about the spaces because you're working so hard to remember the sounds of the letters. But if you can, try to remember how we leave spaces between words when we write together. It really helps readers to read what you wrote.

Why we chose this book The child had written words without leaving spaces. Then, when shown how to leave spaces, she did. The difference between the two pages was obvious and, we knew, would be obvious to the children.

Suggested other books	• Any published book will show spacing between words.
Other possible lessons	• Capitalizing the word *I* • Using periods to show readers where to stop • Using question marks • Using exclamation marks • Using mostly lowercase letters • Using a capital letter at the beginning of a sentence • Putting quotation marks around the words people say out loud • Continued gentle reminders to the class and individuals to make their writing look the way it looks in books

Beginnings, Endings, and Titles

Beginnings, endings, and titles are elements of craft that, for the most part, children know something about and include in their writing on their own. This is particularly the case when they have developed a sense of story through listening to stories told or read. Their stories often begin with them doing something: "Me and my mom are at Stop & Shop," or "We are driving in the car," or "I went to my cousin's house." They often end with "Then we went home," or "Then I went to bed." Although we value this writing, we want to show children that writers are intentional about how they begin and end and title their stories. As they begin to see that many possibilities exist, they can be more intentional about those things, too.

As adults, we know that the way a story begins is important; we want to be brought into the story, and we want to be compelled to stay. We know that endings are important, too. Ralph Fletcher tells us, "The ending may well be the most important part of a piece of writing. It is the ending, after all, that will resonate in the ear of the reader when this piece of writing has been finished. If the ending fails, the work fails in its entirety" (1991, 92).

As teachers of writing we know different kinds of "leads" and "endings"—we even give names to them—and we want to teach our students about them. This can be tricky, though, because by naming types of leads and endings and providing models of what adult writers have done, we face the danger of imposing an adult view of writing on children and the result is five- and six-year-old writing that sounds like an adult wrote it. We don't want that. We want children's writing to sound like children wrote it.

We have found that one way to give young children information about beginnings, endings, and titles is to go to literature where a child is telling the story, such as *Our New Puppy* (1996), *My Cats Nick and Nora* (1995), *Digger Man* (2003), *My Big Brother* (2005)— literature that sounds like a child wrote it. The writing provides a vision for five- and six- and seven-year-olds.

We also go to the work of other children for a vision of what is possible. For example, a child may veer from the typical beginning—

"I am going to Stop & Shop"—and step right into the story as Jarren does—"In Florida, there are palm trees"—or as Christopher does when he sets out to take us on a journey: "Day 21. The chicks are not hatching yet."

In those cases, we name what they've done—first for them and then for the other children.

This next lesson addresses ending the story and is based on the work of one writer in the class. Our goal is not for other children to end their stories in a similar way, but to begin to see possibilities for endings.

Lesson Endings: Thinking About How to End Your Story

What's going on in the classroom

- Children are writing stories regularly, most often on topics that matter to them. Some stories tell of an event, such as "When I Went to the Beach," "My Cousin's Birthday," others tell of things they like to do, such as "When I Ride My Bike," "Me and My Sister Play with Dolls," and some explain about something they know well: "Trucks," "How Chicks Hatch," "Bats."
- In all but the last category, most of the stories end with "and then we went home" or "then we went to bed."

What's next

- They know that stories need endings, but we're not sure how appropriate it is to expect kindergartners to consider the type of ending that best fits their story and craft it accordingly. Sometimes, however, whether intentionally or by chance, that's exactly what happens, and when it does, we want to show the child what she has done and show the other students as well.

Materials needed

- a sample from a child who wrote an unusual ending
- *Matthew and Tilly*, by Rebecca C. Jones, and *Ginger*, by Charlotte Voake, which the children know well

This is what I noticed . . .

"Today I want to talk to you about endings of stories. I noticed something Jarren did when he wrote the ending to his story called 'What It's Like to Be in Florida.'" I read his story:

"'Thers pom teers.	There's palm trees.
"'Ther's how'sis.	There's houses.
"'Thers aepartms.	There's apartments.
"'Thers beshis.	There's beaches.
"'Bet most of all thers no sno!	But most of all, there's no snow!

"When I got to that last page—'But most of all there's no snow!'—I just knew the story had ended. Those words, 'But most of all . . .' let me know the end was coming. They seem to say, This is the last thing. And on the last page, Jarren gave us one last, very important piece of infor-

Talking, Drawing, Writing

mation: 'there's no snow!' It's like he's saying, 'Okay, readers, here's the most important thing.' On all these other pages"—I flip back as I retell—"it seems he tells us about how Florida looks, about the things that are the same in Florida—apartments and beaches—and about things that are different—palm trees and bright colored houses. Then, just by the way he says, 'But most of all, there's no snow!' he lets readers know there is one more thing about Florida that's really important to him. He could have said, 'In Florida, it's warm and sunny,' but he didn't. By writing 'But most of all,' I can tell that having no snow in Florida is what he likes most about it. And you know, the way he wrote it sounds like the books we read.

"So, telling what is most important is one way of ending a story. But there are other kinds of endings, too."

Let me show you what I mean . . .

"Another kind of ending is the one Rebecca C. Jones uses in *Matthew and Tilly*. In that story Matthew and Tilly have a fight, remember? And we hope they become friends again, and right there, on the last page, we see that they do. Here, let me read it to you:

"'"I'm sorry," he called.
"'"So am I," said Tilly.
"'And Matthew ran downstairs so they could play.
"'Together again.'

"The story ends happily, the way we hope it will.

"In *Ginger*, there is a different ending. When we get to this page—'And now Ginger and the naughty kitten get along very well . . .' we think the story is over. We think they lived happily ever after, but these three dots tell us something else is coming, so we know it's not over yet. And when we turn the page, we learn that they get along very well. . . most of the time! The author surprises us by showing us that they are good friends, but that sometimes they still annoy each other. It is a surprise ending."

So, today as you write . . .

"Boys and girls, there are a lot of different kinds of endings. You can leave your readers with one really important piece of information, as Jarren did. You can end your story with a good feeling, like everything is okay again, the way Rebecca C. Jones did. Or you can end your story with a surprise, like Charlotte Voake did in *Ginger*. There are other ways, too. I notice some of you end your stories like this: 'And then we went home.' Or like this: 'And then I went to bed.' And those might actually be the best endings for your stories. But as you start to pay attention to the ways authors end their stories, you might think of other kinds of endings and you might want to try one for your story."

Why we chose these books

These books have different kinds of endings that beginning writers can understand and do successfully. As you are looking more closely at the books you read to your students, you'll find these kinds of endings and many others to share with your students.

Suggested other books

- *My Best Friend Moved Away*, by Nancy Carlson
- *Roller Coaster*, by Marla Frazee
- *Leon and Bob*, by Simon James
- *The Stray Dog*, by Marc Simont

Other possible lessons

Beginnings

- Making decisions about how to begin a story (Teacher thinks aloud about different ways to begin her story.)
- Same topic, different beginnings (Look at how three authors who wrote about the same topic began their stories differently—use published books or work of children in the classroom.)
- Sometimes the simple beginning is best (Sometimes, "I went to my cousin's house" is the best way to begin.)

Endings

- Making decisions about how to end a story (Teacher models different types of endings for her story.)
- Revealing how you felt, what you thought, etc., things that readers wouldn't know unless you told them
- Refering to conversations you had during read-alouds, about different types of endings

Titles

- Titles make the reader want to open the book.
- Titles tell the reader something, but not everything, about the story.
- Titles are usually short. (In just a few words—sometimes one or two or three—the writer gives readers an idea of the story.)

Making Characters Come Alive

The writer Joan Didion once said, "I don't have a very clear idea of who the characters are until they start talking" (1986, 87), and truly, when a character says something, we get to know them better. Five- and six- and seven-year-old writers naturally use characters' words, and it usually happens first with actual words coming out of a character's mouth and out into the air. Usually, if the face is looking to the left-hand side of the page, the writing coming out of the mouth goes from right to left! Eventually they put the words in a bubble, as they've seen speech bubbles in books. But they also put a character's exact words in the text. Sometimes they do it because I've used exact words in the text of my story or they've paid attention to how exact words are used in the stories they've read, or we've talked about it during read-alouds, interactive writing, or other times during the day.

Sometimes, they include exact words in their texts because when they tell the story during a conference and use someone's exact words, we catch it and show them what they've just done: "Those words that your mom said, 'Get in the car, kids!' the way you just said them got me feeling like I was right there with you, listening to your mom calling to you and your brothers and sisters. If you put those words in your story, the way you just said them, it will make your mom seem more real in your story."

What we don't want is for everyone to start putting words in their stories if it doesn't make sense. You can always tell when children are doing that because it's what they think we want them to do, and it sounds artificial. Instead, we want to show them how they can put words down on paper to make the person come alive. This isn't something we expect all kindergartners to do; what's important is that we begin the conversation and that we notice it when a student has done it in his or her writing, as in the following example.

Lesson Including Exact Words People Say

What's going on in the classroom	• Children are writing stories and including specific, detailed information in the illustrations and in the words. • Sometimes as they explain the story verbally, they use the exact words the character said.
What's next	• We want to show them that when you write the exact words a person said, readers get to know that person a little better.
Materials needed	• *My Big Brother*, by Miriam Cohen, illustrated by Ronald Himler • two or three different ways that students use characters' exact words
This is what I noticed . . .	"In *My Big Brother*, Miriam Cohen and Ronald Himler help us to know the boy and his brothers and his mother. In the illustrations, Ronald Himler shows us what they look like. Right here on the first page we see the boy who is telling the story, and his brother. Then on this page we see there is another little brother. And on this page, where they're getting ready for church, we see the mother. From these illustrations, we learn something about what they look like and where they live and how they dress when they're doing different things. Not only do we get to know them by seeing them, but we also get to know them by hearing the words they say."
Let me show you what I mean . . .	"Like on this page, where the older brother is helping his little brother shoot the ball in the basket, he says, '"Good shot, little brother!"' When I hear the words the big brother says, I feel like I know him a little better. Just by hearing the words he said to his little brother, I know that he's a kind, older brother. "Then here on this page, where the boy is remembering to appreciate the mother for cooking such good food, he says, '"Mmm, Mama. It was GOOD!"' By hearing those words the boy says, we get to know him a little better. I hear him being thankful to his mother, and I know something about him that I didn't know just by looking at the pictures or reading the words the author wrote.

"Then, on this page, where the big brother is packing to go to the army, we hear the mom's words: '"Take your warm socks!"' Those words and the expression on her face let us know how she's feeling, don't they? She wants him to be safe and not be cold. We know she's worried: we can see the worry on her face and hear worry in her words.

"Some people in this class do the same thing. They let us hear the people in their stories by including the words they say. In Taleaha's story, there's this part about when they had to leave the pizza place. Here it says, 'I went to leave because my mom said, "Come on kids, it's time to go!"' I can just hear your mother saying that, Taleaha! You could have written, 'I went to leave because my mom told me it was time to go.' That's what happened, isn't it? But instead of telling us about it, you let us hear the words she said, and by doing that, you make her seem more real.

"And here, in Marisol's story, we see Marisol and her cousin and the girl in bed, and someone is peeking through the doorway and there are words coming out of the person's mouth: 'You can't catch me!' Later on, again, when Marisol is leaving her cousin's house, we see her head in the window of the car, and in the speech bubble it says, 'Bye you guys!' Instead of writing, 'I said bye to my cousin and the girl,' she puts the words she said in there."

So, today as you write . . . "As you work on your stories, think about what these writers did. If the people in your story are saying things, you might want to include their words. Because sometimes, just hearing the exact words people say help us to know them better."

Why we chose these books Each of these stories gives simple examples of characters' exact words.

Suggested other books
- *Good Boy, Fergus!* by David Shannon is a book of commands and callings and "one-sided conversation" with a dog. It may be a way for children to begin thinking about using someone's exact words.
- *Ginger*, by Charlotte Voake
- *My Cats Nick and Nora* and *Our New Puppy*, both by Isabelle Harper, illustrated by Barry Moser

Other possible lessons
- Using speech bubbles to show people talking
- Two people talking: dialogue

Although we have situated each of these lessons in context, we've still presented them as isolated lessons. Readers neither see how one lesson leads to the next, nor how, very often, we stay on a particular topic, presenting many lessons in a variety of ways to help our students understand. In the following chapter, we bring you into a classroom where one teacher addresses the same topic over a series of days.

CHAPTER 9

One Teacher, One Classroom

It is early April, and the children in Caitlin McArdle's kindergarten are writing. Most are writing stories in booklets of about five pages, and a couple are choosing to work in their Drawing & Writing Books, but whatever the medium, there is a happy feeling in the room, a sense of investment in meaningful work.

Now that the children are writing independently and extending their stories through pictures and words, Caitlin's mini-lessons tend to focus more on aspects of the craft of writing. Mostly, her students are writing narratives that relay a series of events: going grocery shopping, playing in the park, a cousin's birthday party. They have done a good job of learning what their teacher has taught them: to include information. Lately, Caitlin notices, they are including EVERY BIT of information, much of which isn't necessary. Their stories sound something like this:

page 1: We are driving to Stop & Shop.
page 2: We parked the car.
page 3: We are going in Stop & Shop.
page 4: We bought the food.
page 5: We went home.

Caitlin wants to help them see that you write about what is most important. She wants them to know that writers make decisions about what information to include and that they try to tell things readers wouldn't necessarily know, which means leaving out what readers can figure out on their own. In other words, she is teaching them about selecting the details that make the writing effective.

Because she knows that you don't address a topic just once, she revisits it for days in a row. We take you now into Caitlin's classroom for four consecutive lessons in which she is helping her students understand what's involved in being more "specific."

Including Specific Information That Readers Wouldn't Know

 Lesson Giving Readers Important Information

What's going on in the classroom	• Children are writing independently.
	• There is evidence in their writing that they're incorporating some of the information being presented in the mini-lessons.
What's next	• Students need concrete examples of what it means to be specific, to give readers "important information."
Materials needed	• *The Paperboy*, by Dav Pilkey
	• *Dim Sum for Everyone!*, by Grace Lin
This is what I noticed . . .	"Today I want to talk to you about something two authors have done that I think will help you in your writing." She holds up a copy of *The Paperboy*, by Dav Pilkey.

"In this book, *The Paperboy*, Dav Pilkey could have said, 'I woke up. I went downstairs. I delivered the papers. Then I went home.'

"But he didn't say just those few things. He said, 'The mornings of the paperboy are still dark and they are always cold, even in the summer. And on these cold mornings, the paperboy's bed is still warm and it is always hard to get out, even for his dog . . . but they do.'

"He made sure to tell the reader these important things about the story. He wanted us to know how the paperboy felt about getting up— that he got up when it was cold and still dark out and that it was hard to get out of his nice, warm bed—because he figured those were things that the reader might not know. Like what Grace Lin does in *Dim Sum for Everyone!*. On the pages of the book, she didn't just write,

"'We went to a restaurant.
"'We went in.
"'We sat down.

"'We ate food.
"'We went home.'

"Instead, she wrote,

"'Dim sum has many little dishes.
"'Little dishes on carts.
"'Little dishes on tables.'

"She thought about what was important to her about eating dim sum. She thought about what someone reading this book might not know. And in our writing, that's what we try to do. We want to tell the reader the important things—things they might not know.

"So, if you were writing a story about, say, going shopping with your mom, do you need to say,

"'We drove to the store.
"'We got out of the car.
"'We walked into the store'?"

The children call out, "No!"

"No, because readers probably would know that you did that. Instead, you tell all the important things that readers might not know. For example, Bryan is writing about going to the park, and what his readers might not know is that when he went to the sandbox, he built a BIG mountain. Or Kiara is writing about going to Build-A-Bear, and she's describing the clothes she chose; readers might not know why she chose those clothes."

So, today as you write . . .

"Today I want you to be thinking about some things that are important to you about your story, things that your readers might not know. When you go back to your seats to work, make sure you put those important parts in your stories."

As in most of the lessons we've presented in this book, Caitlin is giving information that she believes will be helpful to her student writers, but she's not expecting everyone to go back and incorporate it that day. She knows better. She knows that learners need lots of examples, lots of time to experiment, and lots of opportunities to see in order to understand.

Which is why, on the following day, she addresses this same topic.

Lesson Including the Important Parts: Being Specific About One Part

What's going on in the classroom

• There's an ongoing conversation about what it means to include specific information that might not be obvious to the reader.

What's next

• Students need to see an example of writing that includes specific information that is closer to the writing that they're doing.

Materials needed

Standing against the easel next to her Caitlin has placed

- Deandre's booklet that he's working on, because he included a specific piece of information the previous day;
- a piece of published writing by a child from the previous year, who was also specific in the information she included in the story;
- *The Paperboy*, by Dav Pilkey, and *Dim Sum for Everyone!*, by Grace Lin.

This is what I noticed . . .

"Kindergarten friends, remember yesterday we talked about *The Paperboy*, and *Dim Sum for Everyone!*, and how these writers chose to write about the important things? These writers are writing about things they know. It seems like Dav Pilkey knows something about being a paperboy, and we know that Grace Lin likes dim sum because we read about it back here." She turns to the back pages and recaps some of the author information she'd previously read. "The thing Grace Lin did in this story was, she chose to tell us things we *might not know*. And in your writing, you have a chance to tell people something about you—things that other people might not know.

"So when you're writing about going to the movies, do you need to say, 'After the movie, we got into the car?'"

"No!"

"No, because most readers could probably figure that out. But if, after the movie, you stopped and got a slushie, like Deandre did . . .," she says slowly and with excitement, as she holds his book up. "In his story, Deandre told about going to see *The Incredibles*, but at the end he added a part. Right here he says"—she points and reads—"'We got a Slushie.'

"He did what Dav Pilkey and Grace Lin did: he included something that was important to him, that readers might not know. When you are writing, you want to be thinking about that, too."

She stands his story against the easel and takes the other piece of children's work in her hands and says, "I have another story to read to you." She holds up a child's published story. "It was written by someone who was in this class last year. Her name is Taleaha Browne. I want you to listen to the story and see that she included parts that seem important, things we might not have known if she hadn't put them in."

Caitlin reads the story called "A Day at School," pointing out parts of the illustrations as she goes along, such as the overhead lights, particular bookshelves, doorways, and certain fixtures such as the aquarium and the kidney-shaped table—things in the classroom that these students would recognize.

"Taleaha could have said:

"'We came to school.
"'We ate pancakes.
"'We had a good day.'

"But she didn't."

Yanniel speaks out: "She made another choice. She told the words slower and told the whole story."

"Yes, and in slowing the story down, she told the really important parts about this day at school."

So, today as you write . . . "So when you go to your workplace, think, What are the important parts that I should tell somebody about my story? And when you think of something important, make sure you put that part in."

Caitlin returned to the same topic, used the same language, kept it short and focused, and connected the lesson to her students' work. What was significantly different in this lesson was how she drew on the work of a published writer *their* age. In doing so, she helped them see what it looks like when kindergartners incorporate what they learn from professional writers. By sharing Taleaha's published story, she moved them a step closer to what they are capable of—from professional literature to literature that five- and six-year-olds can produce. If they didn't understand on the previous day when she talked about how Dav Pilkey and Grace Lin included what was important to them, they might understand it a little better now that they saw what Taleaha did. And if that still seems like too much of a reach—after all, Taleaha had lots of words and was very precise in her drawings—they may be able to imagine doing what Deandre did. By sharing his work, Caitlin's message was this: a boy sitting right here in this class was able to learn from Dav Pilkey and Grace Lin, and this is what it looks like when he tried it in his writing. Although Caitlin doesn't expect every child to go off and incorporate the information from the lesson, she looks for ways to present it that make it possible for them to do it. And she watches to see how they understand.

They show her how they understand when they incorporate the information in their writing, as Deandre did. They also reveal their understanding through their responses. Yanniel's comment, "She made another choice. She told the words slower and told the whole story," helps Caitlin see how he is making sense of *the ways of a writer*. His words seemed to imply that Taleaha slowed her story down by taking readers into one short part of a bigger day, telling about that one part in more depth rather than trying to include all the parts of the day. This is what engaged him as a reader. His comment also acknowledged the essence of what Caitlin is trying to teach, that the writer is in charge and that each writer makes decisions for her own story.

 Lesson Including the Important Parts: Deciding What to Put In and What to Leave Out

What's going on in the classroom
- An ongoing conversation about what it means to include specific information that might not be obvious to the reader.

What's next
- Revisit the conversation, using the work of other kindergartners, this time with an even simpler story.

Materials needed   • a published book, written by a former kindergartner

This is what I noticed . . .   "Boys and girls, you know how, for the past two days, we've been talking about how writers tell the important things about a story?"

They nod and say, "Yes."

"What are some books we've read that show how writers do that?"

They recall *The Paperboy*, *Dim Sum for Everyone!*, and "A Day at School."

"Well, today I have another story to share with you. This is called 'Taleaha and Nysia Went to the Movie Theatre,' and it is written by another kindergartner from last year." She points and reads: "'Written and Illustrated by Nysia Monét Romain.'"

Children notice the drawing on the cover and comment, "Oh I saw that movie!" and "It's *The Cat in the Hat*!"

"We know right away that it's going to be something about *The Cat in the Hat*, don't we?"

"Yeah, because you can see the hat!"

"Well, this is a story about how two little girls went to the movies together." Caitlin reads the story and the children interact during the reading (see Figure 9.1).

The story ends and Allison immediately asks, "Is there more pages?" She could see through the paper to where more text was showing through.

FIGURE 9.1 Nysia's published book: "Taleaha and Nysia Went to the Movie Theatre."

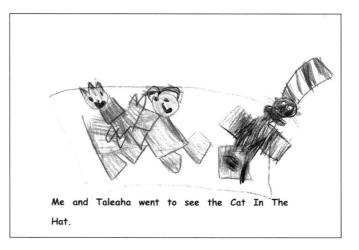

We bought gummy worms and popcorn with butter and something to drink.

Taleaha found the door for us.

I found the seats. We watched the movie.

Then we went home.

Boston

About the Author

This is Nysia. She is five years old. She likes when Ms. McArdle laughs. She likes to play on the computer. Nysia likes to paint. She likes to do science. She likes to do morning work. Nysia likes to do work board. She likes to do independent reading.

FIGURE 9.1 Nysia's published book: "Taleaha and Nysia Went to the Movie Theatre" (continued).

MYNAMISNysla.

I AM FiveYrZOWD.

I llkeWiNMS.MCAr
dletLEF.
Illiketopiron
ThecMPutr

Illiketopat.
Illiketodos IHYTZ.
IlliketoDO MONEWK.
IlliketoDoWRKBon
IlliketoD®ADPn

Caitlin turns to the About the Author page and reads it. In the author information it says, "She likes when Ms. McArdle laughs." Kiara calls out, bemused, "How do you laugh, Ms. McArdle?"

Caitlin engages in some informal talk with them, then turns back to how this story applies to them as writers.

"Boys and girls, it was important for Nysia to say that she went with Taleaha and their moms. It was important for her to say that they got popcorn and gummy worms. It was important to say that Taleaha found the right door. It was important for her to say that Nysia found the seats. Those are things that were important to Nysia and things she wanted her readers to know—things we wouldn't know unless she told us."

"But we didn't know what they had to drink!" Allison says.

"No, she didn't tell that part."

"Maybe it was a slushie," Najee suggests.

"Maybe," Caitlin says. "Or maybe something else, but that's not a part Nysia chose to tell."

So, today as you write . . .   "We have seen a couple of kindergarten authors who have written books and worked really hard to tell the important things. Today, when you go back to your writing, think about what's important, what you want to tell somebody about your story. Those are the things you want to put in."

The children interacted more during this lesson than they did on previous days, and Caitlin let them. It was almost as if she needed to hear their responses because the responses revealed their understanding of telling the important parts. When Allison suggested, "But we didn't know what they had to drink," most likely she was referring to the example from Deandre's story that Caitlin had shared the previous day, where he had written, "I got a Slushie." Clearly, it was not this piece of information that Caitlin intended to emphasize but the fact that Deandre had made a decision about a part that was important to include. Allison's response revealed her interpretation (when you write about going to a movie, you tell what you got to drink), a reminder to us to make sure we vary the examples we use while assuring our students that each writer decides what to include in his or her writing.

Yet Caitlin *had* varied the examples of student work she shared. The content of Taleaha's story was different from Nysia's, and they both were different from Dav Pilkey's and Grace Lin's. Both Deandre's and Nysia's stories were about going to the movies, yet in using those two examples, Caitlin was helping them see that although writers may write about the same topic, what is important to one writer may not be important to another. By going back and explicitly naming each part of Nysia's story as she did in the mini-lesson, Caitlin reinforced the idea of being specific about what you include.

In the lessons presented over these three days, Caitlin moved from the broad vision of where we're headed as writers (published authors), to examples that are attainable (*kindergarten* authors). Vygotskian in her approach, she helps them see that this is not just for famous authors, and it's not just one student who can do this; we can, too. She makes it possible for them to get there.

Lesson Including the Important Parts: Being Even More Specific in a Published Piece

As the music that calls the children to the rug ends, Allison is sitting on the chair—Caitlin's usual place—and Caitlin is sitting on the rug at Allison's feet. Caitlin begins:

"You know how we have been talking a lot about how writers tell the important things in a story? Just like Grace Lin did in *Dim Sum for Everyone!*, and Dav Pilkey did in *The Paperboy*, and Taleaha did in 'A Day at School,' and Nysia did in 'Taleaha and Nysia Went to the Movie Theatre'? All those writers thought carefully about what was important about their stories. They thought about what they wanted readers to know. Well, I have another published story that *the author* is going to read!" She gives a little smile in Allison's direction, and Allison looks pleased. Caitlin holds up Allison's published story as she speaks.

"Allison had written a bunch of stories, and I asked her to choose the one she thought was her best. She chose this one, and then I typed it on the computer. She illustrated it again and here it is!"

Caitlin holds up the published book and Allison reads, "'When I Went to the Doctor's.'"

"Tell us about this border," Caitlin says, pointing to the frame around the title.

"It's all doctor stuff," Allison says, pointing out the tiny stethoscopes, thermometers, and blood pressure cuffs that form the border on each page, similar to the way Jan Brett, an author/illustrator whose work they had studied as a class, used elements of her story to create a border.

Allison reads the story, page by page (see Figure 9.2). When she finishes, Caitlin turns to the class and says, "Let's think about what

FIGURE 9.2 Allison's published book: "When I Went to the Doctor's."

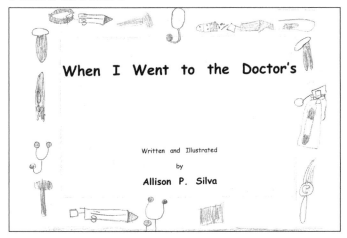

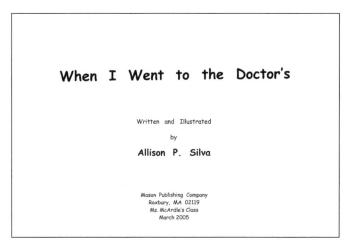

I was waiting for the doctor. I was making a card. It was her last day.

She was calling my name.

I was getting ready to go home. I was starving!

Figure 9.2 Allison's published book: "When I Went to the Doctor's" (continued).

I was waiting. I was writing and watching t.v.

We were walking to the hearing room.

About The Author

This is Allison. She is six years old. She is in K2B. Her birthday is in January. She likes the art center. Her favorite friend is Najee. Her favorite book is 10 Minutes Till Bedtime. Her favorite food is apples. She likes to play on the computer. She likes to play with magnetic letters. She likes to read new books with Ms. McArdle.

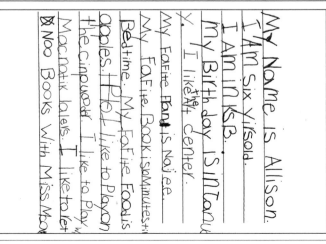

Allison did. She didn't just say, 'I went to the doctor's. The doctor checked me. I went home.' She told things that were important to her: how she was watching TV while she was waiting, how she made a card for the doctor, and why she made it—things we wouldn't have known if she hadn't put them in her story.

"Who thinks they're ready to go back and think about including the important parts in their story?"

This series of mini-lessons, presented in the spring of kindergarten, illustrate how one teacher tried to help her students move forward in their understanding of the craft of writing. She didn't vary her words much. She kept coming back to the same language: *important parts*, and *what readers might not know*. What varied were the examples she used to illustrate those words. At the end of the week, not every child had incorporated the idea of telling the important parts, but there were signs that some children were internalizing the concept. For example, during share time at the end of one of the writing sessions, Joshua told the group that he had included something his readers wouldn't have known, and proceeded to read: "After we watched the movie we ate the food. It was chicken and rice." It was the first time he had extended the thought on a page in a way that revealed something more specific.

On another day, Mia, who is visually impaired, moved her fingers along her page as she read: "Me and Skye and Kiara are pretending in the house corner" as a voice from the rug cheered, "She's reading Braille!"

When a student asked, "What were you and Skye and Kiara pretending?" Mia responded, "We were pretending to cook," which led to other questions asking for more information about what else she and her friends cooked.

If, as a result of the response from her peers, Mia adds more specific information to her story, then hooray for Mia. But if not, we still celebrate the small steps forward that our students take with five- and six-year-old charm. What matters here is that the idea of making decisions about what to include and what to leave out was becoming part of the conversation in this classroom. This teacher and these students now share another bit of information about how writers work that they will refer to again and again.

What may be the most important element reflected in these lessons is that they were presented with a generosity of spirit, high expectation, and belief in students. In each of these lessons, Caitlin's manner says, Here's something that writers do to make their stories good enough that we want to keep reading them. Since we want *our* stories to be worth reading, let's give it a try. Here's one way you might think about doing it in your writing, and I'll be here to help you along the way.

These lessons illustrate one teacher's progression of thinking about teaching—-her teaching her students. Mini-lessons come from our thinking about our teaching. On each of these four days,

Caitlin presented mini-lessons to her students in response to what she had observed. She spoke from a place of knowledge about the art and craft of writing, and the art and craft of teaching, from what she knows about how young children learn, and from a place of knowledge about these particular children as people, learners, and writers. Because of that, her lessons were pertinent and succinct.

Because of their day-to-day living and learning together, teachers and students establish points of reference to which they turn throughout the year. For Caitlin and her students, books like *The Paperboy*, *Dim Sum for Everyone!*, "A Day at School," "Taleaha and Nysia Went to the Movie Theatre," and "When I Went to the Doctor's" came to represent much more than the stories themselves. Along with valuing the individual stories, these children were also studying how these published authors, whom they viewed as fellow writers, were practicing their craft. These books became points of reference about writing, as did their own stories—those they shared orally and those they wrote—along with their ongoing conversations about how they work as a community of writers. Only the teacher who is with students day after day can draw on the history of that group of writers. Only the teacher who has watched these students over time can recognize a breakthrough for a particular child, celebrate it, and turn it into a learning opportunity for the others.

Closing Thoughts

IN SOME WAYS TEACHING WRITING has become easier now that there are so many books and resources out there, but in other ways it has become more difficult. Teachers are now being given writing curricula and told *what* to teach, *when,* and *how.* What we had in those early days—because of principals like Jean Robbins, then principal of Atkinson Academy, who accepted the invitation of Don Graves and his researchers to come to her school—was professional freedom to look, to wonder, to use what we know about young children, teaching, and writing, thereby allowing children to show us how to help them learn. We weren't teaching a premade writing curriculum; we were creating it based on watching our students.

In a sense, Boston gave us that same freedom. We weren't given a curriculum to follow. Instead, people like Maryanne Martinelli and Syd Smith, curriculum leaders in Boston who asked us to do this work, trusted our expertise and allowed us the room to learn alongside the teachers and children. We watched teachers come alive as they saw what their students could do. We heard them saying things like, "This makes so much sense," and "I never knew I could expect this quality of writing from my kindergartners." In turning to those teachers, and with them, to their students, we've come to better understand what young writers *can* and *want* to do.

Our hope is that no teacher is expected to use this book as a manual; in fact, we tried to write it so that wouldn't be possible. What we hope instead is that it gives teachers a sense of how it can look, what can be possible when young children talk, draw, and write. Most important, we hope it gives teachers license to watch closely those brilliant teachers who have so much to teach us: our students.

Bibliography of Children's Books

A Note About the Bibliography

The titles we've included in this bibliography are those we've referred to in the lessons presented in this book. They are by no means *the* books but some we have come to know and love and find useful in our work with children. There is always a danger in suggesting books to use for a particular lesson: people sometimes think they need *this* book to address *this* topic. In fact, for years teachers asked for a list of books to use to teach various elements of craft. We resisted, explaining that there is no one book or set of books, but that each of us needs to go to the books that we and our students know well, and look closely at them with an eye toward the writing.

Perhaps a better response would have been to share how we go about choosing the books we use. There are, after all, things we look for, look at, and pay attention to when browsing through books in bookstores or libraries or at conferences that influence our choices. Here, we've begun a list of some things we do, think, ask, and notice as we look at books with young writers in mind. We don't think it is complete, but we hope it helps you think about the books you choose for your work with your students. And we hope you add your criteria to this list:

Illustrations

Because drawing and writing are the vehicles through which children tell their stories on paper, we look to see how the stories are told through the illustrations and how they work with the text so that there is a wholeness between the two.

Amount of Text

Because we work with young children who, at least at first, write a sentence per page, we want books with a similar amount of text. We read aloud many books to our students that have lots more text, but as we look for books to use as models of writing, we want some that look and sound like what our students can do. We try to find at least some that stay close to the amount of text our students might be able to put on their pages.

Are the Characters Human?

We ask our students to tell stories of their lives. Because they are human, and because many, if not most, of their experiences happen with other human beings, we want them to have some good models of stories written in a human voice, about human encounters.

Ordinariness of the Topic

We're always on the lookout for ordinary, everyday topics. Stories about extraordinary things are wonderful and we need to have them in the classroom and read them, and yes, refer to them in mini-lessons when it seems right to do so. But stories written about ordinary things, such as getting a haircut, going to the park, having a little brother or sister, playing with trucks, and taking care of a pet, trigger students' own stories. They make it possible for all students to see that they have things to write about, too.

Topics That Represent Our Students and the Broader Population

We look for books that represent people and situations that our students can relate to, in terms of race (African American, Asian, Hispanic, Native American, Caucasian, and so on); family cultures (such as one parent, two parents, two parents of the same gender, extended families living in one space); and diversity of class, culture, ethnicity, and so on, and there is a greater selection in some of these categories than in others. For students to feel safe enough to reveal themselves in their writing, they need to know that who they are and where they're from will be valued. One way we do that is by reading books in which they see others like themselves.

Written in First Person

Not all the books we choose are written in first person, but many are. When children tell stories about what they know, they do so in the "I" voice. Therefore it is important for them to have models of writers who do the same thing. If they are to write *their* stories, they need the sound of the first-person voice in their heads.

Favorite Authors

In bookstores and at conferences we seek out our favorite authors and illustrators. We're always looking to see what their new books are and reading to see if we want to add them to our collection. When students get to know one author's or illustrator's work deeply, they come to see patterns, stylistic similarities, and differences, and can develop a writing relationship with the person behind the work.

Genre

We need to make sure that our collection is filled with books from a variety of genres—personal narrative, poetry, informational texts, notebooks/diaries, reference guides, letters, songs, plays, and so on—and that we read them aloud or look at them together during various times of the day, as well as refer to them during mini-lessons.

Connections to Others

When we know about a particular student's passion, we keep our eyes out for books on that topic.

Emotional Connection

Probably the most important thing that causes us to stay reading is that the book touches us in some way. It makes us laugh, reminds us of someone or something, brings tears to our eyes, and gets us thinking, The kids will love this! We don't have to love every book we share with our students, but we do need to see its value for the purpose of working with student writers.

The following two lists include the same books; the first is arranged alphabetically by author, the second is arranged alphabetically by title.

We hope these criteria give you a way of thinking about the books you'll choose for your work with your students.

Children's Books by Author

Ballard, Robin. 1999. *When We Get Home*. New York: Greenwillow Books.

Brandenberg, Alexa. 2002. *Ballerina Flying*. New York: HarperCollins.

Burleigh, Robert. 2001. *Goal*. Illustrated by Stephen T. Johnson. New York: Harcourt.

Carlson, Nancy. 2001. *My Best Friend Moved Away*. New York: Viking.

Cohen, Miriam. 2005. *My Big Brother*. Illustrated by Ronald Himler. New York: Star Bright Books.

Cooper, Elisha. 2006. *Beach*. New York: Orchard Books.

Coulman, Valerie. 2004. *I Am a Ballerina*. Illustrated by Sandra Lamb. Montreal: Lobster Press.

Crews, Donald. 1978. *Freight Train*. New York: Greenwillow Books.

———. 1991. *Bigmama's*. New York: Greenwillow Books.

———. 1992. *Shortcut*. New York: Greenwillow Books.

———. 1998. *Night at the Fair*. New York: Greenwillow Books.

Davies, Nicola. 2001. *Bat Loves the Night*. Illustrated by Sarah Fox-Davies. Cambridge, MA: Candlewick.

———. 2001. *One Tiny Turtle*. Illustrated by Jane Chapman. Cambridge, MA: Candlewick.

Emberley, Ed. 2002. *Trucks and Trains*. New York: Little, Brown. There are many other drawing books by Ed Emberley.

Frazee, Marla. 2003. *Roller Coaster*. New York: Harcourt.

George, Jean Craighead. 1997. *Look to the North: A Wolf Pup Diary*. Illustrated by Lucia Washburn. New York: HarperTrophy.

———. 2001. *Nutik, the Wolf Pup*. Illustrated by Ted Rand. New York: HarperCollins.

Harper, Dan. 2001. *Sit, Truman!* Illustrated by Cara Moser and Barry Moser. New York: Harcourt.

Harper, Isabelle. 1994. *My Dog Rosie*. Illustrated by Barry Moser. New York: Scholastic.

———. 1995. *My Cats Nick and Nora*. Illustrated by Barry Moser. New York: Scholastic.

———. 1996. *Our New Puppy*. Illustrated by Barry Moser. New York: Scholastic.

Hesse, Karen. 1999. *Come On, Rain!* Illustrated by Jon J. Muth. New York: Scholastic.

Huneck, Stephen. 2000. *Sally Goes to the Beach*. New York: Abrams.

———. 2001. *Sally Goes to the Mountains*. New York: Abrams.

———. 2002. *Sally Goes to the Farm*. New York: Abrams.

———. 2004. *Sally Goes to the Vet*. New York: Abrams.

Isadora, Rachel. 2005. *Luke Goes to Bat*. New York: G. P. Putnam's Sons.

James, Simon. 1997. *Leon and Bob*. Cambridge, MA: Candlewick.

Jenkins, Steve, and Robin Page. 2006. *Move!* Illustrated by Steve Jenkins. Boston: Houghton Mifflin.

Jones, Rebecca C. 1991. *Matthew and Tilly.* Illustrated by Beth Peck. New York: Dutton.

Katz, Karen. 1999. *The Colors of Us.* New York: Henry Holt.

Lin, Grace. 1999. *The Ugly Vegetables.* Watertown, MA: Charlesbridge.

———. 2001. *Dim Sum for Everyone!.* New York: Alfred A. Knopf.

———. 2002. *Kite Flying.* New York: Alfred A. Knopf.

Low, William. 1997. *Chinatown.* New York: Henry Holt.

Milich, Zoran. 2002. *City Signs.* New York: Kids Can Press.

Narahashi, Keiko. 2000. *Two Girls Can.* New York: McElderry Books.

Nevius, Carol. 2004. *Karate Hour.* Illustrated by Bill Thomson. New York: Cavendish.

Paulsen, Gary. 1995. *The Tortilla Factory.* Illustrated by Ruth Wright Paulsen. New York: Harcourt Brace.

———. 1995. *La Tortilleria.* Illustrated by Ruth Wright Paulsen. Translated from Spanish by Gloria de Acagón Adújar. New York: Harcourt Brace.

Pilkey, Dav. 1996. *The Paperboy.* New York: Orchard Books.

Prince, April Jones. 2006. *What Do Wheels Do All Day?* Illustrated by Giles Laroche. Boston: Houghton Mifflin.

Rao, Sandhya. 2006. *My Mother's Sari.* Illustrated by Nina Sabnani. New York: North-South Books.

Rosenberg, Liz. 2001. *Eli's Night-Light.* Illustrated by Joanna Yardley. New York: Scholastic.

Rylant, Cynthia. 1985. *The Relatives Came.* Illustrated by Stephen Gammell. New York: Bradbury.

———. 2000. *In November.* Illustrated by Jill Kastner. New York: Harcourt.

Schaefer, Lola M. 2006. *An Island Grows.* Illustrated by Cathie Felstead. New York: Greenwillow Books.

Shannon, David. 2006. *Good Boy, Fergus!* New York: Blue Sky Press.

Shelby, Anne. 1990. *We Keep a Store.* Paintings by John Ward. New York: Orchard Books.

Simont, Marc. 2001. *The Stray Dog.* New York: HarperCollins.

Steen, Sandra, and Susan Steen. 2001. *Car Wash.* Illustrated by Brian Karas. New York: G. P. Putnam's Sons.

Stuve-Bodeen, Stephanie. 1998. *Elizabeti's Doll.* Illustrated by Christy Hale. New York: Lee and Low.

———. 2000. *Mama Elizabeti.* Illustrated by Christy Hale. New York: Lee and Low.

———. 2002. *Elizabeti's School.* Illustrated by Christy Hale. New York: Lee and Low.

Suen, Anastasia. 2004. *Subway.* Illustrated by Karen Katz. New York: Viking.

Tarpley, Natasha Anastasia. 1998. *I Love My Hair!* Illustrated by E. B. Lewis. New York: Little, Brown.

————. 2002. *Bippity Bop Barbershop*. Illustrated by E. B. Lewis. New York: Little, Brown.

Voake, Charlotte. 1997. *Ginger*. Cambridge, MA: Candlewick.

————. 2003. *Ginger Finds a Home*. Cambridge, MA: Candlewick.

Zimmerman, Andrea, and David Clemesha. 2003. *Digger Man*. New York: Henry Holt.

Children's Books by Title

An Island Grows, by Lola M. Schaefer, illustrated by Cathie Felstead. Greenwillow Books, 2006.

Ballerina Flying, by Alexa Brandenberg. HarperCollins, 2002.

Bat Loves the Night, by Nicola Davies, illustrated by Sarah Fox-Davies. Candlewick, 2001.

Beach, by Elisha Cooper. Orchard Books, 2006.

Bigmama's, by Donald Crews. Greenwillow Books, 1991.

Bippity Bop Barbershop, by Natasha Anastasia Tarpley, illustrated by E. B. Lewis. Little, Brown, 2002.

Car Wash, by Sandra Steen and Susan Steen, illustrated by G. Brian Karas. G. P. Putnam's Sons, 2001.

Chinatown, by William Low. Henry Holt, 1997.

City Signs, by Zoran Milich. Kids Can Press, 2002.

The Colors of Us, by Karen Katz. Henry Holt, 1999.

Come On, Rain! by Karen Hesse, illustrated by Jon J. Muth. Scholastic, 1999.

Digger Man, by Andrea Zimmerman and David Clemsha. Henry Holt, 2003.

Dim Sum for Everyone! by Grace Lin. Alfred A. Knopf, 2001.

Eli's Night-Light, by Liz Rosenberg, illustrated by Joanna Yardley. Scholastic, 2001.

Elizabeti's Doll, by Stephanie Stuve-Bodeen, illustrated by Christy Hale. Lee and Low, 1998.

Elizabeti's School, by Stephanie Stuve-Bodeen, illustrated by Christy Hale. Lee and Low, 2002.

Freight Train, by Donald Crews. Greenwillow Books, 1978.

Ginger, by Charlotte Voake. Candlewick, 1997.

Ginger Finds a Home, by Charlotte Voake. Candlewick, 2003.

Goal, by Robert Burleigh, illustrated by Stephen T. Johnson. Harcourt, 2001.

Good Boy, Fergus! by David Shannon. Blue Sky Press, 2006.

I Am a Ballerina, by Valerie Coulman, illustrated by Sandra Lamb. Lobster Press, 2004.

I Love My Hair! by Natasha Anastasia Tarpley, illustrated by E. B. Lewis. Little, Brown, 1998.

In November, by Cynthia Rylant, illustrated by Jill Kastner. Harcourt, 2000.

Karate Hour, by Carol Nevius, illustrated by Bill Thomson. Cavendish, 2004.

Kite Flying, by Grace Lin. Alfred A. Knopf, 2002.

La Tortilleria, by Gary Paulsen, illustrated by Ruth Wright Paulsen, translated from Spanish by Gloria de Aragón Andújar. Harcourt, 1995.

Leon and Bob, by Simon James. Candlewick, 1997.

Look to the North: A Wolf Pup Diary, by Jean Craighead George, illustrated by Lucia Washburn. HarperTrophy, 1997.

Luke Goes to Bat, by Rachel Isadora. G. P. Putnam's Sons, 2005.

Mama Elizabeti, by Stephanie Stuve-Bodeen, illustrated by Christy Hale. Lee and Low, 2000.

Matthew and Tilly, by Rebecca C. Jones, illustrated by Beth Peck. Dutton, 1991.

Move! by Steve Jenkins and Robin Page, illustrated by Steve Jenkins. Houghton Mifflin, 2006.

My Best Friend Moved Away, by Nancy Carlson. Viking, 2001.

My Big Brother, by Miriam Cohen, illustrated by Ronald Himler. Star Bright Books, 2005.

My Dog Rosie, by Isabelle Harper, illustrated by Barry Moser. Scholastic, 1994.

My Cats Nick and Nora, by Isabelle Harper, illustrated by Barry Moser. Scholastic, 1995.

My Mother's Sari, by Sandhya Rao, illustrated by Nina Sabnani. North-South Books, 2006.

Night at the Fair, by Donald Crews. Greenwillow Books, 1998.

Nutik, the Wolf Pup, by Jean Craighead George, illustrated by Ted Rand. HarperCollins, 2001.

One Tiny Turtle, by Nicola Davies, illustrated by Jane Chapman. Candlewick, 2001.

Our New Puppy, by Isabelle Harper, illustrated by Barry Moser. Blue Sky Press. 1996.

The Paperboy, by Dav Pilkey. Orchard Books, 1996.

The Relatives Came, by Cynthia Rylant, illustrated by Stephen Gammell. Bradbury, 1985.

Roller Coaster, by Marla Frazee. Harcourt, 2003.

Sally Goes to the Beach by Stephen Huneck. Abrams, 2000.

Sally Goes to the Farm, by Stephen Huneck. Abrams, 2002.

Sally Goes to the Mountains, by Stephen Huneck. Abrams, 2001.

Sally Goes to the Vet, by Stephen Huneck. Abrams, 2004.

Shortcut, by Donald Crews. Greenwillow Books, 1992.

Sit, Truman! by Dan Harper, illustrated by Cara Moser and Barry Moser. Harcourt, 2001.

The Stray Dog, by Marc Simont, from a true story by Reiko Sassa. HarperCollins, 2001.

Subway, by Anastasia Suen, illustrated by Karen Katz. Viking, 2004.

Tortilla Factory, by Gary Paulsen, illustrated by Ruth Wright Paulsen. Harcourt, 1995.

Trucks and Trains, by Ed Emberley. Little, Brown, 2002.

Two Girls Can, by Keiko Narahashi. McElderry Books, 2000.

The Ugly Vegetables, by Grace Lin. Charlesbridge, 1999.

We Keep a Store, by Anne Shelby, paintings by John Ward. Orchard Books, 1990.

What Do Wheels Do All Day? by April Jones Prince, illustrated by Giles Laroche. Houghton Mifflin, 2006.

When We Get Home, by Robin Ballard. Greenwillow Books, 1999.

Sample Teacher Plans:
Introducing the Drawing & Writing Book

THE FOLLOWING NARRATIONS offer three different approaches that teachers have used to introduce the Drawing & Writing Books to their students. Certainly, there are more possibilities.

Teacher One

It was the end of the second week of school that we began working in the Drawing & Writing Book. For the first eight days, during the forty-five minutes or so that we called writing time, I read a story aloud and then we told stories. I told mine on the first day and didn't need to tell another—they "got it" and couldn't wait to tell theirs. We'd end with an interactive writing lesson, which led right into our word-study work. I didn't introduce the Drawing & Writing Books right away because I wanted the students to hear lots of stories and to tell lots of stories. They also needed opportunities to work independently before I gave them their Drawing & Writing Books. We also did a sketching lesson first thing in the morning, right when they came in. It was a nice way to start the day, so it's not that they weren't putting things on paper. They were.

Then, on the eighth day of school, I introduced the Drawing & Writing Books to a third of the class as the others were working at choice. I showed them the books and gave them a chance to work on the first page. I did that again on the ninth day with another third of the class and again on the tenth day with the rest. By the end of the second week, they had all had a chance to use their new books, which made it much easier for me to then model a lesson in my own Drawing & Writing Book on the following Monday, the eleventh day of school. Since then, our writing time begins with someone telling a story, me presenting some piece of information that I think will help them as they work in their Drawing & Writing Books.

Teacher Two

We started right in on the second day of school. I showed them how I would start to draw a picture from the story I had told them the day before, and then gave them their books, but I let them work for only about seven minutes. I stopped them before they were finished because I knew I wanted to show them how to go back to the work they started and continue with it. Also, I knew that seven minutes was just about right, because my real goal for that time was to teach them how to "be" during writing time. I found that for some of them, the Drawing & Writing Book was appropriate; for some, it seemed like it was their first opportunity to use colored pencils and paper. They were just going back and forth across the page with the colors, making swirls. When I asked them to tell me their stories, they didn't seem to know what I meant.

In retrospect, the short writing time worked well at first, but that has something to do with my experience. I had done this last year (with disastrous results!) and I knew how I wanted to structure it—beginning with a small amount of time and gradually extending it. For the first month or so, we worked in our Drawing & Writing Books for three days (beginning with a read-aloud, then listening to a couple of children tell their stories), and we did a sketching lesson on the other two days. By the second week of October, they were working in the Drawing & Writing Book all five days. I moved the sketching to another part of the day.

Teacher Three

This year I'm moving more slowly than ever. I think it's because I know I'm going to have these kids again next year in first grade and I want to make sure we've established a way of being in this class-room. So they're spending a lot of time learning to work with each other in these different areas of the room. I'm allowing them to be more playful than I have in the past [she points to a child working at the art table who is using a hole punch to make "snow" out of pieces of colored paper], and as I talk to them and listen as they "play," I'm learning so much about them. We do interactive writing every day—at this point it's mostly labeling things in the room—and we do sketching at least twice a week. They tell stories every day, and once a week I choose one of those storytellers to draw the story they told on an 18-by-24-inch piece of paper, an idea I learned from my colleague Barbara Nowell-Haines. It usually takes them a few days to finish their drawing because there's so much room on the page, but we spend time talking about what they'll put where, and they end up filling up the page. Then, during interactive writing they come up with sentences for their pictures. They decide what they want the words to be, and as a class, we write the sentence interactively. I also give them opportunities to write and draw, so I'm guessing that by the end of September, which will be three weeks into school, when I introduce those Drawing & Writing Books, they'll know what they're for and how to spend their time working in them.

Some Materials for Young Writers

- lots of *children's literature* displayed beautifully and made accessible to children
- *writing* written and illustrated by children (original work and published pieces)
- a *carpeted library area* where the class gathers together

- *Drawing & Writing Books*—one for each child (with a few extras for the children who fill up the first one)
- *writing folders*—two pockets, three fasteners (one for each child; use four colors)
- *writing folder inserts* for record keeping (copy one set for each child)
- *Princeton files* to house everyday folders (four—one for each color of folders)

- *writing paper*—lines of different widths, unlined, etc.
- *different colors of paper* for covers (the same size as writing papers)
- *stacking paper trays* for writing papers and covers (at least eight)

- *hanging file folders* to hold accumulating writing (one for each child)
- *crate* or some other container or file drawer to house hanging files

- *work caddies* (containers that house writing tools):
  ◦ *crayons* (thick and thin)
  ◦ *pencils* (thick and thin)
  ◦ *multicultural crayons* (thick and thin)
  ◦ *black felt-tip markers* (thin)
  ◦ *colored pencils* (mostly thick, some thin)
  ◦ *multicultural colored pencils* (mostly thick, some thin)

- *staplers* (at least two)
- *staple removers* (at least two)
- *cup/container* for used staples (at least two)
- *scissors, rulers, glue sticks*
- *tape*
- *correction/cover-up tape*
- *sticky notes*
- *date stamp* and *ink pad*
- *chart paper* for when the teacher writes in front of the class
- *markers* for when the teacher writes in front of the class
- *pencil sharpener* that children can use

Materials for a Drawing Center
- *drawing/sketchbooks* (one for each child)
- *pencils* (thick and thin)
- *Ed Emberly books on drawing*
- *other "how to" books on drawing*
- *bendable wooden figures of humans*
- *three-dimensional shapes* (cubes, pyramids, etc.)
- *interesting objects to observe and draw*

Publishing Materials
(some possibilities)
- *bookbinding machine plus supplies* (covers, backs, coils)
- *three-hole punch and brass fasteners*
- *bookbinding tape*

Cumulative Writing Record Form

Date D/W Book or Booklet Topic/Title	Knows About Craft (sense of story, organization . . .)	Knows About Conventions (spelling, punctuation, etc.)	Needs to Learn	When to Teach

Cumulative Writing Record for _____ **School Year** _____

Talking, Drawing, Writing: Lessons for Our Youngest Writers. Martha Horn and Mary Ellen Giacobbe. Copyright © 2007, Stenhouse Publishers.

Talking, Drawing, Writing

Small-Group Writing Record Form

Small-Group Writing Record: Assessing and Documenting
Date: _____

Child/ Writing	What I Notice Before Reading	What Writers Are Doing Craft/Conventions	Information Writers Need to Learn	When to Teach

ML= mini-lesson IW = interactive writing Conf = conference RA = read-aloud Conv = conversation MM = morning meeting WS = word study RI = reading instruction

My Finished Writing Form

My Finished Writing

1	2	3	4	5
6	7	8	9	10
11	12	13	14	15
16	17	18	19	20
21	22	23	24	25
26	27	28	29	30

Talking, Drawing, Writing: Lessons for Our Youngest Writers. Martha Horn and Mary Ellen Giacobbe. Copyright © 2007. Stenhouse Publishers.

Writing Folder Inserts

My Finished Writing

1	**2**
3	**4**
5	**6**

My Ideas for Writing

1	**2**
3	**4**
5	**6**

My Proofreading List

1. I can write my **name** on my writing.

2. I can write a **title** on my writing.

3. I can write the **date** on my writing.

4. I can **number** my finished writing.

5. I can write the title of my writing on the page called **My Finished Writing.**

Talking, Drawing, Writing

From "The Writing Workshop: Support for Word Learning" by Mary Ellen Giacobbe. In *Word Matters* by Gay Su Pinnell and Irene Fountas. Copyright © 1998. Heinemann.

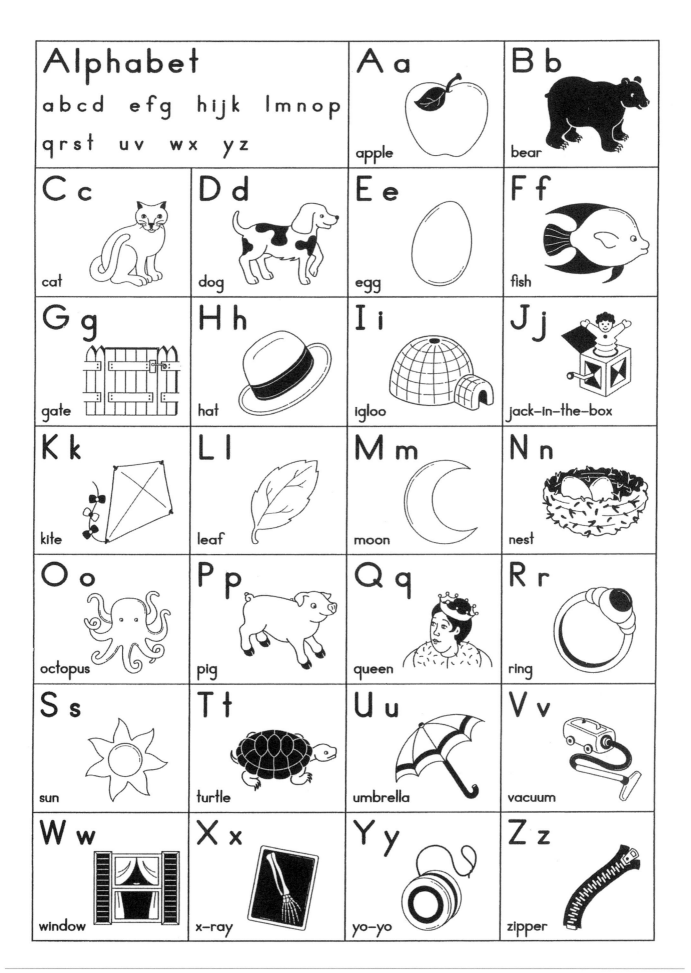

Alphabet	A a	B b
abcd efg hijk lmnop qrst uv wx yz	apple	bear

C c	D d	E e	F f
cat	dog	egg	fish

G g	H h	I i	J j
gate	hat	igloo	jack-in-the-box

K k	L l	M m	N n
kite	leaf	moon	nest

O o	P p	Q q	R r
octopus	pig	queen	ring

S s	T t	U u	V v
sun	turtle	umbrella	vacuum

W w	X x	Y y	Z z
window	x-ray	yo-yo	zipper

American Heritage College Dictionary, 4th ed., S.V. "proofread."

Berthoff, A. E. 1982. *Forming, Thinking, Writing: The Composing Imagination.* Montclair, NJ: Boynton Cook.

Bodrova, E., and D. Leong. 1996. *Tools of the Mind: The Vygotskian Approach to Early Childhood Education.* Englewood Cliffs, NJ: Merrill.

Britton, J. 1967. "The Speaker." In *Talking and Writing: A Handbook for English Teachers*, ed. J. Britton. London: Methuen.

Brookes, M. 1996. *Drawing with Children.* New York: Jeremy P. Tarcher/Putnam.

Cummings, P., ed. 1995. *Talking with Artists.* New York: Simon and Schuster.

Delaney, F. 2005. *Ireland.* New York: HarperCollins.

Didion, J. 1986. "Characters." In *Writers on Writing*, ed. J. Winokur. Philadelphia: Running Press.

Dyson, A. H. 1986. "Transitions and Tensions: Interrelationships Between the Drawing, Talking and Dictating of Young Children." *Research in the Teaching of English* 20 (4): 379–409.

Fletcher, R. 1991. *What a Writer Needs.* Portsmouth, NH: Heinemann.

Graves, D. 1978. "How Children Change as Writers." Atkinson, NH: NIE Funded Study.

Johnston, P. 2004. *Choice Words*. Portland, ME: Stenhouse.

Kohn, A. 1998. *What to Look for in a Classroom: And Other Essays*. San Francisco: Jossey-Bass.

McCarrier, A., G. S. Pinnell, and I. Fountas. 2000. *Interactive Writing: How Language and Literacy Come Together, K–2*. Portsmouth, NH: Heinemann.

Moore, H., and K. Clark. 1998. *Henry Moore's Sheep Sketchbook*. New York: Thames and Hudson.

Murray, D. 1984. *Write to Learn*. New York: Holt, Rinehart and Winston.

Newkirk, T. 1989. *More Than Stories: The Range of Children's Writing*. Portsmouth, NH: Heinemann.

Ray, K. W., and L. B. Cleveland. 2004. *About the Authors: Writing Workshop with Our Youngest Writers*. Portsmouth, NH: Heinemann.

Sowers, S. 1991. "Six Questions Teachers Ask About Invented Spelling." In *Literacy in Process: The Heinemann Reader*, ed. B. Power and R. Hubbard. Portsmouth, NH: Heinemann.

Vygotsky, L. 1978. *Mind in Society: The Development of Higher Psychological Processes*. Cambridge, MA: Harvard University Press.

———. 1986. *Thought and Language*. Edited by A. Kozulin. Cambridge, MA: MIT Press.